T0313021

To the Prophet Mohammed, peace be upon him,
who teaches his followers to respect women.

And all those men in the entire world, including
my father and son, who respect women.

You don't get frightened of these furious, violent winds, oh Eagle! These blows only to make you fly higher.

—Allama Iqbal, 786

Contents

Contents

CHAPTER I
Learning to Say No

I FIRST LEARNED OF THE POWER in the word "no" from Father. I was no more than seven years old, sitting in the drawing room of our home in Karachi on a Sunday morning, doing what I was the best at—reading—when I heard voices in the other room. Two men were at the door of our house; they were insisting that they speak to Father, whose name was Mian Mahmood Ali Chaudhry, about an important matter. He greeted them and invited them into the room where I was reading.

On Sundays, we were all at home. My sister worked in the kitchen helping Mother, who never asked me to help in the kitchen, as if she had a sense of impending doom that something bad would happen to me if I were to be around fire or water. On that particular day, I was engrossed in my favorite book, *The Adventures of Sherlock Holmes*. My brothers were outside playing cricket in the street. Usually, I would be outside too, playing and running with my friends. But earlier, I had brought many books from the Frere Hall library, so I was inside reading.

I loved listening to Father speak about his business. Father never asked me to leave the room when that happened, and now I sat attentively at the far end of the drawing room as he spoke to the two men. Father practiced criminal law, and he often defended men falsely accused of crimes. These men were here to discuss one of his clients, a man who had engaged Father's services to defend himself against serious accusations. Their voices were low, even friendly. They wanted to convince him to do something. One of the men Father knew already because that man also practiced law. They spoke in familiar tones.

Father was a man of iron will, whom I greatly admired. Father scrutinized his guests with the wary glare of an experienced advocate as I had often seen him do with others. His jaw set, hard as a rock, as he listened. When they were finished, he spoke.

"No, I cannot do that," Father said without anger; instead, his voice was filled with a determination that he would never acquiesce to their requests. The details of their mission became clear to me as they further presented their arguments. Father was defending a politician against charges of corruption. Father had taken the case only because he believed the man to be innocent. This much I already knew. But these men wanted the fraud charge to stand; they wanted Father to lie in court, or to make his case so weak he could never prevail.

Evil politicians in our government often used false accusations to defame and discredit honest politicians who stood in their way. This way of doing politics was deeply rooted in my country, from top to bottom. Honest people became obstacles to those who unjustly wanted to have their way, so they must be pushed aside.

The men offered Father a large sum of money to prejudice his client's case, to make sure he did not win. Later, Father told me that the two men offered him more than twelve times what his client had agreed to pay him.

"No, I won't do that," he repeated, his voice as firm as ever. He was known as a man of his word. "Don't you people know that those who give and those who take bribes will go to *Jahannum*? Now, you must leave my house."

One of the men laughed brusquely. "Ha Ch. Sahib, you don't look like a religious person. You have no beard, you wear Western clothes, but you talk about religion."

"Islam is in my heart," Father said. "I don't need to pretend."

Father rose to his feet. He was tall, toned and athletic, clean-shaven, with neatly combed black hair, and the clear brown eyes that could break stone when he stared at you. Even at home, working in his office down the hall, he wore a suit and tie, because neighbors often came over to ask for help.

It is most unusual for a Pakistani to ask a guest to leave his home, particularly in our home, where hospitality was central to our life. Father had said no to these men's fraudulent scheme, and now there was no more welcome here. At that moment, when Father insisted they leave, I felt a surge of warmth. I was proud of his courage, of his willingness to stand up to corrupt men. Though I was only seven, I understood the strength it must take to say no. I felt as if I stood on a mountaintop, breathing clean, fresh air.

The men left, and Father closed the front door. He strode by me, through the room, and into the kitchen, where Mother prepared our dinner. There was confidence in each of his steps, his shoulders squared and unburdened; his conscience was not burdened.

A few days later, I was again reading. Mother, the beautiful Ridha, always gracious and kind, settled into the kitchen to cook the family's favorite foods for the evening meal. She did not ask me to help her in the kitchen, though many of my friends were in their mother's kitchens learning to cook, helping to clean. Father never allowed me to clean the house, to wash the dishes, and Mother did not want me around the fire we used to prepare food. She wouldn't even let me open the oven door. She insisted that I see to my books and continue my studies. I was the top student in my grade at school.

Guests arrived at our door, and Mother rushed by me. She ushered several women into the living room, where she greeted guests. They were polite and kind. They had brought her gifts—gold necklaces, gold rings, bangles, and bracelets along with other exquisite jewelry. Their laughter was familiar and inviting, and they were friendly and gracious with their gifts. Mother wanted to know why they would bring her such gifts when she did not like to wear any of this.

In reply, they asked a small favor of her. She only needed to persuade Father not to help his most important client with his fraud case. It was a little thing, they said, that Father should help them in this way. These visitors wanted her to influence him, to get Father to understand how beneficial it would be for her family if his client lost his case. They promised that their husbands would refer more cases to Father in the future.

Mother was silent. I surmised she considered how she would respond. In her quiet way, she told them she could not do what they wanted. But they were persistent. They laid out many pieces of gold on the table in front of her. One woman placed a few sparkling pieces in her hands, "Ridha, look here. All this jewelry is made of twenty-two-karat gold."

There was a firmness in Mother's voice. "I would never ask my husband to lie about anything. I will never go against what my husband has decided. Please take your gifts and go."

What she did burned in my memory. Women greatly treasure gold. To wear gold necklaces, bangles, and jewelry in one's hair and on one's fingers and toes gave one great prestige. And prestige, like appearance, was critical in our society, which was so fractured by ignorance of the teachings of Islam and illiteracy. Mother was unyielding. Their dresses rustled as they rose. They pulled their dupattas over their heads and readied themselves to leave.

Another tried one last time. "Ridha, your neck is very long and beautiful. Look at this necklace."

Again, Mother said no.

The women left. The door closed. Later when Father arrived home, my parents talked in the kitchen, alone. Father was unhappy that they approached Mother in his absence and his family was in danger from these people. But I never felt in danger. Instead, I felt safe knowing Father was a man of his word and that Mother stood by him, not budging, even for gold and jewels. My parents were true Muslims who could not be bribed or swayed to shirk their duty, even by influential people.

I was very young when I heard all of these conversations; still, I understood what they meant: we must be strong in the face of those who would try to corrupt us. I admired my parents for their loyalty to each other, to their children, and to their religion. From an early age, it was easy for me to see the difference between what was right and what was wrong. There was never an argument in our home over doing the right thing, or treating another person fairly—Father and Mother expected that of us.

Saying no to evil schemes seemed so simple, something that others around us would see as honorable. What I did not know then was how much trouble saying no would cause me as an adult.

Ridha, my mother, grew up in a village in Toba Tek Singh town in Punjab, near Faisalabad City, which was famous for its cotton and textile industry. Mother was known in the area surrounding Toba Tek for her natural beauty, fair skin, long black hair, and pleasant manners. Even though the community had no electricity or running water, education was an essential part of every child's upbringing. She was one of eight daughters, and even in her simple clothes, her beauty stood out—tall, slim, and with a warm smile, she attracted a lot of attention.

Because of her beauty and sterling reputation, my father's mother sought her out for a wife for one of her twelve sons. When Grandmother visited her home, Father was already away at college. Grandmother was so taken with the sixteen-year-old Ridha that she proposed an engagement between her and Father right then.

Grandmother summoned Father home from Karachi, where he attended law school, to meet his future bride. Because of her age, Father waited three years for Ridha to finish school.

Father, one of twelve sons, was tall, as were all the men of his family. They were mostly fair, although some had olive complexions, and they were all educated. My paternal grandfather owned a vast tract of land, and while he easily made a lavish living off his property, he wanted a better life for his sons. He and his hired men labored their entire lives on his farm to provide an education for all twelve of them.

My grandfather sent each of his sons to school to nearby Faisalabad, and then on to either Lahore or Karachi for boarding school. My father also studied at the prestigious Aligarh University in Shimla, India. He was forced to leave after the partition, so he came to Karachi and completed his degree at the Sindh Muslim Law College. One of my uncles became a doctor, two were engineers, and several, like Father, became attorneys.

Father's oldest brother, Uncle Shafi, settled in Karachi where he became a prominent labor lawyer. He was instrumental in passing our current labor laws. Father's youngest and second oldest brother, who married Mother's oldest sister, both decided to live with my grandparents in their village.

Father and Mother were married when she was nineteen and he was twenty-six. At that point, Father had a legal practice already established in Karachi. The very next year my brother was born, then I came along two years later, delighting my father.

Father was pleased his second child was a daughter. In our culture, it wasn't unusual for a man to divorce his wife when she gave birth to a daughter. But not my father. He always showered me with affection and attention, at times more than my brothers, and even pampered me. When I was born, he distributed Ladhu, the customary sweets, in our neighborhood and to the family. He arranged a party for the traditional Gurhty ceremony of placing honey in an infant's mouth, and for the religious ceremony of reciting of the Azan in the newborn's ear. As my parents waited for the respectable person they had invited to perform the ritual, a girl entered our house, took up the bowl of honey, and put a dab in my mouth. Mother was stunned this uninvited girl would do such a thing. The guests gasped.

The story behind the Gurhty ceremony is that the qualities and fate of the one who places the honey in the mouth of the infant is transferred to the child. This girl from the neighborhood, Laila, was a college student who had married for love, without her parents' consent. Her husband was a classmate who was the son of a prominent politician of Lahore. After a few months of marriage, she became pregnant, and her husband disappeared. And now because of her unsavory reputation, no one would have anything to do with her, except my parents, who were always kind to her.

No one knew what she was thinking, barging into the ceremony the way she did, but this incident became an omen to my mother, a portent of what lay ahead for me. For a long time afterward, our neighbors kept asking Mother why she didn't stop the girl. Mother always took a deep breath of sorrow when asked that question. She did not have an answer.

Shortly after that incident occurred, Mother's bad dreams began. In them, she saw visions of me drowning in the sea; I shouted and screamed for help that never arrived. Other times, I was trapped in a burning fire, and no one came to my rescue. These dreams reoccurred consistently, frightening her. Though she wasn't superstitious like so many others, she began to believe them.

I didn't learn about Mother's dreams until I was in class two. From my earliest memories, she never allowed me around fire or water out of this dark fear that stalked her dreams. She encouraged me to stay by myself, not to talk to strangers, and not to make too many friends. She feared the people I met could be a danger to me.

With all of her admonitions, I became introspective, studious, and a voracious reader. I visited the library every few days, bringing home armloads of books. I developed an imaginary world, which was fueled by my constant reading. Mine was a happy life, full of characters, adventures, mysteries, and wonderful parents who doted on me. Books became my world.

Throughout my childhood, Mother refused to let me bathe or shower alone, fearing the vision of her dream of me drowning in the sea would come true in our own home. I often joked with her, "Ammi, how can I drown in my own house?"

Consequently, I never learned to swim as a child.

In spite of my Mother's fears, I was a lively child, friendly with all my schoolmates. I spent my school day laughing and playing with my friends. But I could not have anyone over after school. I always returned home by myself. I felt surrounded by kind and friendly people, but I was always alone. My favorite companion was my imaginary world.

At the time I didn't understand her preoccupation with my studies. I thought her instructions to focus on reading was the result of my precociousness as a student. None of her fears stymied my enthusiasm for life. My days were busy with school, and learning, and having fun with my siblings.

Rahat, my younger brother, was my best friend and confidant. We talked about everything, and we were always ready for adventure. Together, we would jump from high roofs and trees to test our strength. My younger brother Rashik was the one I loved the most of my seven siblings. I happily looked after them for mother. My sister Pinky loved me very much.

Many evenings around the dinner table, I was so absorbed in an imaginary world of a story that I continued reading through the entire meal. Often I would forget to eat my dinner. Father would remind me to eat. My siblings weren't so generous, often ribbing me, trying to break my attention. But it didn't matter how much noise they made; I kept my focus on the book.

After my father successfully defended that politician against the fraud charges, he decided not to take criminal cases any longer. He started taking civil cases, but then his clients began emotionally blackmailing him to avoid paying his fees. Sometimes, they sent their wives and children to my mother, telling her their reasons why they could not pay their fees. They did not want to pay his charges, and he concluded that many of his clients could not be trusted.

He then took up patent and trademark law, and quickly became a preeminent attorney in his field, working with many international clients who wanted to do business in Pakistan. Once he secured the trademark for a Russian client for tanks and a rifle.

On occasion, he let me accompany him to court. I remember one time in particular. The judge adjourned the noisy courtroom with his command, "Order, order." When everyone settled down, he heard the case of an old woman seeking justice. It was apparent she was very poor. When he decided in her favor, she began laughing and crying simultaneously from happiness. I remember thinking I should become a judge who could give a fair outcome to people seeking justice. That would be a noble life, one worth working hard to reach. But to become a judge, I would first need to become a lawyer.

I told Father that I wanted to become a lawyer like him. He said that to practice the law, I would have to deal with cruel and criminal people, many who are not reputable. I should not have to do that my entire life. Instead, he encouraged me to study hard. My uncles, who often visited our home, told me I was smart enough to practice medicine if that was what I chose. To treat the needy is also a noble cause.

I decided that I wanted to help people get well and live long, prosperous lives, so I chose to study medicine. That meant I had to be top in my class, and make the best marks to be accepted into medical college. I applied myself with extreme determination, in the same way that the boys fought and competed on the pitch. Schoolwork came easily to me. I wanted to understand the world around me. So I read everything I could find. If I could absorb the world through the written page, I would have as a child.

My father kept a *salwar kameez* in his office so he could go directly to Friday prayers at the mosque every week. Since girls did not attend the mosque to pray and learn the Quran, we were sent to a Maulvi's (imam's) house to learn our religion. We were taught to recite the Quran in Arabic, which none of us understood. Our native language was Urdu. But still, we memorized and recited, especially during Ramadan, when I, like every Muslim, tried to pray namaz five times a day, and I recited the whole Quran seven times in one month during my childhood. After so many recitations, my natural curiosity took over. What were these words we recited? What did they mean? What was written in the Quran? Why could not we read them in our native language?

After years of rote repetition, I became unsatisfied. So I saved my pocket money and on my own purchased a copy of the Quran in Urdu, along with the six-volume set of *tafseers* (interpretations) by Maulana Syed Abul A'la Maududi, the great expositor of the Quran. He was one of the notable men in Pakistan who supported creating the Islamic Republic of Pakistan during Zia-ul-Haq's presidency.

I wasn't more than eleven years old when I began reading the *tafseers* and the Quran in my own language. It took me many months to get through his translation of the Quran and to read all Maududi's *tafseers*.

Over those months, I learned that the Quran granted many rights equally to both men and women. Along with those rights, it required many duties.

Our responsibilities toward God are called *Haqooq Allah*. They are to believe in one God, pray five times a day, to fast during the month of Ramadan, and to perform Hajj in Mecca.

And likewise, we have as many responsibilities toward others, called *Haqooq ul Ibad*. As Muslims, we were to care for one's family, our neighbors, and those in our community—no one was to go hungry if we could help them. In all our dealings with others—our relationships, our business, our marriage, and at the time of a divorce—we are to always practice respect and honesty and seek guidance from the Quran.

When I read this, it impressed me that religion was not about the words we speak, but the duties we kept, and it had a solution to every problem if we had a strong faith in God. The *tafseers* opened the doors to a whole new world to my young mind. I stood in awe of our simple and beautiful religion. Most of the time religious personalities presented Islam as so difficult to learn and practice that it produced fear in people. But after reading the *tafseers*, I did not fear Islam. I loved it.

Education for both girls and boys is the first rule of Islam. The first message from God to Prophet Mohammad by Gabriel was "Read." This has been interpreted to demonstrate how essential education is, and so children were to be educated equally.

Additionally, as stated in the Quran killing is *haram*—forbidden. Killing even one innocent person means killing all humanity. Rape and extramarital relations are also *haram* according to our religion. So I was surprised to learn as an adolescent that infidelity and rape were common occurrences. I read about them in the newspaper and media reports. It seemed to my child's mind that these crimes were continually increasing.

The Quran also taught something important about forgiveness: it is required to ask forgiveness. Before one's death, to be accepted into heaven, a person has to ask forgiveness from the people they had harmed. If someone dies without asking for forgiveness, Allah will not forgive them after death. This made me think of all the killing that went on in the name of God, both in my own country and abroad.

After my study of the Quran, I became convinced, even at my young age, that most Muslims only knew about their duties toward God and did not practice their responsibilities toward others. All the killing and hurting people in the name of Allah is not from the Quran.

I was always surprised to see those who were considered good Muslims because they kept a beard and attended the mosque in their *shalwar kameez* to show off their devotion to prayer in the *Masjids* (mosques). Their thoughts, tongue, mind, eyes, and everything else were corrupt. They were dishonest, unkind to orphans, cruel to their wives and children, greedy for materialistic things, and power hungry. What kind of Muslims were they?

I often spoke to Father about what I learned. He was impressed with my knowledge of the Quran, and he frequently asked me questions about Islam and the meaning of the Quran. I was always glad to "teach" him, but I felt he knew it already.

One day, I was sitting on the stairs outside of the main gate of our house with my little sister. I must have been about nine, and my sister four. A businessman who owned a printing shop across the street from our house, stopped to speak to me. I recognized him immediately as the owner of the shop, who came to our neighborhood occasionally in his big expensive car to manage his printing press. He was much older than my father, fat and ugly, but well dressed.

He stopped his big shiny car at the corner of the street. After he finished his business in his shop, he approached me.

"I would like to take you for a ride." He flashed his expensive watch full of diamonds as if he could entice me to ride with him because of his fancy jewelry. *What a show-off*, I remember thinking.

"Come here; I want to give you this Rolex watch with diamonds if you go with me for a ride."

I stayed seated on the steps with my sister. "Uncle, I don't like watches. My father always takes me in his car to see movies at the Capri Cinema and to the Perl Continental Hotel for brunch. I don't need to go anywhere with you."

He kept insisting, so I stood to go inside. "Let me ask my father."

He suddenly had a confused look on his face, and quickly rushed toward his car. Inside the house, I told my father what the man had said to me. Father strode outside a stormy look in his eyes. The man had already started his car. Before he could pull away, Father stuck his hand in the car window and held the steering wheel to stop him from leaving.

"What are you saying to my daughter?"

"I just wanted to take her—"

Father cut him off. Speaking firmly but calmly, he said. "I don't want to see you again in this neighborhood—ever."

The next day that man moved his printing press out of our neighborhood, and we never saw him again.

CHAPTER 2
Magic Spells

Mother's admonitions were constant. She wanted me to stay to myself, never to allow myself to become too close to any friend, except for my siblings. Left to myself much of the time, I dwelled in a world of imagination from detective stories, historical novels, *Reader's Digest*, the Quran, and just about any other book I could get my hands on, even if I did not understand its content. All of these ideas and characters and stories ran through my thoughts, giving me a strong sense, if an utterly romantic one, of how my world should operate. All this reading and intellectual discovery imbued me with the courage think on my own, to speak on my own, and to be my own person.

I dressed like my own person, too. Mother always stitched beautiful frocks for me. I did not like the standard prints because they were too familiar. I enjoyed different patterns, rather than the typical ones worn by most girls. I preferred geometrical prints, stripes, and checks in vibrant, but not outlandish, shades. Mother perused the foreign fashion magazines and sewed frocks that were trendy in the West. I kept my hair short with bangs that covered my forehead. In general, I enjoyed standing out and being different by wearing modern clothes.

I remember one day, I was eight years old, when an elderly man, whom we called Mama (mother's brother), who usually walked my siblings and me to school, was too sick to help us. He had lost both hands during the fighting when Pakistan was partitioned from India, and so his primary job each day was to escort the neighborhood children to school. Because he could not walk us to school that day, I set off on my own. I passed Sind Muslim Law College, where father had studied law, when a car slowed down beside me as I walked. Several of my friends were in the car, and one of the girl's fathers drove. He asked me to get in, and said he would drive me to school.

I knew all the girls in the car, but still, I did not want to join them. I could make my own way to school. I did not need a ride. I thanked the man and told him I would rather walk.

"Thank you, Uncle, but this is the way I walk to school every day."

He continued to drive very slowly beside me on the road. Again, he asked me to get into the car. I thanked him and kept walking. The girls leered at me, smug looks on their faces, but I refused to be part of their drama. He followed along for another few blocks and then sped on his way.

A few evenings later, I overheard Father telling Mother how a father of one of my school friends had approached him at the mosque. He had related the incident on the way to school to Father and said. "Ch. Sahib, your daughter has a strong ego. She would not get in the car."

Father responded, "No. It is self-respect."

Father's voice was filled with pride as he related the story to Mother. "She is like me," Father said in front of me. "Yes, and like me," Mother added and hugged me.

When I was twelve, Sharif, my father's cousin, visited us from my father's village. He was roughly dressed, ordinary-looking, and almost eighteen years older than me. Because of my parents' reputation for hospitality, we often entertained relatives from Punjab. Sharif visited us regularly during that year, and paid particular attention to me. One day my mother told me that Sharif had asked my parents to marry me. From my expression, she knew I did not like his proposal. She told me not to worry. Father already turned him down. My father had told him that I planned to become a doctor and would not marry for many years. Besides, he was not a compatible match for me in any aspect.

Sharif was furious, my Mother told me. He was very upset when Father told him to leave.

Days later, I learned from Father that Sharif had stormed over to my Uncle Hamid's house, and begged him to convince Father. Uncle told him again about my desire to become a doctor. Sharif would not stop his arguing, so Uncle removed his shoe and began beating Sharif over the back and head.

Uncle told Sharif, "If Brother Mahmood has refused you, how dare you come to me?" It is a great insult to be slapped with another man's shoe.

I did not think much of Sharif after that, since I was secure in Father's protection. Only later did I learn that sometimes women are forced to marry, even if they don't want to. Father would never allow that of me. But some men, if they do not get their way, will lash out in anger to obtain by force, by conspiracy, or by magic, what they cannot attain by asking. It is regrettable that many women's lives are ruined this way.

Later, Sharif sent me a message through relatives that he would make great effort to force me to live alone. Since his proposal had been rejected, no one would be allowed to marry me—ever. As shocking as this attitude was to bear, I realized much later that it is very hard on some men's egos to experience rejection, so they must find a way to strike back.

I thought nothing of his threats. In those days, I had so much to look forward to, and marrying an unsuitable man was something Father would never allow. Above all, I wanted a marriage like Mother and Father had, one arranged, but not forced; one bound together in love, where two walk side by side, supporting each other's strengths and passions. That, I thought as a child, would be the greatest happiness.

As much as I loved reading, I also had a passion for drawing and painting. I constantly drew sketches of anyone who happened to be in sight. I saw myself as an artist. Father did not encourage that ambition; he never allowed me to study painting or to take up any other hobby that took away from my schoolwork. He wanted me to focus on my grades so I could get into medical school. But that never diminished my desire to paint, and when I reached high school, I talked Mother into interceding for me. After many requests, Father finally allowed me to join the Arts Council, a local college that offered a variety of art classes. But I could only attend after I had completed my intermediate college examinations.

The Arts Council was only a fifteen-minute walk from our house. I did not enroll as a full-time student, but just took casual evening classes. I was very excited sitting in my first class, waiting for the teacher, Miss Zonera, to arrive, when a good-looking young man about my age came to me and introduced himself.

His name was Furqan. As he talked, it became apparent to me that he was a man of little ambition. His late father had been wealthy, and with that cushion, he did not seem to take anything seriously, even these art classes. He attended them to pass the time, and because he believed he would find a girlfriend. I tried to be pleasant with him, but I made it clear I had no interest in him.

I attended classes for two months, and he continuously tried to get my attention. One time he said he was only trying to protect me from other students. I told him to stop wasting his time; the other students were all very decent.

After a while, he got the message and left me alone—at least in person. He began sending *Tavezes* to me at home by post. These are magic spells written out on square pieces of paper. Superstitious people in Pakistan use them because they believe magic will get them what they could not otherwise obtain. Mainly they are used as love potions. The sayings written on the cards are supposed to make a person love. To me, using *Tavez* was a distinct act of desperation on Furqan's part. What he could not purchase with his father's money and what he lacked in personality and character, he thought he could make up for through using magic. He honestly thought paying someone to perform these magic spells would make me love him. I could not imagine a person wasting their time on such nonsense. Not all the magic in the world would ever convince me to like him, much less love him.

I thought this was the most stupid behavior imaginable.

Before the end of our classes, he asked me again if my feelings toward him had changed after receiving his letters. I felt sad for him. I told him, "Look, God does not want us to use magic. It is forbidden in Islam; you know that. You can never force someone to love you. I don't love you, and I will never love you, even if you were born seven times." I encouraged him to use his time and energy to do something useful, to get an education, and to try to help people.

I didn't see him again for a long time, and I learned that he had applied and was admitted to a Homeopathic College, and started calling himself Dr. Furqan.

The next month, the results of my Higher Secondary School exams were out, and I learned that I was admitted to the Sindh Medical College in Karachi. A few years before I was accepted in Karachi, a new all-girls medical college had been opened in Nawab Shah. It was founded by Mr. G. Mustafa Jatoi, who was an influential and popular leader of Pakistan People's Party. Therefore, it was an important school. I was one of the twenty-one students who were transferred from Karachi to Nawab Shah Medical College, and twenty-one Sindhi students were transferred from Nawab Shah to Karachi.

Nawab Shah lay in the heart of Sindh province's agricultural districts and was an eight-hour train ride from cosmopolitan Karachi. My parents were hesitant to send me that far away on my own. I knew Mother feared something tragic would happen to me, and Father possibly thought I was too innocent to live independently. But I was determined to live with other girls my own age, who were focused on the same goal. So, when my parents told me they didn't want me to travel so far away from home, I began crying that they had to let me study and live in Nawab Shah. I had to convince them this would be good for me, so I told them if I had to stay in Karachi, I would also attend regular classes at the Arts Council. I did not see this as a threat or manipulating them. My artistic talents were beginning to blossom, and I was thinking about developing them to a professional level.

I told Father that the Principal of the Arts Council, Mr. Masood, had said that I should not go to medical college; instead, I should become a full-time student at the Arts Council. "There is an artist inside you," he said. "You were born an artist. You need some guidance and training."

This recognition delighted me. I was beginning to gain some mastery and enjoying it. With Mr. Masood's encouragement, I started thinking of myself as an artist.

I also told my parents for the first time about the journalist from *Mirror* magazine who wanted to publish my interview and photos of

my paintings to encourage me as an emerging artist. They were astonished to hear that.

Father especially did not like this. Yet he of all of the people in my
life understood my determination to reach a goal once I set my mind
to something. I believed I could have become an accomplished artist
if I applied myself. In the back of my mind, I knew that I could do
both—medicine and art.

After discussions with Mother, Father permitted me to move to
Nawab Shah. But he had one condition—I could not return home
to visit for six months. He did not want me traveling back and forth
because I was homesick. If I went out on my own, I had to stick it out
for the duration. In a way his condition was a vote of confidence—not
only could I leave, but I would be all right without them. I would
figure out my life as I went along, and in time, I could return home to
the people I loved.

I immediately agreed, and within the month, I was packed and
ready to travel away to college. While preparing to leave, I realized
that my crying was the first time I had ever shed tears in front of my
parents, especially Father.

I did not think of my tears as a form of manipulation, but as a
desperate expression of my most profound desires. I needed to be on
my own, out of their sheltered protection, in order to find myself. That
he listened and relented to my request pleased me. That I had parents
who were willing to help me realize my dreams, gave me a sense that I
possessed a beautiful life. I had every reason to expect a happy future,
and that with my parent's support and guidance, I would find lasting
love and happiness.

Even though Mother had spent her entire life worrying about me,
I felt ready to be on my own. If I needed help, Father would stand by
me. Surrounded by my loving siblings, my life ahead appeared secure
and bright. I thought God was my best friend; He so far had listened
to all my deepest desires.

In the days before my departure, my Uncle Hamid (the one who
had destroyed his shoe on Sharif's head) came to see me off. He sat me
down and began to speak earnestly, offering me some advice, which I
was glad to receive, since I respected and enjoyed my uncle's company.

"Baby," he said, "now that you are going to live in a different city independently, you will meet many boys. You have to be careful and—"

At this point, Mother, who was sitting with me, cut him off. "Hamid, my daughter is very intelligent. She does not have any interest in boys. She will only focus on her studies. We do not need to give her any advice about boys. We trust her."

Uncle looked frustrated, but he would never contradict Mother or Father. He said slowly to Mother, "Ridha Bhabi, Sharif says he will use magic to destroy your daughter."

Mother's face turned pale, and she started having difficulty breathing. I said confidently, "Magic has no power to harm me. Believe me, I read the Quran every day, so I know it will protect me from magic, Satan, and evil. I am not afraid of Sharif and his magic."

Mother relaxed after that.

The next day I boarded the train to Nawab Shah and rode away to begin my five years of medical study. I was very sad to leave the house. I would especially miss my youngest brother Rafhan, but at the same time I was very happy; I felt free and independent, on my way to becoming a doctor.

On the long train ride, the abbreviated conversation with Uncle Hamid came to mind. Before Mother cut him off so abruptly, he was going to give me some practical advice about boys. The fact that Mother thought I did not need practical advice struck me in a way I had never thought of, for as beautiful as my childhood had been, so full of cherished and loving moments, I had not been given much training in practical matters. To my embarrassment, I still had not ever taken a shower without Mother's strict supervision. I never understood her doting on me as a lack of trust in my abilities, but rather a manifestation of her fear that somehow water would destroy me if she did not carefully supervise me.

I knew many things from my studies and reading, but I had little experience with everyday life. Despite Mother's beliefs that I had no interest in boys, I was nineteen and needed to know certain things. What if I met someone and I wanted to open my heart to him? How would I know what to do and say?

As the train swished along, hurrying me toward my new home for the next five years, I could not help wondering what Uncle Hamid would have told me. Would his advice have prepared me for what I knew would happen inevitably? What girl my age did not want to meet a handsome, charming, intelligent man who would love and protect her? One who would appreciate her intelligence and ambitions? How would I know whom to trust without some guidance? Mother's advice simply to ignore the reality that boys existed, though impractical, was the only guidance I left home with.

At Nawab Shah, I quickly fell into a routine of classes, study, and various social activities with new friends and classmates. Living in the dormitories was very different from living at home, but I enjoyed every minute of it. I felt free of Mother's fears, and liberated from the men who were pestering me, such as Sharif and Furqan.

After a few months, I received a letter from my mother that my youngest brother, Rafhan, who was only two years old, missed me. He had contracted a fever that did not respond to medicine. She wanted me to come home to visit him. I took emergency leave and rushed home. As soon as I hugged him, his fever went away.

When I was leaving, I saw Furqan at the train station. I was distraught that he was still following me. Seeing me, he mistakenly believed that I had changed my mind about him. But I had not.

He told me that he loved me.

"This is not loving. Don't you understand? Mutual feeling is love," I said. He did not listen. He said he planned to use magic spells until I no longer wanted to live in Nawab Shah. He wanted me to move back to Karachi where he could see me easily. I was relieved when the train pulled away from the station that I lived far away from Karachi.

After that, I began to dream that I was set to travel somewhere, and I always arrived at the train station late, with my train just leaving the station. I hear the whistle and begin to run, but it is useless. The train moves swiftly and disappears into thin air. These dreams continued to plague me for years until they finally stopped when I completed my medical study.

I did not think there was any connection, but in real life, I did begin to miss trains, buses, and later, when I started traveling abroad, missing flights, which was unusual for me. I was normally so punctual. Something was wrong.

Student life opened me up to so many new experiences. I began playing table tennis and regular tennis. These new activities were fun and challenging, but I still wanted to learn more skills.

I joined the Girl Guide Training Association. The instructors taught us to shoot a rifle and to march. At the end of our training, the President of Pakistan, Zia-ul-Haq, visited to award us our certificates of completion for Girl Guide Training. One by one, we marched up to him. When I presented myself, he asked if I enjoyed living and studying in Nawab Shah, a small town compared to the bustling Karachi. I replied that I liked this college. He appeared surprised and said that he received many requests from students to transfer to Karachi. I said, if I returned to Karachi, I would focus more on becoming an artist, and Father would not like that.

He laughed, and asked, "You want to become an artist?"

"Yes, I do."

He was very friendly. He put his hand on my head during the conversation, the same way in our Punjabi culture that my uncles and grandparents did. It was a sign of affection. In a fatherly tone, he said, "You are a very sweet and intelligent girl. If you ever need help transferring to Karachi, contact me."

I smiled and nodded, and I moved on.

Later, when my classmates asked me what the president had spoken to me about, I explained about his offer to grant me a transfer. They were astonished that I wanted to stay in Nawab Shah and not return to Karachi. I was happy here. The distance from Karachi allowed me to focus on what I wanted most—becoming a doctor. In every way, I considered myself fortunate to have this opportunity. My school was also far away from certain men who continued to pester me.

In letters from home, my sister told me that Furqan had shown up in our neighborhood, talking to some of my friends. He wanted more information about me. He mainly wanted to know Mother's name. I was curious why he would want Mother's name. Later, I discovered that those who practice magic need specific information about the person they want to put a curse on or want to influence. To cast their spells, they need the name of a person's father and mother, date of birth, and often want clothes and other personal items. I did not believe in any of this, but it further convinced me of Furqan's ignorance. While I worked hard to make a future for myself, he wanted to use the forces of the supernatural to get his way.

One day a colleague handed me a letter outside of class. It was a love letter from one of my professors. This same professor began sending letters to my dormitory room quite regularly, until I did not know what to do. I expected more from my professors, a mentoring relationship, not a romantic one. This professor was a young man, who had just recently graduated and been appointed to teach. The whole situation seemed odd to me, and I no longer wanted to attend any of that professor's classes.

It got to be too much, and I finally complained to the dean of the college, Dr. Ahsan Karim. The dean asked me, "What do you want me to do? Should I fire him?" After thinking, I said, "Tell him we need to have a teacher-student relationship. And he needs to apologize." The next day, Dr. Karim called me into the office and informed me, the love-letter-writing professor, after listening to my complaint and request, had decided to quit. That uncomfortable episode was over.

CHAPTER 3
Becoming a Doctor

Several of my friends from Karachi found out that I had had a conversation with President Zia, and he had offered to help me transfer to Karachi if I asked. They pestered me until I agreed to help them. Twenty-one girls in total wanted to transfer. Even though I wanted to stay in Nawab Shah, I decided to help them. We planned to approach him the next time he came to Nawab Shah or Karachi, which was closer to us than Islamabad. We read in the newspapers that he planned to attend a ceremony marking the birth of Pakistan at the mausoleum of Mr. Mohammad Ali Jinnah, the founder of Pakistan, in Karachi.

All twenty-one of us took a train to Karachi and arrived at the mausoleum to look for him. When I spotted him striding across the grounds surrounded by a military guard, I approached him. He was by the grand marble staircase, which ascended a steep rise to the towering mausoleum, and gleamed in the sunshine. The twenty-one-cannon salute for Mr. Jinnah had already been completed, and now he strode to the tomb for the recitation of *Darood* and *Fatiha*.

I felt the urge to speak to him. His guards tried to stop me, but I avoided them and was able to get close enough to get his attention by calling to him loudly. A big soldier with a rifle blocked me, threatening to arrest me if I did not go away.

"President *Sahib*," I said again loudly.

The president turned to face me, a blank expression on his face.

"Do you recognize me? We met at the medical college several months ago for the Girl Guide Training."

He considered for a moment. "Yes, yes, I do remember you. Is there some trouble?" He motioned for the guards to release me and allowed me to approach him.

"Yes, sir. You said I could contact you when I wanted a transfer to Karachi."

"Yes, yes, I remember. But this is not the time or place to discuss those matters. You must come to Islamabad. There I will consider your request." With that, he turned from me and ascended the gleaming white stairs leading up to the mausoleum to attend the Fateha Prayers.

We all returned to Nawab Shah by train, disappointed, but still hopeful that he would grant the request of the girls who wanted to transfer. My friends were quite amazed at my courage, that I would approach President Zia despite the threats of his bodyguard. They wanted me to go to Islamabad and meet with him at his presidential palace. They were confident that if I showed up, he would grant all twenty-one of them their request to transfer.

I did not want to travel to Islamabad, and I did not need to transfer. I refused to go, but some of the other girls finally convinced me that I should take a group of four girls and travel to Islamabad. The girls collected money. With only enough for four of us, we took the train to Islamabad.

The older sister of one of the girls lived in Islamabad. She was a CSS officer. We stayed with her, and in the evening, three of her colleagues visited us. Two of them were Ashraf and Tahira, and the other looked exactly like my favorite movie star, Waheed Murad, who was known for his engaging personality and romantic roles.

This man was introduced to me as Mansoor Suhail, a CSS officer of the Ministry of Foreign Affairs. His appearance struck me because he also dressed like Waheed Murad, in a dark suit and tie, with a starched sky blue shirt. He had a real sparkle in his eyes and a surprisingly pleasant, high-pitched singing voice. When he began singing a popular romantic song, the girls gathered around him. His voice sounded sweet and soft, which made him pleasant to listen to.

As he sang, his eyes fell on me, searchlights seeking for something in me. Between his romantic words, his charming smile, and glancing looks, I began to feel a real attraction. This was something I had not felt for any other man before. Did he know that he stirred such feelings in me? Was he doing this on purpose?

With everyone talking and having fun, I felt suddenly speechless, as if anything I said might seem trite. I did not even know him, but it was apparent that he could charm a snake out of its skin.

After one song, he leaned toward me and asked. "How old are you?"

"I will turn twenty soon," I replied, wanting to sound older and worldlier than I was.

"When?"

Did he want to purchase a gift for my birthday? Was he trying to gauge whether I was old enough for romance? I was too tongue-tied to ask. "October 25," were the only words that came out of my mouth.

"Don't you talk?" He leaned back, flashing me an inviting smile.

I returned his smile, but I still could not speak.

He began singing again, and telling jokes, making everyone laugh. After a couple of hours, the singing was over, and we were all exhausted. My friend's older sister, who was our hostess, did not appear entirely happy with me. Later, my friends told me Mansoor and my friend's big sister were more than colleagues. Did she think Mansoor was interested in me? I did not know what to think of any of this. I hardly knew the man.

The next day four of us waited for hours at the gate of the presidential palace, but President Zia did not appear. That evening Mansoor and his group came again. Mansoor resumed singing his romantic and tender songs, and between the songs, he tried to engage me in more conversation. He spoke slowly and softly, gradually drawing me out. His attention sparked a genuine sense of attraction. This was so new to me. It was like nothing I had never felt before.

Was he flirting with me? Did he mean anything by all of this attention?

I could hardly sleep that night, all of Mansoor's words running through my mind, trying to figure out what all of his attention could mean.

Over the next four days, us girls waited by the gate until the president finally appeared. A long black limousine approached; I stepped up to the car, and his chauffeur slowed. President Zia rolled his window down and smiled at me. He was with his wife and his daughter, Zain Zia.

"You have made it here!" There was a real surprise in his voice as he instantly recognized me.

"Yes, sir. You requested that I come here so we can speak about the transfers."

I had in my hand the applications for all twenty-one students who wanted to transfer. I tried to hand them to him, but he would not take them. Instead, he glanced behind me to the girls who stood with me.

"I will transfer all four of you."

My heart began pounding. We had come this far. I had to plead my case. "Sir, there are twenty-one of us who want to transfer to Karachi. They collected money and sent us here to represent them. Can you please transfer all of us?"

Behind me, my friends were saying to me we should accept what he offered.

President Zia motioned with his hand for me to come close so he could speak to me. He stared directly into my eyes and spoke in a low voice with a big smile. He spoke so softly; I had lean down to hear him, to the point he was whispering in my ear. "I will give you two options. First, you can agree with me and all four of you transfer. Or, second, all four of you can go to jail. Those are your choices. Which will you have?"

I felt a cold chill down my spine. Maybe I had pushed him too hard. I had thought of him as fatherly, but now I sensed his cold side. I quickly turned toward my friends and related the president's choices. Their faces turned white with fear. None of them wanted to go to jail.

I turned back to him. "No, sir. We don't want to go to jail."

His mood lifted, "Good girl! Well then, go to Murree for a few days. Enjoy the sights of the beautiful resort, and then return home."

"Yes, sir. That is a good idea."

He smiled and disappeared behind a darkened window. The limousine rolled on, leaving us alone in stunned silence. All that night we fretted about what to do. I did not intend to transfer, but now I was in the middle of a big mess.

The next day we took a bus to Murree. We debated during the entire ride what to do—would he actually send us to jail? We arrived at the resort town, high in the mountains to the north of Islamabad in a deep quandary. We were still shaken from our brief meeting with the president. None of us knew for sure what would happen.

We had enough funds to stay two days. The next day we forgot the threat and enjoyed our stay. We had not taken any warm dresses with us, so we wrapped ourselves in bed sheets and went horseback riding. Mansoor and his friends did not go with us because they had to work. After a short holiday, we returned to college. The other students were disappointed, but they were satisfied that we refused to transfer because of them. What more could we do?

Besides the president's threat, I had other things on my mind. As soon as I arrived back at school, I received a very romantic greeting card from Mansoor. The photo on the front had a couple walking hand in hand. The caption read, "A beautiful era has started." I was surprised but happy. He had given me a lot of attention over the four evenings I listened to him singing and charming everyone. I still did not know how I should respond to him. Should I write to him? Would that be too forward?

Then on my birthday, October 25, I received a beautiful birthday card. He had been asking me questions for a purpose. He must be interested. Shortly after that, he began writing me love letters, telling me how much he wanted to get to know me. Then he started calling.

All of his attention overwhelmed me. He was a handsome, edu-cated, accomplished, and sophisticated man who knew how to sing and say romantic things. I suddenly could not focus on my studies. Then I had trouble eating, and I even stopped laughing. Everything seemed a bit surreal to me; I walked around campus in a daze. I was a little girl again, absorbed in a romantic story, but only this time it was my life, not the life of some fictional character. I was young and in love, and filled with crazy but beautiful thoughts.

One day I wrote him a letter—my first love letter. I did not know what to write, so I told him a story. It was long and more than a little melodramatic.

My two friends who were in Islamabad with me kept insisting that

Mansoor was actually in love with another friend's oldest sister. That made sense to me and would explain why she acted jealous at all of Mansoor's attention toward me. That also confused me. If he were in love with another woman, would he be writing me all of these letters, making these phone calls? I did not understand why he was pursuing another women and me at the same time. In my thinking, reputable men, men like my father, did not do such things.

One day I asked him about his feelings toward my friend's big sister. He replied that she was only a friend and colleague. We often talked over the phone, but he never once mentioned a future together. But he continued to speak romantically to me.

I may not have known much about men, but I knew what I thought about marriage: that I would only marry a man who I loved who loved me and me alone. I was not interested in a romantic adventure that would lead only to heartbreak.

On a break from college, I returned to Karachi thoroughly confused about what to do with how I was feeling. At home, Mother was worried to see me so thin and weak. I had lost some weight, which shocked her. I did not tell her about Mansoor out of fear it would heighten her worry over me. Instead, I visited my eldest cousin, Farida Baji, a student at Karachi University. She was older and more experienced. She listened to my entire story about Mansoor—how we met, how he looked like the famous movie star, Waheed Murad, his singing and sweet words to me, his letters and phone calls. She then read all his letters and cards.

Finally, she said, "There is not one word here about a future together. I don't think he's serious." She thought he was just flirting with me. She advised me to forget him, to tell him not to call me any longer. "You are just infatuated with a man who reminds you of a movie star. Consider this," she went on, "he is seven years older than you. He is very sharp and experienced. He is not sincere with you. What if he had a drinking problem too? You never know. I think he sees that you are innocent and can be easily swayed."

Why would he do that? That is what I did not understand. All during my visit home, I wanted to stop hearing his voice, his sweet words, and musing on his charming memories. But his words and songs played in my mind like a recording. He had stirred something deep in me. Farida Baji thought I was only infatuated, in love with an idea, not a person.

Was that all I was feeling—infatuation?

Then I had to consider my friend's sister. She had been so gracious to us, allowing us to stay in her home in Islamabad. I had no desire to hurt her. If they were in love, and planning to marry, then I had to put a stop to his calls and letters. I did wonder though why he would be contacting me with such loving letters and calls if he loved another woman. Did he have any intention at all of proposing marriage to me? Or was I just too innocent to understand this man's true intentions, whatever they were?

I sat down and wrote him a letter. I explained that I did not want to receive cards, letters, or phone calls from him any longer. As hard as it was to write that letter, it was even harder to forget him. It took me a year to get him completely out of my thoughts.

The next year, I heard through a friend that Mansoor had married his longtime fiancée, Lubna, and moved to New York. So he had been toying with two other women while engaged to another. What a big flirt. I was very surprised but glad I had cut off communicating with him.

At my graduation convocation, I was honored by President Zia-ul-Haq, who presented me with a silver medal for academic excellence. President Haq had traveled to Nawab Shah for the convocation ceremony at the college. The national TV broadcast the ceremony live. I felt so proud to be among so many accomplished students and to be honored before my parents with this beautiful medal.

Afterward, I mingled with my peers to say our farewells. We would all soon disburse across the country to various residencies. I packed for home. Some of the Karachi students hired a *tanga* (horse-drawn carriage) to enjoy for our final ride to the station. I was excited to return to our sweet city of Karachi. On the railroad platform, men from the nearby engineering college waited for their girlfriends from the medical college.

One of the male students had made a habit of waiting for me on the platform whenever I would return to visit home. He would then carry my luggage from the *tanga* to the train. That day, for the last time, he moved my bags onto the train and set it in the racks above my seat. He then sat in the same compartment right across from me. Though this routine had been going on for a year or more, we never spoke. He never introduced himself, and so I did not think it my place to be forward and offer my name.

He knew we were all leaving for good, and several of his friends had approached me on the platform to tell me he had waited for many hours to see me, so I should talk to him. He was shy around girls, and my silence was out of confusion. I was used to men talking to me, not me talking to men, so I did not have a clear idea of how to open a conversation. For the next eight hours, we sat across from each other in total silence, an excruciating experience. I struggled to think how to begin a conversation with a stranger. Also, Mother's admonition that I should stay to myself and not get too close to strangers was foremost in my mind. Some of my thoughts also went to Mansoor, who was wise in the way of a woman's heart, though he had used that knowledge cruelly to enflame my infatuation. This young engineer in comparison was an unformed man, a mere boy who could not even open his mouth to ask me one question. So I felt cautious. If he did not know what he was doing, I did not want to get in another situation like the one I had with Mansoor, opening myself up to a stranger with smooth words.

But if this boy had any smooth words, he was not using them on me. Thinking back, we could have talked about anything—the weather, our plans for the future, becoming a doctor, an engineer, movies, religion, politics—any question from him would have opened the floodgates of our untapped curiosity about each other. Instead, we sat in silence.

Eight hours later, he helped me unload my luggage at the Karachi train station and into a taxi. He then sat in the front seat and directed the driver to my home. On the way there, I wondered what would become of him. Would his shyness cut him off from any chance of happiness? I certainly did not feel that way about my life. My life dripped with happiness. I dwelled on the cusp of great adventures; I felt it in my bones.

After we arrived, he helped me unload my luggage. He looked at me one more time. We watched each other for a few minutes, neither of us speaking. He then turned and got into the cab. As he drove away, I realized if I wanted to look him up later to track his success, it would be impossible. I did not even know his name.

At the door, my youngest brother, Rafhan, saw me with luggage, and he ran to inform my mother. She came and hugged me. "Rafhan told me that a guest arrived our home. It looks like she has a plan to stay with us for long. She has several suitcases with her." We both laughed. I had been away so long my brother had forgotten what I looked like. But now I was home, and ready for the next step on my way to a happy life.

That evening, Father arrived home from his office. He greeted me warmly, with open arms and a proud smile. "My daughter, the doctor. Welcome home."

Things had changed in the time that I'd been away. Two of my younger brothers, Rahat and Rasikh, were away, studying at the Cadet College Petaro.

My sister, Pinky, was especially happy upon my return. She was a student at D.J. Science College, and still lived at home. One day soon after my return, we decided to go shopping. She wanted to meet a friend downtown, so we went to Zaibunnisa Street in Saddar Town, which is a very exclusive area. Many of the buildings are from colonial times and are elaborate in their construction and ornate in their decorations. The buildings are filled with clothing and shoe stores, jewelry shops, bookstores, restaurants, and other merchants, all with the finest merchandise.

After we strolled through some of the clothing stores, my sister wanted to visit another friend, who worked as a secretary for a businessman. She met us in the lobby outside her boss's office. While my sister, Pinky, and her friend talked, three men stepped out of an office and walked toward the door for elevator. One of them stopped in the hallway and stared at me. He was heavyset and well dressed, in a handsome suit and white shirt and tie, and neatly groomed. I began to grow uncomfortable with the man's gaze on me.

Was there something wrong? Were we in the wrong place? I caught my sister's friend's eye, and she noticed the man in the lobby.

"Oh, let me introduce you," she said to us. "This is my boss, Zia Ullah Khan. This is my friend's sister, Dr. Raana. She has just completed medical college."

He looked rather excited and replied, "Don't let her go," before he went back to say farewell to his guests. He shook hands with his guests, sent them off, and then ducked back into his office. In a few minutes, workers began entering his room with big packages and then leaving empty-handed. Then he called on the intercom to his secretary to send me into his office.

I was reluctant at first, remembering my mother's fears. Inside his spacious office, he had jewelry displayed in open boxes, a few dresses laid out on a chair and hung on hangers.

"This is for you," he said, spreading his hands over his wares.

I had just turned twenty-four, and this man must have been in his late forties, maybe his early fifties. At any rate, he was far from my age. Why would he want to give me these gifts, which were probably worth many thousands of rupees? What was he trying to prove?

"Why are you giving me these?" I asked, wanting to hear his reasons.

"Please," he said a gracious smile on his face. "Take what you want." When I hesitated, he said, "You can take everything. Whatever you like, take it."

I sat down in a chair across from him, trying to understand his generous gesture. It was a bit overwhelming, but I still did not know why he would be making me this offer after I had only met him a few moments ago.

"You are very kind," I said, "but my mother has always taught me to dress simply. I do not wear much jewelry. These clothes of yours are very expensive and fancy, but not my style." I normally wore cotton dresses, and the ones he offered were made of expensive silk. On that day, I wore a bottle green dress from a designer called Peter Pan.

"You look very nice in your dress. Give me fifteen minutes, and I will have the dresses you like to wear." He spread his hands toward the jewelry. "Take what you want."

I asked him what he meant by his generosity.

"I would like to hire you as my secretary," he said, unashamed at his request.

I said very calmly, "Fauzia told you I am a doctor."

He immediately offered a handsome salary of one lakh rupees a month and a car. (One lakh was more than USD $3,000). This amount was beyond what I could ever make as a resident physician every month. My first salary as a resident was about USD $14 a month. As considerable a sum he offered me was, it held no attraction to me.

"Zia Sahib, I have worked hard to become a medical doctor. I'm starting my residency soon, and then I will practice on my own." I wanted to say, *how could you think I would give up my dream for all this?* Money had never been a consideration in my becoming a doctor. I wanted to serve humanity. I did not even feel a need to explain myself any further to this man. Without even knowing me, he wanted to purchase me, as if I were another piece of fine jewelry for him to collect.

I needed to leave, and rose from my seat.

"Why are you leaving?"

"I must go. I am going to start my residency soon."

"How much will you get from your residency each month?"

"It will be a nominal amount, sir."

He came around his desk and stood beside me, a look of genuine shock on his face that I had turned down all his expensive gifts and a lucrative job offer.

"So many girls would have sold out for only a bottle of perfume, but you won't take even one thing from me. Why you are showing me this attitude?"

"Go and buy those girls; don't waste your time with me." I turned from him in disgust and moved toward the door.

"Please, don't go. I have something to ask you."

I hesitated.

"I want to marry you. Will you be my wife?"

"Sir, you are a very mature man, surely you already have a wife."

He paused. "I will divorce her."

I smirked at him, trying to hide my revulsion.

"I had already planned to divorce her, but I couldn't find a beautiful and educated girl like you."

"Thank you, but I am not interested."

"Take some of the jewelry to your mother. Maybe she will convince you to accept my offer."

I started laughing, remembering that incident from my childhood. "Mr. Zia, I learned everything from my parents. I know she will also refuse to take your expensive gifts."

What is there to think about? You are a married man! I wanted to shout at him. I would never marry a man like him. In my mind, only an educated and loving person, who would be faithful for my entire life, would interest me. If he would divorce his current wife for me after a chance meeting, what would he do to me once he found another young and attractive woman?

I practically ran to the door. I stood in the lobby, seething at this man's impudence. He followed as I hurried down the hall. Marriage meant little to a man like him. If he saw a woman he wanted, he could buy her and dump his current one in an impulsive moment. What disturbed me most was that he could so easily betray his wife. And then for him to think he could induce me to give up my dream of being a physician, for just some pretty clothes and expensive jewelry, was even more disturbing.

Was everything in my country for sale so cheaply?

Once I settled back in at home, my focus was to search and apply for residencies. I was very excited to receive an interview appointment for a residency from the local Singh government. MQM leader Dr. Farooq Sattar conducted the interview himself, and after asking me many questions, he said, "I would definitely offer you the residency if you are Muhajir. I must admit you are a brilliant doctor."

"No sir, I am not Muhajir. I am Punjabi."

"Then I am sorry. This position is only for Muhajir."

Punjab is a large province of Pakistan with major cities such as Lahore, Faisalabad, and Islamabad, and most people who live there speak Punjabi. My parents moved from Faisalabad to Karachi, which is a cosmopolitan city of Sindh province. While the majority of the population in the area are Sindh, many Muhajir live there too, having emigrated from India after the partition. The Muhajir speak Urdu. Since the Muhajir were a minority with no political power, they were excluded from jobs and government positions. In the early 1980s, Altaf Hussain founded the political party MQM to advocate for the rights of the Muhajir people. Later, the MQM turned to terrorist tactics to implement their agenda. Altaf Hussain fled to London, but he continued as the leader from his party from abroad, becoming a symbol of terror and power.

I was very disappointed with this injustice. But as I arrived home, Father handed me an acceptance letter for a paid residency through the Karachi Metropolitan system.

"I have to start my residency at Abbasi Shaheed Hospital in a month," I said, reading from the letter. I could hardly contain my excitement at beginning my residency. It was the beginning of a new era of my life.

CHAPTER 4

Reluctant Wife

I stood alone at the bus stop near the Abbasi Shaheed Hospital, waiting for a bus to take me home. It was my first time in the North Nazimabad area of Karachi, and I could hardly contain my excitement. I was beginning my pediatric residency at Abbasi Shaheed Hospital. The day before I was to begin, I rode a bus to the hospital to meet the staff, and to view the wards I would work on.

By late afternoon, I had toured all the wards and met the staff, so I left to return home. I had returned to the same bus stop I had used earlier in the day. A crowd had gathered. Since I was new to the area, I just figured the buses were late. An hour passed, and I began to worry how I would get home.

Suddenly, a white car pulled up, and the man inside waved at me. I did not know anyone with a white car, so I ignored him. Finally, he pulled over to the curb, got out, and approached me. He was medium height and build, and dressed in an immaculate white *salwar kameez*. His olive complexion, thick mustache, and dark, expressive big eyes were very inviting. He smoked a pipe that he held in one hand, and smelled of expensive perfume. He was handsome.

"What are you doing here in the late evening?" he asked, in his heavy voice. "Waiting for the bus? There are no buses, rickshaw, or taxis." He motioned toward the crowd.

"Why?"

"The transport companies called a sudden strike a few hours ago to protest against MQM workers who have burned some of their buses and taxies."

It was true that people were milling, waiting. Some were beginning to leave. Buses, which usually came frequently, were nowhere in sight.

"Thank you. I will get a taxi."

"Nothing is working at this time. And taxis are not safe for you. Sometimes the drivers take women passengers to their own homes."

I shook my head confidently. "No one would do that to me. I am too brave to let that happen."

He only smiled. I surveyed the streets, and he was correct. There were no taxis, buses, or even the ubiquitous rickshaws.

"You must let me help you." His smile was warm and ingratiating. "I can drop you anywhere you'd like. I realize you are a courageous person, but it's not good for you to stand here too long." He motioned toward his car with his long slender fingers.

I told him I did not want to get into a strange man's car.

"I am not a stranger. My name is Erfun."

I glanced up and down the street again. He stood there smiling at me, wanting to help. Did I dare trust a stranger like this? He moved slowly toward his car.

"Please, let me drop you." He opened the passenger door. His white car appeared clean and new, and he was so convincing. "Where do you live?"

I told him. He said that was not far. He would be glad to drop me. He was right. I could not stand on the street and wait until it was dark. What would I do then with no taxis or buses? He looked trustworthy.

"Remember! I am fearless, so don't ever think—"

He cut me off with a laugh. "Yes, I know, don't worry."

I gathered myself and stepped into his car. He closed the door. His car smelled of sweet tobacco and flowery perfume."

"Is it Azzaro?"

"Yes, how did you know?"

"It's my brother Rahat's favorite."

"And what does Rahat do?"

"He will be going to the Royal Naval College in the UK very soon," I said proudly.

"That's impressive."

He began to drive, a broad smile on his face as if he had indeed lucked out at something great. He was a young entrepreneur, he told me, with several businesses in the old area of Karachi and the countryside.

"What class are you in?"

"I just finished my studies."

"So you are like me," he said jovially.

"Like you? In what way?"

"I'm not interested in studies, so I dropped out of school."

"I didn't mean that. I am a doctor."

He turned and stared for a moment, then pulled the car to the side of the road and stared some more. "A doctor."

"Tomorrow I begin working at Abbasi Shaheed Hospital to complete my residency in pediatrics."

"I can't believe it. You are so young and innocent. I thought you were a school girl."

I laughed.

"How old are you?"

"This October, I will turn twenty-four."

"I will be twenty-four this December."

Now I was surprised. "You look much older."

"How is this? I look older than my age, and you look younger than your age." We both laughed, and soon we were talking back and forth as if we had known each other for a long time.

I surprised myself, as I found that I enjoyed talking with Erfun. During that conversation, Mother's admonitions to not trust strangers went out the window. He wanted to know all about my new job. He was very excited that I was a medical doctor. I did not think about it then, but later I realized that this was the very first time I had felt comfortable talking with a man about my private life, my goals, my career, and such.

That day, I had worn a simple beige cotton dress and high heels. He looked me over, "Your dress is very elegant and fashionable. Do you always dress like that?"

"Of course."

"The color suits you. Is this your favorite color?"

"No, red is my favorite."

"This is my favorite color," he said, pointing to my dress. "Your hair is still long and black." It had not faded through all of my hard studies. "You like your hair down?"

"I always wear it down like this. I like to be simple like my mother." Also, I can't use hairpins or clips; they all fall out my hair is too straight.

He wanted to know all about me, my personal and professional life. Which department in the hospital I would be working in. What I would be doing. What I enjoyed doing on my days off.

"There is no ring on your finger? So, you're not engaged?"

"Nope," I said.

"What about your boyfriend?"

I shook my head.

Now he seemed genuinely surprised that I did not have a boyfriend.

"What are your plans after your residency?"

I had big plans. I wanted to travel to the United States to complete some postdoctoral study in my specialty. My uncles had always told me that the best way to become a top physician was to learn the latest techniques and medical theories from the best teachers. I did not think it strange at all that I would want to travel and learn. I told him I preferred to study in New York because the United Nations is there. When I detailed my plans, he seemed surprised again by my ambitions.

As Erfun dropped me at my house, I had to admit, he was handsome, well dressed, and appeared to take care of himself. He was polite and respectful, two qualities that were very important to me. But he was not educated. Even then, I came away with a good impression of him. I left his car with a fresh glow of enjoyment. I had never talked so freely with a stranger before, and it felt refreshing to be open and engaging. I did not think the conversation would lead to anything more, but I did enjoy it.

I had only been working in the pediatric ward a few days when one of the nurses came to me and said a man was here to see me. Who could that be? Only my parents and family knew I was here.

In the hospital lobby, I found Erfun with a wide grin, holding a basket. He handed it to me. "Food for you." He had packed a lunch of roasted chicken, fruit, and some bottled water.

"Why have you come here?" I asked. "I haven't stopped thinking about you, but you shouldn't come here to the ward."

"My house is very close. I thought maybe you didn't get a chance to have lunch, so I brought this to you."

"That is very nice of you." I hesitated to take it from his hand. His attention flattered me, but I did not know this man. But I could not stand in the lobby forever arguing with myself in front of him. However, caution won out. "I'm sorry, but I can't take it. Besides, I have just eaten. But thank you anyway."

Erfun was not a man who was easily dissuaded, "Please, Raana, take the food. If you do not take it, then I will leave it for the nurses."

His determination was attractive. He had a natural way about him, as if life was not difficult for him. He was used to getting what he wanted. His handsome features, nice clothes, expensive perfume, and warm dark eyes were hard to turn away from. But I had plans to travel to the United States to continue learning in my field, and I knew Pakistani men. I knew what they expected of their wives.

"I must return to work, but if you want to leave it for the nurses, I'm sure they will be very pleased." I thanked him for his kindness and returned to my ward.

Later the nurses were all in a twitter, talking about the handsome man who left such lovely food for them. Every day that week, he appeared around noon and left delicious food. On one day, I ate one of his sandwiches. After a week of making daily lunch trips, Erfun began telling the nursing staff that he was my fiancé.

I did not think this man would give up easily, but this was beyond reasonable. He was not my fiancé. I had had nothing more than a few conversations with him. His daily visits, along with telling the nurses that he was my fiancé, went on for about a month. Soon the doctors and nurses began to wonder why I seemed to be avoiding him since he was my fiancé. I told them that the man imagined things: he was not my fiancé.

I was surprised that he had found a way to enter the wards after visiting hours. Later I discovered he was distributing gifts and money to the gatekeepers and staff.

Erfun refused to be ignored. He chased me everywhere I went. We talked on several occasions. Once he asked me why I ignored him if I didn't have any friends. I asked him how he knew I did not have any friends.

"I have thoroughly investigated you. Many of the doctors are after you, but you do not have any interest in them. I know that for sure."

"That doesn't mean I will start liking you, or that we will become friends."

Nothing I said dissuaded him. He continued to bring food and treats to the hospital.

One day, he finally declared his intentions. "I want to marry you."

Again, I told him of my plans to travel to the United States. After that, I did not have any idea where my medical training would take me. The last thing I wanted to do was to be pushed by marriage into an unfulfilling life.

I always imagined that I would have a marriage like my parents, one of equals. They supported each other in ways that spoke of love and acceptance and equality. Even though Mother didn't finish her education in order to marry Father, after they were married, he supported her so she could complete college, and then earn her master's degree. And when Father wanted to open a new practice, Mother sold her wedding jewels to finance his ambition. My entire life, I had observed that they walked side by side, respectful, loving, and kind to one another. That's what I wanted.

Every time I saw Erfun, he told me how much he loved me. I repeatedly asked him not to come to the hospital, that he was causing a scene by saying he was my fiancé. I tried to dissuade him from visiting anymore by warning him that Professor Dr. Akbani did not like his presence in the ward. But he just ignored what I said.

He then once again reiterated that he wanted to marry me. I asked how he could enter into marriage so quickly. He replied, "Money."

That reply bothered me, but after a while, I learned that he meant that he had the resources to pursue me until I relented. I had to put a stop to his pestering me, and it was evident that he would never accept a no from me. Finally, I said if he was serious about marriage that he would have to speak to my father. I knew my father would never agree to our marriage because we were from different castes. Erfun had little education, nothing beyond secondary school. I had my medical degree, and soon I would be on my way to performing postdoctoral work. I knew Father would not be pleased with Erfun's proposal. If I could not dissuade him, then Father could. Father was the most persuasive man I knew.

When Erfun visited my home, Father turned him down. Father told me that Erfun fell on his knees and begged, but Father stood his ground. Later when we talked, Father asked me if I knew that Erfun was a Muhajir. I said, yes, I knew. He must have said that to remind me that our family was Punjabi, and it was the tradition in most Pakistani families to marry spouses from the same caste. But that wasn't the reason I had rejected Erfun.

After his conversation with Father, Erfun came to me one day after I left work. I could tell that he was upset. He waited for me on the sidewalk by the bus stop where I had first met him. He was dressed in black jeans and a blood red T-shirt; he looked athletic and handsome. But his eyes were troubled and brooding, as if he were contemplating dark things. It was evident he was not used to being denied what he most wanted.

"You know I love you and want to marry you. But your father rejected me."

"Yes, I know what he told you."

His eyes grew darker; then his face turned up, a proud grin on his mouth. "If you don't marry me, I have friends in the MQM who will kidnap you."

Formed as a backlash against the ethnic exclusion of the Muhajir from Pakistani government and society, the MQM (a political party) had many followers who had turned violent, running roughshod over entire neighborhoods in Karachi—beating, stealing, extorting, and even kidnapping the innocent and their enemies indiscriminately. They aimed to have a greater say in the government. Instead, the MQM had become a gang of thugs who used brutal tactics to intimidate their adversaries. Many people considered them terrorists.

I was shocked that a man would use MQM intimidation tactics against me. How could I love such a man? Whether he would do such a thing or not, I did not know. What he wanted was for me to fear him. That I would not do.

"I don't care," I said. "No one can kidnap me."

"If not you, then they will kidnap your sister. You should be afraid of what they would do to her if you don't marry me."

Somewhere between shock and disbelief, I caught my breath. The MQM were the epitome of evil, raging in the streets like criminals. How could I submit to this blackmail, this betrayal? I was so angry. I had to be careful with this man. I had to stand up to him.

"So this is how you show you care?" I stared into his big dark eyes, a look of displeasure on my face. "You are a bad person. I would never marry you."

He must not have been used to such strong words. His haughtiness turned instantly sheepish. A mortified look washed over him, and he turned from me, striding quickly away. I did not see him again for a few days, when unexpectedly, he called me one evening. He sounded apologetic and wanted to know if I would have time to meet someone, a friend of his.

"Why should I meet one of your friends?"

"His name is Haider Maududi."

Erfun tried to explain, but I knew the man's name instantly. He is the son of the late Moulana Maududi, a renowned philosopher and imam. Erfun's contrition sounded sincere. He knew he could not intimidate me. I wanted to push him away, but in the same breath, I wanted to meet the son of that person I admired most.

"How do you know him?" I asked.

"He is my longtime friend and is visiting here with his family from Lahore for private flying lessons. He will convince you to marry me."

"I consider you a nice man, one I could be friends with. But I am not thinking about marriage." I had a deep fear that my dreams would somehow become derailed by marrying Erfun.

Later that week, I met with Mr. Haider Maududi and his wife. I explained to him how I had read all of his father's books as a child. We spent some time speaking together during an enjoyable afternoon. I was impressed that Erfun knew the son of the famous Maududi. If he knew Haider Maududi, then that must mean that Erfun had a good circle of friends. Maybe I could trust him to be a good man.

The rest of the afternoon, Erfun continued to apologize for threatening me. During the day, Haider Maududi took me aside and told me that he could see from talking to me that I was educated and religious. He also knew Erfun wanted to marry me, but that I had doubts about him. He said I should not let Erfun's lack of education dissuade me. That if we did marry, I would be good for Erfun. I would help him to settle down and become a good man. I did not think too much of Haider Maududi's statement then; I had never thought of Erfun as a bad person, just not the right person for me. Haider told me that Erfun knew my heart, what I cherished and valued, and so he must love me.

The day overwhelmed me with a flood of good feelings about my life and even about Erfun. Meeting the son of the late Maududi, whom I greatly admired for his scholarship and religious devotion, and that Erfun knew this man, gave me great hope. Up to that moment, I had not allowed myself the freedom to trust a man.

I had spent so much time with Father, who was ever skeptical of men's intentions, and Mother, who had drilled into me since I was a child never to trust anyone. All these years of schooling, I had been so intent on achieving my goals, and certainly marriage and family was one of them, but hardly the only goal of my life.

Now here was a man who had gone to such great lengths to show that he really loved me. He wanted me in his life, and he wanted to embrace my life with all my ambitions.

That evening after we left Maududi, I told Erfun that he must speak to my father again. Without Father's blessing, I would not marry him. Erfun readily agreed. In the next few days, he came to visit Father, and I knew they talked for quite a while. Father, afterward, seemed irritated at me: why would I want to marry a man with no education? Why a man from the Muhajir?

I told Father that Erfun had promised to allow me to continue my postgraduate education. He had promised to take care of me. He loved me. Isn't that what Father wanted for me? A man who would love me unconditionally, as he loved Mother.

I knew Father was reluctant, but he finally gave his blessing. Despite giving me his consent, he was still sad. He knew something was not right. For the next three days, he did not come home, sleeping alone in his law office.

Erfun and I were officially engaged in a small ceremony. We had dinner a few times to get to know each other better, including a romantic candlelight dinner. At that dinner, he gave me a gold chain and a leather handbag. I felt safe with him, and at peace.

We were married in Karachi in January of 1985. The ceremony was beautiful. My entire family attended, along with all of Erfun's family and friends. Sometime during the large celebration, my father came to me and said, "Never come to me with any complaint about your husband." Then Erfun swept me away to a fairytale honeymoon. He took me to Murree, a resort town northeast of Islamabad, in the mountains of Punjab. I had been here once before as a medical student, and I enjoyed the beauty of the mountains and the scenery. Now happily married to a loving husband, every view appeared enchanted, as if I had never seen it before. In Karachi, the weather is hot and humid most of the year, but here the roofs of the shops, restaurants, cafes, the trees, the grounds, and the surrounding mountains, were all coated with a layer of pristine snow. Everything glistened white, and the crisp, fresh air was invigorating.

I wore a green dress that delighted Erfun as we strolled among the shops. We ate our meals in a reverie of our new love. Relaxed on boat rides on Lake Murree, floating along by ourselves on a quiet winter day.

One day I wore a white dress, my hair divided into two long braids hanging over both shoulders. We drifted on a small rowboat in the lake. The sunshine on the tranquil lake glistened on the surface, little diamonds of light that reflected on my face. Erfun kissed me on the cheek, and then on the forehead, and said I looked like a princess in a fairytale dress. Our guide laughed at the unusual sight of a man kissing a woman in public. This was something that Pakistani men did not often do. But Erfun was overcome with the sights and feelings of love, and I was too.

That day he said, "I love you." I replied for the first time, "I love you too, Erfun." He was very excited to hear that, and said, "That is the best thing I have ever heard."

We stayed in a lavish hotel, and enjoyed blissful days that were free of cares and worries. For eleven days, we were untethered from our busy lives, free to enjoy each other's company. These were perfect days. I had imagined what married love would be like, but these eleven days were even better than what I had imagined, and this was only the beginning.

Erfun seemed even more relaxed and open, and enjoyed the stay so much he proposed that we move to Murree permanently. Here, he said, we could be free from the pressures of his life, his family, and all the responsibilities on his shoulders. He talked about opening a business for himself and a clinic for me in Murree. Our life together would focus on our happiness.

If he was serious, I needed to consider his proposal carefully. He was the oldest son in his family, and his father needed him to run the family businesses. Moving up here would deprive his family of Erfun's efforts. As we talked, he seemed earnest in his desire to walk away from his life in the city. What I did not know was why he feared to return home. I thought he wanted to escape the pressure of his long hours and the demands of his business. I did not discover the true nature of his fears until later. But at that moment, I felt that his place was with his family. And my place was to return to Karachi and to take up my life as a physician. Not agreeing to Erfun's desire to start a fresh new life on our own became one of the biggest blunders of my life. It probably would have saved both of us from what awaited us in Karachi. But it would take time to fully understand just how big a miscalculation I had made.

After eleven days, we left the bliss of Murree, and drove down into the Punjab flatlands, which were wrapped in a hazy cold. We were on our way to the city. I felt convinced that our days in the mountains were only a taste of the bliss to come. How could I think otherwise? He had worked so hard to convince me that he was true.

Upon our return to Karachi, Erfun's family greeted us with great excitement. We distributed gifts to them. His sister, Gezala, was especially pleased to see us. She was estranged from her husband, so she lived in the family home, surrounded by an accepting family, and with a loving husband, I felt content.

After a few days of settling into the family home, I began working at Nasim Clinic. I had a renewed sense of purpose. The routine was the same. But I was now a married woman, buoyed by love, secure in my new life, confident that my husband would protect me the way Father had taken care of Mother.

Everything I had ever wanted lay right in front of me. After a week Erfun spoke very politely to me. "Quit your job and stay at home for a while. You are a newlywed. You should have time here at home."

I agreed.

CHAPTER 5

Naïve Wife

I MOVED INTO ERFUN'S PARENTS' HOUSE full of the euphoria of the closeness that had saturated my life on our honeymoon in Murree. Steeped in my own vision of marriage, I naively believed that the love we experienced and felt for each other would grow deeper, just as my parent's love and companionship had blossomed and grown fuller over many years. My parents had become best friends, confidants, and, in every respect, partners in a contented life. Their relationship existed in my mind not as an ideal to live up to, but as typical of marriage, the way husbands and wives were with each other. I did not realize how naïve that was.

Erfun's family welcomed me warmly, including Gezala, Erfun's only sister. She made an effort to make me feel comfortable. We got along well, and I appreciated her kindness.

Our initial days as a married couple were everything I expected, full of love and satisfaction. His younger brothers and parents were considerate and caring, very respectful of me. Either his family, mine, or his circle of friends invited us to dinner almost every evening. Yet Erfun always wanted me to attend without him, and go instead with his parents and Gezala. When I was asked his whereabouts, I made sure they knew that he shouldered many responsibilities in his family's business.

Gezala always went with me to the social events. She was young and charming, even though she stuttered when she spoke. However, she was overweight and wore old-fashioned, tight-fitting embroidered dresses with jewelry and heavy makeup that made her look older than her age. When we were together at a gathering women thought I was the daughter of the family. I always wore simple, fashionable cotton dresses, no makeup, and little or no jewelry. I continued the same practice after I married.

After a while, I began to wonder why Gezala didn't return to her husband. She seemed ashamed of her situation, and I started to feel sorry for her. She walked around with a long face, and looked lost and confused. It became apparent to me that Gezala and Erfun had always been close, and now she took every opportunity to rekindle their bond. She often greeted him at the main gate when he returned from work, the way she had done since he was a little boy. Whenever she saw us together, talking or eating, she came and sat by us. Then she began coming into our room, and she wouldn't leave. It was very uncomfortable for both of us.

My mother-in-law sensed this uneasy situation, and one day she suggested that we should try to accommodate her. She was very lonely, and our laughing and talking made her feel worse. For the first time, I learned that Gezala was demanding a divorce from her husband and she would now be living with the family permanently.

I believed that in the early days of our married life, we needed privacy to develop and grow our love. But Gezala, with her weeping and tears, began to pull us apart. She took every opportunity to play on Erfun's emotions, claiming that he didn't love her anymore because she was now a burden on him.

I believed this was the major reason Erfun began coming home late, to avoid her drama every evening. It didn't matter how late he arrived, as soon as she heard Erfun's car, Gezala would run and wait for him at the main gate. She often followed him into our room and began talking to him, complaining about her day, or how lonely she was, or just breaking down in tears. Then she began joining as us at dinner. When she could, she drew him into her room, where they talked for hours.

She was pathetic.

After a few weeks, I told her that Erfun and I needed space as newlyweds to be together alone. As pleasant and gentle as I was, she was adamant that it was her right as a sister to spend time with her brother. She even warned me to stay away from them when they were talking together. In her perverted mind, she believed the order of life should be sisters first and wives second.

She began pushing her way between us at meals and during our time together as if it were a settled matter that I was the interloper intruding on their relationship. Gezala took over our lives, and before I realized the grand mistake which allowed it, I was on the outside looking in.

Gezala had little motivation to improve her situation. She spent her days inside reading romance novels and watching dramas on TV, whiling away the hours as if nothing outside the doors of her home could possibly interest her. Her way of being friendly included her offering me her trashy novels to read and gossiping. I was always gracious to her, thanking her for her offers, but I had other things to do. I had spent years of study and preparation for my life as a doctor. I could not easily idle my mind on the sofa watching soap operas. I had plans for my future.

I began planning for my postdoctoral studies in gynecology. I had all the materials and books I required. Erfun and I had discussed my desire for further research, and he had agreed to support my academic pursuits after we married. So, I spent my free time the way I had always spent it: studying.

This did not sit well with Gezala. She kept coming into my room where I had my books, pleading with me to keep her company. When I told her I was too busy, she was astonished that I could live alone in my room and be happy. I tried to explain to her that I was used to this way of life. I was brought up in a world of books, and study was essential to me. Besides, I informed her, I was a poor conversationalist.

One morning before he left, Erfun chided me for not being more friendly to her. He wanted to know why I couldn't read her books and spend time with her. I shouldn't spend so much time reading my medical books, he told me.

I remember slouching on my bed thinking, *this is my husband, and I love him. I need to listen to him.* But this is not what we agreed to. Yet it was never in my thoughts to defy him, especially not openly in front of his family. I had worked incredibly hard, studying long hours to pass my classes, to graduate at the top of my class, and finally to sit for my medical exams. Now he was asking me to engage in something frivolous to make his sister happy.

Secretly, I hoped Gezala would reconcile with her husband and move back in with him. But that didn't happen. Once Erfun suggested I talk to her, and I tried, but it was a disaster—I don't do well with small talk.

During the week, Erfun always had an excuse for coming home late. I knew he had business meetings. But when he came home late on the weekends, his breath smelled of alcohol. I had never been around anyone who drank regularly. My father never drank, neither did my uncles and brothers, and we never had alcohol around the house.

Then there were Erfun's moods. Some days he would hardly talk, as if he carried weighty matters around in his mind. I knew his business consumed him, but there seemed other concerns that he hadn't spoken about to me; not yet anyway.

Despite all this, which I considered minor nuisances at the time, we enjoyed our new unrestrained passions at every opportunity. After he left for work, lying in bed, all I could think about was the sense Erfun and I were growing apart. What could I do to bring us closer? This wasn't the marriage we had spoken of during our engagement. I wanted to use my years of training and learning to work as a doctor, and here I was stuck in the clutch of a mean-spirited woman's manipulation.

Gradually, the glow of our honeymoon dimmed. I started developing headaches that I knew would grow into a more profound depression if I didn't find constructive things to occupy my time. I started helping Erfun's youngest brother with his studies. He didn't pay much attention to his school work because he received little encouragement. I worked with him daily on his homework and tried to motivate him to do better. I joined my mother-in-law in the kitchen and took cooking lessons from her, learning about everyone's favorite dishes. Also, I began volunteering at a local hospital in a drug and rehab unit. After a few weeks, Erfun asked me to discontinue my volunteer work because I needed to be home. I was disappointed, but again did as he asked.

Through all this, I never lost my dream of practicing medicine at the highest level I could.

Gezala refused to give up her campaign to get me to pay attention to her. I thought that if I stayed busy, she would leave me alone, but instead, she complained to my mother-in-law that I wasn't talking to her.

At my wits' end, I spoke up to my in-laws. I told them I didn't mind Gezala living here, but that she must stop interfering with our marriage. I was tired of her complaining to Erfun, provoking him to anger against me. Her behavior was wrong, and it had to stop.

They listened, but they ignored my pleas.

Finally, one day when Erfun was in an unusually bright mood, he asked me why I wasn't working. "You have so much free time. You can work as a doctor, why not?"

I did not need any coaxing. I applied to the Imam Clinic and flew through the interview process with Dr. Mrs. Imam. Soon I began working with a noted gynecologist, Dr. Nasreen.

My first day in the gynecology ward, my in-laws brought a delicious lunch for the entire staff. After completing my first full shift as a doctor, I was so excited I could hardly contain myself. My dream had arrived.

I hoped that with me out of the house, Gezala would find something or someone else to occupy her attention. Instead, she became standoffish, evidently resenting my independence. When I returned home every evening, beaming with enthusiasm and self-satisfaction, she decided to put her foot down. While I was gone, she made sure that Erfun knew about her dissatisfaction.

Before the completion of my first week at the clinic, Erfun stormed into the ward in the middle of my shift, demanding to see me. When he spotted me across the ward filled with patients, he rushed toward me. His eyes were bloodshot, and he reeked of alcohol. I stood with several doctors and nurses, staring in surprise, trying to figure out why he was gesticulating like a lunatic. Yelling like a madman, he grabbed my arm as if I were a child and began pulling me toward the door.

"What is it?" I demanded to know. "Why are you doing this?"

"You should not be working here." He pushed me through the door. He turned to the staff and doctor, who all looked shocked, and announced, "She will not come here anymore. She is discontinuing this job." He was in a rage and nearly dragged me into the parking lot.

"Why are you doing this? If you didn't want me to work, why can't we talk about this at home?" He roughly wrestled me into his car, slamming the door. Every part of me felt hot with embarrassment. I was insulted and humiliated in front of my colleagues. I could not understand why he would embarrass me that way. Everyone around me treated me with respect, and this man, who said he loved me, had just disrespected me in the most depraved way.

At home, I rushed into the house past Gezala. Everything was a blur to me, but I couldn't help but notice that she was smiling. I rushed to my room and threw myself on the bed. I stayed there for the next day, too embarrassed to face his family.

Within a month, I was pregnant. I thought his mother and his sister would be kinder to me now. Surely, Erfun would return to the doting man who had chased me relentlessly. A woman's pregnancy is a time for celebration in my culture. Woman are cared for and protected because a new family member is on the way. This would be Erfun's child, and he would be a proud parent, as his father has been.

When I told him I was pregnant, he was strangely quiet. Was he surprised? He looked as if he didn't quite understand how this could happen to me. I thought the idea of fatherhood might be a shock to him, not the fact that I was pregnant.

After a while, he warmed up to the new reality, and one day offered to take me to the doctor. The gentle, kind Erfun returned. He held my hand in the car, and he talked to me softly as he drove through Karachi. I felt protected again, the way Erfun used to make me feel. I wasn't paying attention to where we were going until we ended up in an unfamiliar neighborhood, one that didn't look like where a reputable doctor would have an office. He pulled up in front of the dilapidated looking building.

"What is this place?" I asked.

"This is Karimabad."

I could not imagine why he would bring me to a place like this.

He opened the door for me, and I said, "There's no doctor here."

He said it would be all right, and took my hand and held it warmly as we walked upstairs where he knocked on a door. Something inside me told me that this was not right. I wanted to run, but he had my hand. I thought, *This man loves me, he wouldn't bring me to harm.* A woman in a dirty housedress with stringy unwashed hair opened the door. She showed us in, and her helper, also dressed in dirty clothes, lurked in a corner. In the middle of what was actually a dowdy living room, with an old sofa and chair and a threadbare carpet, was an exam table with stirrups. I gasped and turned to Erfun.

"Why are you bringing me here?"

Erfun's soft brown eyes turned suddenly cruel. He stuck an index finger in my face. "I do not want this baby. You have to get rid of it."

Everything inside me curled into a ball of fury. I did not want to kill my baby. I had never hit anyone, but I wanted to hit him. Instead, I bolted to the door. He grabbed me and spun me around, forcing me back toward the exam table. He then blocked the door so I could not leave. The two women grabbed each arm and forced me onto the table. I kicked my legs and screamed at the top of my lungs as they tied my hands down so I could not move.

"Quiet, girl," the old hag said. "This will be over quickly if you hold still."

"This is my baby," I yelled repeatedly. "Don't touch me."

Someone stripped me below the waist, and a filthy hand over my mouth stifled my screams. I refused to let the woman touch me, so I kept kicking and squirming until they tied my feet into the stirrups.

This was insane. No anesthesia. No sterile technique. No hand-washing. No soap to clean me. No gloves. They were going to kill me along with my baby.

I looked down to see what she was doing, and a wave of terror raced through my entire body when I saw a sharply pointed, rusted wire in her dirty ungloved hand. She intended to shove that unsanitary crude instrument of death into me. It would tear everything inside me apart.

I had to resist this murder. I squirmed, moving my hips to keep it from the cervix.

"Stop moving, or this will perforate your uterus," the dark woman with stringy hair said. "Then you will never have babies." I knew that she was telling the truth. The dangers she threatened were real. I wanted to have more children, but if it damaged my uterus, my chances of conceiving again would be over.

With my feet and hands tied, she penetrated me and then pushed the wire inside my cervix, and an intense shooting pain ripped through me. I turned to Erfun, pleading with him with my eyes to stop the cruelty. He refused to look at me. When he finally did, his eyes were cold and uncaring. My husband who claimed to love me and who promised to protect me stood aside, his arms crossed over his chest in utter resolve to see this through. I closed my eyes, tears running down my cheeks. I had to stop resisting. I had no choice.

When the tip of the sharp wire started scraping and detaching my fetus from the endometrium of my uterus, the pain was so intense I thought I was going to die. I imagined it was Erfun's hate coursing through me, an evil purgative. Why did he hate my child, if he said he loved me?

What kind of man would do this? A shooting pain sprinted through me as if I'd been shot. At the point I thought I would die, everything went black.

When my eyes fluttered open, I thought I was dreaming. I was back in my old bedroom at my parent's house. Then I heard weeping, and felt the thick cloth between my legs, and throbbing pain in my abdomen, as if someone had attacked me with a knife. I lifted the sheet. The cloth was thick with blood clots. I shook with fever. I could not stop shivering. This was no dream; this was my worst nightmare.

My mother sat beside me, weeping. The look of fear in her eyes was palpable. The worry on her face almost made me cry.

"What happened, my child?" she asked. "Why did Erfun drop you here? You are bleeding and shivering."

I wanted to tell her everything, but I couldn't. If that woman hadn't perforated my uterus, she had at least given me septicemia. My head and face were on fire. The pain in my uterus told me the entire story. Already, the infection could be spreading through my organs. I knew it was an incomplete abortion. I could bleed to death if I didn't get help. And Erfun, the man I insisted on marrying, had done this to me. How could I tell her all this and burden her further?

"I have called a doctor; she will be coming soon."

"No. Take me to a good gynecologist, now."

"What happened to you?" She placed her cool hand on my forehead, then my cheek. "You are burning up, my child. Tell me."

I turned my face to the wall.

"I'll call your father. He'll know what to do."

"Please don't," I insisted. "Just take me."

She rose to take me to the hospital.

About then, the monster Erfun called. I could hear my mother's tearful voice saying that I could be dying and she was taking me to the hospital. After she hung up, she came and told me that he would be here soon.

It took him another agonizing hour to come over. He carried me to the car, and set me down in the back seat. We didn't speak on the way to the hospital. Staring out the window at the passing city, I still could not fathom what he had done to me.

We pulled up in front of the Fatima Hospital, and he carried me inside. Someone rolled out a wheelchair, and I was soon in a bed. Dr. Fatima attended to me. After an examination, she confirmed that the uterus was intact. The profuse bleeding and clots were due to an incomplete abortion. First, the sepsis had to be controlled, and then she would complete the abortion with a D & C. She ordered an infusion of powerful antibiotics. The next day she performed the procedure. After another day of rest, I went home. With all my years of study and preparation for a medical career, I never imagined this taking place.

I didn't see Erfun for my entire hospital stay. He only showed up to take me home.

The house was quiet and looked strange when I arrived. I convalesced. In the mornings, I lay staring at the ceiling for hours. My life had turned into one long, languid moment. Nothing I ate tasted good to me.

Since Gezala always answered the phone, when Erfun called, she never told me. In the first weeks of our marriage, Erfun had complained to me that I was always too busy to come to the phone when he called. I told him I didn't know about his calls. I suggested he ask his sister why she never told me he had called. But he wouldn't confront her.

Now Erfun refused to let me use the phone to talk to my mother. She seldom visited, and I couldn't call to invite her over. I was cut off from my professional colleagues and contacts.

Gradually, I regained my strength, and for a while, at least, I resigned myself to my secluded life. My energy returned, and I found it easier to dress and care for myself. And in my room, when I could close myself off from Gezala, I returned to my studies. I believed one day, Erfun would change his mind again and remember what he had promised me, that I could practice medicine.

One day a visitor arrived at the door. A woman whom I had never met was here to visit me. She introduced herself as Erfun's friend, Roohi. I invited her in, served her tea, and made her comfortable. She was dressed very nicely, like a modern businesswoman. I could tell she was a nice person.

Our first visit was congenial. She asked me how Erfun and I had met. I didn't know what to think of her at first, but she was so friendly. She assured me that she and Erfun were only friends, and she just wanted to know more about the woman Erfun did marry. I told her about how Erfun had chased me for two years until I relented to marry him. She seemed amazed—not that Erfun would chase me, but that I actually married him.

Over several visits, we became friends.

One time she asked where Erfun was. I said that he was out of town on business and would be away for a few days. Right after my forced abortion, Erfun had begun traveling for business, and he was only home a few days a week, and even when he came home, he arrived very late.

She laughed, holding her hand over her mouth. Then her look sobered up, and she gazed at me strangely, almost sadly.

"You are so innocent," she said. "He has no businesses outside Karachi. He is not out of the city. Maybe he is staying in another house he is renting. Or maybe he is staying with another woman in a hotel somewhere."

I did not know what to think. If he was not out of town, then where was he?

"You have to put your foot down with him. You have to be strong," she said. "You have to demand that he come home every day after closing his business. You have to insist he stop drinking and make sure he takes care of you. You are his wife."

I told her, confidently, that I trusted Erfun. If I saw it with my own eyes that he was doing something objectionable, then I would confront him.

"You are surely very different from other women. Your husband comes home late, and you don't accuse him and yell at him. You are so calm."

My father's remonstrations over my marriage to Erfun surfaced in my mind. "Why would you marry him?" he had asked once. I remember saying that I loved him. And that was still true, even after what he did to my baby and me.

I shook myself out of my memories and thanked her for her advice. We chatted for the rest of her stay, and after I closed the door behind her, her words began to sink in, and I began to wonder.

Where exactly was Erfun? I tried not to think about what Roohi told me.

After three more months, I became pregnant again. This time I planned on being very careful. I made sure that his parents and brothers were home when I told him the good news. I said to him, "This time I will not go for an abortion." He said he was happy, and appeared genuinely interested in the baby.

Before the week was out, he came home and said I had to go with him. He took my hand and began pulling me toward the main gate.

"We need to go see the gynecologist."

I knew his intentions. I refused to leave the house, but he was stronger than me, and violently pulled me through the hallway. With one hand, I held onto the doorpost. He continued dragging me.

"No, no, I need this child. If you didn't want this child, why didn't you tell me?" I continued yelling and screaming in the house holding onto anything I could find as he pulled me toward the gate.

Thankfully, my mother-in-law and father-in-law came running to see what all the shouting was about. I said he was taking me to have an abortion.

My father-in-law stood up to him. "We are happy to have a grandson," he said to Erfun. "Leave her alone."

With that, he released me and left. I ran to my room to compose myself. I wanted to cry, but I knew that it was essential for the health of the child for me to remain calm and not get too upset. I felt safe for now in his parents' house. They wanted this child as much as I did, so I had at least their assurance that Erfun would not force me to have another abortion. I didn't think I could survive another episode of killing my own child. I expected that with a child on the way, I would have the care and attention of my husband and his family. My husband did not see things that way. I did not see a gynecologist for the first seven months of my pregnancy. Erfun did everything he could to keep me isolated. If he couldn't make me abort my child, then he would do everything in his power to let me know he was an unhappy man. He didn't come home for stretches of days, and when he did come back, it was so late that I was asleep.

One day Gezala called me to the phone. The woman on the phone didn't tell me her name, and I didn't recognize her voice. She told me the strangest tale: She said Erfun was living with a woman over on Tariq Road. I told her I had asked Erfun about his girlfriends, and he said he wasn't seeing anyone else since we married. She let out a mocking laugh.

"Here, go and check it for yourself." She then gave me an address.

After she hung up, I stood there for a long moment considering her words. I decided that I would trust what Erfun had told me. Despite my efforts to forget that call, I didn't eat for a whole day. No one said a word to me about my lack of appetite.

A few days passed, and the woman called again. She knew I hadn't followed up on her story. I still did not know her identity. She must have decided that I didn't believe her, so she began calling my mother and telling her the same tale.

My mother and my sister came to see me one day. My mother looked so frantic I thought she was going to have a heart attack.

"Who is this woman? What does she want? Why is she calling me?" She had such fury in her voice over this woman's accusations. After I calmed her down, "Mother, don't worry about it. I don't know who she is, but it's all a lie. I know it's a lie."

Before they left, my sister told me that Mansoor had sent me a birthday card from New York, as usual. I told her to throw it away.

When Erfun did come home, I asked him about that woman. He said, "Don't worry about her, she is just jealous because I married you." For the first time, he told me the truth. He had become sexually active when he was thirteen, and he'd had sexual relations with lots of women in the past. But after marriage he stopped seeing everyone.

Our conversation made me heartsick. I had trusted him. But with this revelation, so many pieces of the puzzle that was Erfun began to fit together. Our discussions at Murree during our honeymoon made more sense now. He truly had wanted to live permanently at the mountain resort where we had spent the lovely days of our honeymoon. He had wanted to start a new life. He had even offered to help me open my own clinic, and he would open a business. He had wanted to escape a life that orbited around his girlfriends and sexual proclivities. At the time, I felt it would be selfish of me to insist on moving away, just the two of us, and building a life together. I had no idea he was running from a sordid past. My only thinking at the time was that he was the oldest son; he had a responsibility to his family and their business.

After he told me of his early sexual exploits, I knew I had made a grave error of judgment. I should have listened to my father, and I should have told him of how Erfun, in the beginning, had tried to intimidate me into marrying him by threatening to kidnap my younger sister. I also needed to tell Father of the great mistake I had made by putting Erfun's family first, and not insisting on what was right for us as a couple. But I knew he didn't want me to speak to him about my marriage problems. I began to think that everything that woman on the phone told me was true. But now I was pregnant. I decided that what was best for my child was that I remained calm, and have a smooth pregnancy.

Then I would deal with my marriage.

I kept myself busy. I took a position as a doctor at Rani Hospital, and Erfun left me alone so I could perform my job. Although Erfun had offered a few times to take me to the gynecologist, it wasn't until the seventh month of my pregnancy that I went by myself for my first neonatal checkup. The baby's development was right on track. I felt good, even though my diet was not as healthy as I would have liked it. Erfun's parents didn't do any special shopping or give me any particular attention. And I couldn't see my mother very often. It was a tough time, but I was so glad that Erfun had left me alone to have my child.

During my ninth month of pregnancy, the nurse at my job informed me that a young man wanted to see me. He had been injured in a motorbike accident. The man who entered my office was a familiar face, Furquan. When I examined his foot, I found only fake blood and no injury.

"Why are you doing this?" I said, angrily.

"I have come to propose marriage to you."

This fool was so infuriating. "Do you see I'm about to give birth to my first child, and that I'm already married?"

He spoke in quiet tones. "I know everything about you. This child will never be born, and you will be divorced soon. You will then marry me. I paid to have powerful black magic performed on you."

"Listen carefully," I said to him. "Even if I were alone my entire life, I would never marry you. Don't you know that Islam says whoever uses magic will go to hell?" I opened the door to my office and motioned to him. "Leave, and I never want to see you again."

I worked right up to my due date and performed my job until the last day.

Soon after, my time arrived to have the baby. I didn't want Gezala with me during the delivery. I would rather be alone than to have that selfish woman with me. Because my younger sister was unmarried, she could not go with me. Erfun was away. I called for a rickshaw and took myself to the hospital. My mother was visiting Punjab because the weather there was better for her chronic asthma. And my mother-in-law wasn't home either.

So, by myself, I packed a small bag and prepared for my hospital stay. I felt ready for this next stage of my life. To bring a child into the world and to raise it in the same manner as my loving parents raised me would be one of the greatest joys I could imagine. What I did not imagine or ever anticipate was that I would be taking this ride to the hospital alone. Erfun, who said he loved me, wasn't at my side.

In time, I believed, he would come to love our child the way his parents loved him. I cherished those memories of the loving and kind man from our time in Murree. But there was no waiting around for him to catch up with the fact that he would very shortly have a new family member. My child was on the way. The rickshaw had arrived and was waiting by the front gate, so I rushed out into the afternoon of the first of January—alone.

CHAPTER 6
Trapped in a House of Hate

I SPENT THE ENTIRE NIGHT IN fruitless labor. The next day, although my contractions were still very strong, my cervix was closed tightly. I was admitted to the hospital on January 1, and now it was the third. I was exhausted and dehydrated. The doctor didn't think I would be able to deliver the child without a C-section. That morning, my mother-in-law and Gezala and other family members had shown up at the hospital. The doctor asked for permission to perform a C-section, but my mother-in-law would not allow it. Pregnant women were not allowed to make medical decisions for themselves, such as to have a C-section. Their husbands had to consent to the operation.

The doctor insisted—I needed the operation right away, or the baby or I could die. Dr. Parveen believed the fetus was in danger. Still, my mother-in-law refused to allow it. Only Erfun could decide. The doctor wanted to know where he was so she could ask him.

He was out of town on business, my mother-in-law told the doctor.

This conversation must have gone on for an hour or more before the doctor informed me that she could not perform the operation since my mother-in-law wouldn't allow it and my husband had disappeared.

I could not believe this state of affairs. How could that woman be so callous as to let me suffer like this? Finally, I called the doctor into my room. I told her, "I don't want to die, and I don't want my baby to die. I permit you to do a C-section."

She knew I was a medical doctor, so she assented, despite my in-law's disapproval. I signed the paperwork, and within an hour, an orderly wheeled me down the hall into an operating room. During the ride on the gurney, I began thinking about my child.

I didn't know the sex of the child. But since my early childhood, I'd always wanted a sister, and when she was born, I thought God listened to my prayers. After marriage, whenever I dreamed of having a baby, I dreamed of a girl. I grew up with five brothers, and even though my father doted on me, I imagined a daughter would be special. But during that long ride into the operating room, my thinking began to change. A girl's life can be very hard in my country, at times cruel. Even for an educated adult like myself, there is so little a woman can control. I always thought that with my education and profession, my situation would be different. But I was just as much at the mercy of a man's whims as any other woman. Erfun had all the power he needed to make my life miserable, and I had no way to stop him. No, I did not want to bring a girl into a world to live among these men who would only dishonor and disrespect her for no other reason than that she's a strong and confident girl. A boy's life is much easier. So as they wheeled me along, I prayed silently for a boy. A boy who would always treat the women in his life with gentleness and kindness; a boy who would see into their hearts their greatness and the gifts they bring to this troubled world.

Soon the anesthesiologist fitted a mask over my face, and already I was drifting off into a twilight zone of painless sleep.

I prayed from the deepest recesses of my heart, *God, please save my child and marriage. Please turn Erfun back to the same loving and caring person I knew before our marriage.*

The doctor stood over me, robed and masked, ready to bring another miracle into the world. I prayed that my child's life would be full of success and compassion.

In the recovery room, I awoke to a new life. The nurse handed me a swaddled newborn. He was all in blue. The three days of strong contractions had taken a toll on him, but otherwise, he was a healthy boy of eight pounds, eight ounces. I held the little angel in my arms, and suddenly he opened his big intelligent eyes. I could not stop staring at him. God had heard my prayers. As I held him to me, he latched on with an eagerness that told me he would thrive, grow, and become strong. I felt secure in that moment. It was just my son and me, a sacred moment that rejuvenated every part of me with the hope that my life was meaningful. While I had every expectation that Erfun would take his place as a doting and caring father, I could not foresee the future. I would care for this child as a treasure granted to me by God.

My father, brothers, my sister, mother-in-law, Gezala, and Erfun all gathered in my room to greet the new family member. Even my uncles who lived in Karachi came to congratulate me. A new birth is such a joyous time for a family, and our time together was no different.

I called Erfun over, and I placed our child in his arms.

"Here is your son." My heart lifted when his eyes grew large as he stared down at the baby boy, his chubby arms and hands waggling with life. What father isn't overjoyed to hold his son for the first time? I could see the transformation in Erfun. His eyes grew wide with surprise and joy at holding his son in his arms. My hopes grew. He would love this child as I did, and he would love and protect both of us.

I was so tired and weak; I couldn't help drifting off to sleep despite the gathering. But through the haze, I heard someone reciting the Azan. I opened my eyes; my father-in-law was saying Azan in the ear of my son. They were performing the traditional Gurhty ceremony without me. I forced myself awake. The ceremony required someone worthy of emulation to place a spoonful of honey in the child's mouth. The child will then take on the personality of the giver. My mother-in-law had the spoon of honey in her hand and was about to place it on my son's tongue.

"No, no, don't do that," I said, firmly. "I will do that."

My mother-in-law held up and stared at me. I knew what she was thinking: *You? But your marriage!* She feared that since my marriage was so miserable, I would ruin my son's life.

"I will give honey to my son," I insisted, reaching for my baby. I wanted to speak encouraging and positive words to him, guiding him to work hard, gain a good education, and have an upbringing in a loving home. I wanted to prove her wrong. Only God has the power to decide my boy's destiny. I didn't care what she or any other person thought of me.

"If Erfun had a better upbringing, my life would be better," I told her.

She didn't say anything as she sheepishly handed me the precious bundle.

Erfun stood at the back of the group and never said a word. I took the spoon from her hand, placed it on my son's tongue, and let the drops of honey run into his mouth. I prayed he would grow strong in kindness and wisdom, and would always be a gracious and courageous man. I wanted him not only to be successful, but to be an example to his father. I had broken tradition by performing this act myself. But it was time for a new tradition, one built on honesty and kindness. After the ceremony, the nurses took my son away, and I lay back and rested.

While I slept, my son received his name from Erfun. Traditionally, the grandparents, elders, and family members sit together and decide on a name that will bring honor to the family. But Erfun didn't want any of their suggestions. He insisted on Taimoor after a famous king from the fourteenth century. Taimoor had been a great king, but was known for being very rigid and cruel. Erfun's parents told him it wasn't a good name for his child, but Erfun insisted, evidently influenced by a friend of his in the army who gave that name to his son.

Three days later, Erfun came back to the hospital to pick us up and bring us home. Instead of home, he took me to my parent's house. My mother was still in Punjab. For two weeks, my youngest brother Rafhan and my sister cared for me. To them, my child was royalty, and so was I. Such fantastic care spoiled me. My father was very kind and looked happy for both of us. He even offered some good suggestions to take care of my newborn.

Erfun visited every evening.

Two weeks passed quickly, after which Erfun came and drove me home. He seemed content with his son, and he made sure I was comfortable, and then he left. I would not see him for days at a time, and when he did come home, many times he was drunk.

I needed to visit the hospital for removal of my stitches. The day of my appointment, I waited for Erfun to take me. But he never came home. I removed the stitches myself.

In Erfun's parents' home, I was treated like a roommate, not a daughter and the mother of their new grandchild. As I gradually regained my strength, and Taimoor began sleeping better and settled into a regular schedule, I returned to my studying. I had not given up on my plans to do a post-graduate study; I just didn't know when I would have the opportunity. Most of my day was taken up with caring for Taimoor. After I fed, bathed, and changed him, and put him down for his nap, I had time to myself. I pulled out my medical books and spent several hours a day reading.

Outside in the drawing room, unbeknownst to me, Gezala fumed. After a while, my quiet, simple life ended. One afternoon, Erfun stormed into my room in a rage, screaming about my behavior, how I was insulting his sister.

"I told you she does not like you doing this." He pointed at my books. "What? Do you think you are better than everyone else because you are a doctor? A doctor is nothing! Nothing!"

I couldn't believe this outburst. He didn't care about our sleeping child. He didn't care about my feelings, or any of the promises he had made to me before our marriage.

I was sitting on the bed with one of my books open on my lap. "You used to think me being a doctor was quite impressive. Why do you all of a sudden think so differently?"

He reached down, grabbed the thick textbook off my lap, and tore it in half. Then he shredded everything until the books were destroyed. I stared at the pieces of the expensive text as the torn pages fluttered to the carpet. I had never seen anyone treat a book that way.

"A doctor is nothing! I can hire ten doctors if I need one." He lunged at the small shelf where I kept my texts and notebooks, and he took them one by one and tore them to shreds, strewing the bed and floor in a shower of confetti. I was too shocked to say a word.

But when I saw he wanted to beat me, I shot up to escape and opened the door. Gezala stood in front of me, evidently leaning close to eavesdrop. She had the strangest expression on her face. Her presence startled me, and her weird grin reminded me of a message from the Quran: "Those who will put hatred between husband and wife will go to hell." I do not wish hell on anyone, but at that moment, I was certain that's what she deserved for provoking Erfun's anger.

Before I could brush past her, Erfun grabbed my wrist and pushed me onto the bed.

"I told you my sister doesn't like it when you always study, and you don't understand." When he finished destroying all of my books and notes, he stood over me. "If I wanted to, I could pay an employee ten times what you make. If I wanted to, I could buy a medical degree for 30,000 rupees, [around USD $350] and I wouldn't need to read all this."

"Go ahead, buy a degree. See if it makes you a doctor. I don't care. Some people do things for reasons other than money."

He glared at me. I thought for sure he would strike me, but he didn't. Instead, he stuck an angry finger in my face. "You are nothing! Just an ugly, stupid woman." Then he stormed out and slammed the door. I heard Gezala's laugh.

Every part of me felt paralyzed, and moments of my past life flashed through my mind. I remembered the first time Erfun and I had met on the street, and he had offered me a ride. When he had found out that I was a doctor, he had been so impressed. He had marveled at how much I had accomplished, the studying I had completed, and my plans for the future.

The Erfun who destroyed my books and tried to annihilate my dreams and my soul was a completely different man. This Erfun wasn't the confident, charming man I had married, but a man riddled with a deep sense of inferiority that his wife had a profession that was more prestigious than his.

I lay down on my bed, among my shattered books, bits strewn everywhere, a confetti of hate. Restoring them to wholeness was impossible. I closed my eyes and felt too weak to move. Every dream about my career and my marriage lay among those shards of knowledge, shattered by hate. It was then I heard the frantic wailing of my son. My feet and hands would not obey my efforts to rise. I had to find the strength to go on, to live for my son.

I kept myself busy caring for Taimoor and trying to stay calm. Physically, I was still weak from the operation, and Erfun's destruction of my books and papers had eroded what little energy I did have. Exhaustion came over me that I couldn't shake, and I suffered from terrible headaches. I fell into silence, not talking to anyone, only to coo at my boy. With him, I could smile and be happy.

I began to understand my father's words of warning to me before I married Erfun. He was disturbed that I would marry a man with so little education. At the time, it did not seem to matter to me, because Erfun had expressed such respect and enthusiasm for my profession. Now, I had to accept that Erfun had lied to me and that he didn't care about me. Then why had he married me? I couldn't understand any of what was happening to me, or why I was trapped in this house of hate.

I had to fight the impulse to lie down, close my eyes, and block out the pain with uninterrupted sleep. My appetite disappeared, and while that was okay for me, it made Taimoor whiny and irritable. I began to bottle feed him to supplement his diet. This meant many trips back and forth to the kitchen, preparing what I needed for Taimoor and myself.

After strict instructions from Erfun to join Gezala and watch TV with her, I went to the drawing room and started watching TV. She turned the TV toward her so I couldn't see it. I felt humiliated and left the room with a heavy heart.

One day Erfun handed me a videotape. "Watch this," he said, "and learn from it." I had no idea what to expect. When I played it, I was horrified. It was a triple-X-rated movie, and the violence to the woman during intimacy by a group of men so shocked me, I shut it off. Anyone who would watch something like that had to be a sexual pervert. I couldn't think of anything I learned from the movie except that Erfun could be a sexual deviant. It scared me what my future would be like with him around my son and me. When he asked me about the tape, I told him, "I hated it. Don't ever ask me to watch anything like that again."

He laughed at me and left the room.

One morning when I wanted to go to the kitchen, it was locked. Erfun's parents had left the house to visit their relatives. I saw Gezala near the kitchen smiling and showing me the keys. In older homes in Pakistan, kitchens are like bedrooms, with doors and windows that can be locked. Gezala had the keys, and without any regard for my health or the health of my child, she had locked it. I refused to let her get the best of me. I didn't ask her to open it. She knew I needed to get into the kitchen to feed my child and myself. She knew I needed to keep my strength up, but her jealousy and envy were too intense for her to do what was right.

I didn't know what to do. Then it came to me; I would go home. My parents lived many miles away on the other side of Karachi, but I didn't care. I would not stay here any longer. I wasn't thinking straight, not realizing how hot it was outside and how weak I was.

I bundled Taimoor up, grabbed my purse, and left the house. It must have been well over 100 degrees outside, and the sweltering after-noon sun beat down on my head as I rushed down the street. I don't know how far I walked, sweat already soaking my clothes, when Erfun drove up and stopped beside me. He rolled down the window and asked me why I was outside with the baby, walking in this heat. I told him what his sister had done, locking the kitchen. We were both starv-ing, and I had to get some food for both of us.

He brought me home, and I was then able to get some food.

But even after that episode, Gezala made it routine to lock the kitchen whenever she got a chance, and she continued to call me names, demeaning me at every turn, telling me that I was nothing, and that I should not think I was better just because I was a doctor. I did everything I could to ignore her, but it was difficult. She lived with us and rarely left the house.

During his time, Erfun's different girlfriends continued calling me. They would tell me they saw Erfun all over town with a woman. Did I know he was with a girl at a restaurant, at a store, or somewhere else? When I asked him about what the callers were saying about him, he just shrugged. They were jealous, that was all. His advice was for me to stop answering the phone.

Erfun continued coming home very late, and most of the time it was apparent he had been drinking. Every day the weight on me became heavier. I wanted to sink into my bed, close my eyes, and sleep all day. I resisted the urge to collapse inside.

Instead, I decided to begin to confront Erfun as Roohi had warned me to do. When he came home late, I started asking him why he was out so late. Who was he with? What was he doing? Why did he drink so much? How was he going to raise a son if he became a drunk?

He was surprised and reacted angrily: "Why are you asking me these questions? How dare you accuse me?" He shouted that he wanted to divorce me, and he would get it done right away. I broke down crying. "Please, no. I don't want a divorce. I won't ask you again."

I had shown him my weakness. I feared being divorced more than I regretted marrying him. So whenever he came home late, he announced that he planned to divorce me. He just wanted to make me cry.

Once, at two a.m., he roused me from a deep sleep, pulled me out of bed, and pushed me outside the front door, and before he slammed it shut, he said, "I'm divorcing you." He left me outside. I stood there in the darkness, and realizing how late it was, I stopped crying, and stopped resisting. *What is the use?* I thought. If he wanted a divorce, then I would agree to it. I stood outside in the darkness, quietly waiting. I did not know what to expect.

An hour later, he opened the door and looked surprised that I hadn't broken down again.

At the approach to Eid, my mother-in-law told Erfun she needed a new dress for the celebrations. He left me some money and told me to have one made. I took a taxi to my favorite seamstress at Bombay Tailor on Tariq Road. I had forgotten entirely about the calls from some strange women before Taimoor was born, suggesting Erfun was living with a woman on Tariq Road. Despite everything I had already experienced, I could not believe that he would betray me by openly living with another woman.

As my taxi drove along the busy boulevard, I remember thinking about the upcoming holiday together with my family. My heart began to revive, thinking of the dinners and celebrations, the exchanging of gifts.

All of my thoughts changed when I spotted a familiar car ahead of me. I asked the driver to stop, and sure enough, it was Erfun. In the passenger seat was a woman I had never seen before. I got out and followed them as they entered an apartment building. By the time, I entered the lobby, they had disappeared upstairs. I knocked on a door.

A woman answered, and I told her I was looking for a friend who lived here, did she know the name of the person living upstairs? I described Erfun.

She said, "Yes, that's Erfun. He lives upstairs with his wife."

When I heard her say "wife," my knees grew weak. I tried to stay composed, and I thanked her. Before I turned away, I grew faint and began to fall. She grabbed my son, and with her free hand steadied me. She led me into her apartment and asked me to sit. I was so dizzy I couldn't stand, and I plopped into a chair. She offered me some water. The words, "Erfun's wife," kept rolling around in my head. How could he do this? How could he betray me like this? I saw them together, laughing and talking, and acting as if they were a couple. I composed myself and left. I stood outside the building for a long time. I was heartbroken, thinking about what to do. I had to confront him. I had to understand what he intended to do. I cannot live like this.

That evening Erfun came home late. I waited for him in the bedroom. As usual, he started yelling for no reason.

"Who was that women you were with today?"

"Why are you questioning me? You know I will divorce you."

"Answer me. Who was that woman you were with today?" I asked firmly.

"Someone gave you the wrong information. I was working all day."

"No, you were with a woman. Don't lie to me."

"Bring the Quran to me. I will swear on it. Bring it right now." When I did not move, he picked one from the shelf. He held it out, placed one hand on it, and began to swear.

"Stop it!" I said loudly. "For God's sake, do not lie while swearing on the Quran. I saw you with my own eyes with that woman on Tariq Road. I went inside the building, and your neighbor said you were living with your wife. Who is she?"

He gave me a haughty look. "She's my girlfriend. I've been living with her for the past year."

"She's your mistress."

"Her name is Shesta, and I'm going to marry her."

"No, I will not give you permission to marry her."

"If you start arguing with me, I'll divorce you and kick you out of the house."

"Today," I said. "Divorce me right now!"

He looked astonished. "You want a divorce?" He was quiet, thinking. "No, no, I will never divorce you. You are too beautiful, and also a doctor. You will marry quickly, and you will have a happy life. I don't want you to have a happy life."

"I am not your property; you should know that." I felt the rage flush my cheeks. "You have destroyed me and my dreams. Do you think I will trust a man again?"

He glared at me but did not say anything.

"Give me a divorce, and then you are free to marry that other woman."

"She drinks with me and you won't. She teaches me so many things, like on that tape you hate."

"She looked like your teacher."

"I will marry her soon, and you both will live together."

"Never. You know that Islam permits me to say no to living with you and your new wife. I'm also permitted to ask for a divorce. Besides, according to our law, you must ask permission from me first."

He stormed toward the door and turned, "I will never divorce you. I will marry Shesta, and you two will live together. Islam says I can have more than one wife, and I want Shesta and you."

"You are manipulating Islam. Islam does not grant you permission for your fun. There are conditions. First, there must be some solid reason. Second, you have to treat both women the same. You have not fulfilled any of these. You never come home after work. You abuse me, lying to me that you are away on business when you are living in Karachi with Shesta and other women. You do not love or care for Taimoor and me as you promised, and as Islam requires. You have to divorce me first if you want to marry her."

He waved his hands in frustration. "I'm marrying Shesta, and I'm not divorcing you. You can live alone, and I will live with her. You will stay married to me for your entire life."

I did not know what to do or say. The only thought running through my mind was that I had to be free of this man. He was not the Erfun I had married. He hated me, and I could not understand why. Taimoor began crying in his crib, so I went and picked him up, cradling him in my arms.

The next day, he asked me what I had decided. I spoke to him in a calm voice, trying to reason with him. But I was set in my heart.

"You have to divorce me first, then you can have Shesta; I will never live with her in the same house."

He stepped forward and snatched his son from my arms so fast I could not react. "I am taking Taimoor to Shesta. She will raise my son, and you will live here alone." Before I could muster the strength to pursue him, he was out the front door, and off in his car. When I heard him drive away with Taimoor, I felt my entire life unravel. The baby was only five months old. He needed feeding and changing soon. I went into my room and slumped onto the bed. I wanted a good life for my son, a life with a loving home. Instead, I had no love in my life, no money, no job, and now my son had been taken from me. And there was little I could do about it. I wanted to cry, but my tears would not come. But the ache in my heart felt like a hammer on an anvil, it throbbed and threatened to burst.

CHAPTER 7
Die in Your Husband's House

ALL I REMEMBER WAS THAT it was a hot summer day, and as it drew closer to the hottest part of the afternoon, my anxiety over my situation began to overwhelm me. I had no money, no job, and no way of leaving Erfun's parents' home, and thus had no hope that my situation would change anytime soon. Erfun came in and out as he pleased, abandoning my son and me to live in this hostile home, fending for ourselves. His behavior made me crazy, and I spent hours trying to figure out why he would do this to me. I constantly searched my mind, trying to piece together what I might have done to turn him against me.

I asked him once why he had married me.

His reply surprised me. I had never accepted gifts from him, and I had refused to marry him. "That made me angry. I married you to teach you a lesson."

My father's warnings came to mind, his surprise and shock that I would agree to marry a man such as Erfun, so uneducated and worldly. He had never said what he disliked about Erfun. But I always assumed it was our enormous differences in education. But it was more than that. I had been entirely naïve in my estimation of the man's character.

Now I could see what I had not seen before our marriage—that apart from our education, there existed a vast difference in our interests and passions. Erfun had, for whatever reason I could not fathom, acted as if he admired how hard I had worked to become a medical doctor. Now it seemed that my degree didn't mean anything to him.

All that mattered to him were money, his work, and his relationship with women. Even our son barely got his attention.

That hot day, I went to the kitchen to feed Taimoor, who had been fussy and crying all that morning. Lost in my thoughts, everything felt like it was coming loose inside me. Erfun's promises of treating me with kindness, respect, and love had held me together during the first two years of our marriage. Now I had lost all hope.

I do not remember why I did it, or even doing it, but I absent-mindedly placed my son on the hot roasting floor outside the kitchen, which was an open area, exposed to direct sun. I was arguing with myself over what to do. I felt so stupid to have believed his promises. I heard crying, but it seemed to come from a great distance. Lost in my painful thoughts, I stopped at the kitchen door. I saw a baby crawling toward me across the burning floor, heated by sun like a hell or oven. Obviously in distress and pain, raising his little hand toward me, his other hand was on the floor, then he tried to switch his hands, his face was full of tears. He wanted me to pick him up, and rest him on my shoulder. I watched him struggle, but I could not move. I had no idea what to do as his wailing grew louder. Somehow, his pleas for help resonated with something inside me as if both of us felt the same pain and were crying out for help.

There was no rescue—for either of us. I stood paralyzed in a state of helplessness.

His wailing must have gone on for a while because it finally became intolerable for others, who usually made it their practice to ignore me, and my mother-in-law rushed from her room.

"What's happening? Why is he crying so hard?" She saw him on the floor, lifting a reddened palm toward her. "My God," she shouted. "Taimoor is burning."

Her shrill voice roused out of my torpor. I quickly snatched him off the floor and tried to soothe him. We stared at each other for a hard minute. She knew my agony, and she didn't have one kind word of solace, and left us without a single word.

I rushed into my bedroom and turned on the air conditioner. Both palms were blistered, his knees were swollen, and his face was flushed red. I applied antibiotic ointment to his blisters and sprinkled heat power on his body, and fed him. Then I spooned some Panadol syrup into his mouth, and he calmed and slept. I still don't understand why I would do this to my son. Or why I had done this to myself. The pain of that moment is still with me to this day.

I wanted to leave the house, but I had no money and no job, and I knew my father would not allow me to return to his home. So, I moved out of our room and began living separately in another part of the house. We became even more estranged. Nearly every time I saw him, I asked him for a divorce. It was my only plan.

One day he came to me with an admission. One that fit together the pieces of the puzzle that made up Erfun. He told me that I shouldn't be surprised at the way he lived. Beginning when he was thirteen, a neighbor down the street left the country to work in the Gulf, and his wife was alone for several years. She seduced him, and he began sleeping with that married woman as a teenager. When he came home very early in the morning, Gezala would meet him at the door and let him in. She knew everything. This went on for several years, and they practically lived together. That's when he lost interest in school. He dropped out before high school, and never went back.

"This is the life I have lived for many years, and you should not be surprised."

If my heart could fall any farther, it did at that moment.

Soon after that, I confronted his mother in the kitchen.

"What should I do about your son? I will never agree to tolerate his second wife."

"You know," she said, "society is very cruel to divorced women." She thought for a moment. "You and your son's life will be difficult if you get a divorce. Why don't you get a boyfriend? It would be much better than living alone. Maybe after a while, Erfun will get fed up with all these other women and return to you."

This woman was as ignorant and immoral as Erfun. No wonder he turned out the way he had. Despite my shock at her repugnant suggestion, I was polite. "No, I can't do that. I'm not that type of person."

"Well then," she said. "You two should live in your own place, away from Gezala. Maybe he will behave better away from her interference."

It was the first practical thing I had heard from this woman's mouth. It was exactly the idea I needed. My hopes suddenly rose—if we lived together alone, away from the menace of his sister, maybe he would be the Erfun I thought I married.

In early 1987, we moved to a lovely apartment in Hoor Palace, a residential district not far from my parents. I was optimistic about our new home, as it was just the three of us and there was no Gezala to taint Erfun's attitude toward me. I made the apartment comfortable, arranging it so it was warm and inviting, hoping to make it a place Erfun would want to come home to.

But the opposite held true. Without the tiny bit of restraint imposed on him by his parents, Erfun instead went wild. I hardly saw him at all; at times, he did not come home for weeks. One day when he did arrive home, he surprised me with an intriguing suggestion.

"Why don't you go back to work?" he said. "You just sit around here with nothing to do."

That night, he stayed home. I had seen the signs and symptoms of an STD in him some time ago, and advised him to go for the treatment. I started living in the separate bedroom. He slept in the other room and left early.

The next day, I applied for a position at Fon Hospital. During that week, my interview went so well they invited me to join the medical staff right away. The hospital was close to my apartment and near enough that I could drop Taimoor off at my mother's before work. She was glad to take care of him, and was relieved that I was able to pursue my profession.

My first day, I couldn't help looking over my shoulder, wondering if Erfun would have a sudden change of heart, and come storming into the ward where I worked, demanding I return home. It had happened before, and it was a most humiliating experience. After a few days without him barging in, however, I calmed down and settled into the routine of seeing patients and interacting with the staff. This was the position I had imagined myself being in since I was a child. Every day, I came home tired, but euphoric to have finally stepped into the physician's life.

The only thing missing from my life was a loving husband. Every day, when I reached the front door of our apartment, I prayed he would be there to greet me with a smile and open arms.

Instead, Erfun showed his true colors. As I unlocked the door of my apartment one day, with Taimoor in my arms, a neighbor across the hall opened her door.

"Dr. Raana, may I speak to you, please?" the woman said.

"Yes, of course." I stepped toward her.

"Dr. Raana, do you know that your husband comes here every day after you leave?"

Why would he do that? I wondered.

"He brought a woman with him." Her look was disapproving.

Erfun had hurt me so many times; I did not think he could do more to me. But this indignity to our marriage, and humiliation in front of my neighbors, was incalculable. I forced myself to smile as I thanked her, hoping she would think there was a good reason for my husband to do this beside the obvious. Inside, I set Taimoor down and looked around the apartment. The living room, the kitchen, and the bathroom all appeared as I had left them. In the other bedroom, the sloppily made bed told a different story. It had been used and remade. I threw back the blankets and sheets, and several hair clips lay on the pillow and sheet.

I almost threw up. I couldn't believe that he would bring that woman in here and use my bed. He didn't care about anyone other than himself.

Almost daily, I found signs that Shesta and Erfun had been in the bedroom. Left behind were her bangles, more hair clips, hairpins, and even some of her clothing. Did she leave here half-dressed? She was taunting me, leaving her things on purpose, like a dog marking her territory.

This went on for weeks. I tried to confront Erfun, but he seldom came home. When he did show up, he only stayed briefly, or he was too drunk to talk reasonably. When I brought up divorce and argued for bringing that horrible woman into my bed, he would fall into a rage, screaming at me that I had to accept him the way he was. He had no intention of changing. I had to allow Shesta into our lives, or I would have to live alone for the rest of my life.

I did not know what to do. He would not give me a divorce, and I would not compromise.

One day, I came home from work, and I was surprised to hear Erfun's voice in the apartment. He was in my bedroom talking to someone. Maybe he was on the phone, and then I heard a woman's voice. I slammed the bedroom door open, and the two of them were in bed. Shesta pulled a sheet up to her chin.

"What is she doing here?" I demanded. "This is my room."

"This is my house, Raana. Not yours." He laid back on the pillow, hands clasped behind his head. The smirk on his face was telling. He wanted me to accept this situation. There was nothing I could do about it. Shesta had a fearful look on her face. She had no idea what I would do. But she also did not have an iota of embarrassment at intruding into my married life. She was a worthless person, as far as I was concerned.

Broken and despondent over this situation, I went to my parents for help. They both sat on the sofa listening, my mother's concern etched on her face. Her health wasn't good, and I hated to bring more distress into her life. My father was resigned. His square jaw set as I detailed the situation with Erfun. He never chided me, as he probably wanted to for marrying a man he did not like. He didn't say anything.

"Maybe if you two come and speak to him, he might change," I pleaded with them.

I made arrangements with Erfun and my parents to meet at our apartment. Erfun had agreed to it reluctantly, but he showed up reeking of alcohol. He slouched into a stuffed chair across from the sofa where my parents sat side by side, taking him in.

I served tea, which no one touched. The cups sat steaming on the coffee table. I took a chair beside Erfun. The temperature felt to me as if it had dropped to zero. My father steepled his hands in front of his mouth, and gave Erfun an appraising glare. My mother began.

"Erfun, we wanted to speak to you about Raana. If you understood her better, and you realized how she felt about marriage, you two could get along better."

Erfun's eyes smoldered, but he was silent. I had seen that look in him before, a gathering of strength before a storm.

"Raana cannot accept a second wife. We did not raise her to think that way. If you come home early and show her love and care."

He jumped out of his chair. "She must accept me the way I am. I will not change. I don't care how she was raised." He beat his chest with his finger and shouted. "I am the husband. She has to accept me. I will have a second wife. That's my decision."

I felt my cheeks burning with shame.

After he stomped out of the apartment, cursing as he slammed the door. The three of us sat in silent disbelief at his behavior. There must have been words of comfort between us, but I do not remember them. When the fuzziness in my brain settled, I knew what I must do for my sanity.

"Father, you must help me get a divorce. You know what to do."

He took a deep breath, leaned forward, and rested his elbows on his knees. My father always chose his words carefully from years in the courtroom, and I could see him thinking my situation over.

"If you divorce him, it will bring dishonor to our family and yourself. Your son will have a very difficult life, and you will be a second-class citizen." He shook his head slowly. "No, I cannot help you."

"Father, please." I had never begged anyone for anything, but he was the only person I could beg for help. "I can't live with this man. I must be free of him."

He stood to leave.

I rose and faced him. "Please, Father, help me."

He tightened his lips. "I'm sorry, Baby. I told you the day you married him; you can never return to our house, and never come to me with any complaints. You must stay here."

"I will die here."

"Then you must die in your husband's house." My father was always serious, and he was never more serious than at this moment. He took Mother's hand and led her to the door. I had never seen my mother sadder than at that moment. Her heart was breaking for me.

When they left, I was alone. I felt that I would be alone for the rest of my life. Erfun would never return to me. I was barely twenty-eight years old. I could not stomach a future with Erfun's hate. I went into the bedroom, fell on my face on the bed, and cried. I cried over my naivety, that I had not taken my father's warning as advice five years before. I cried over my son's future, that he would have to grow up with no father to guide him. I wept for myself, that all my education, all my hard work studying, and all my intelligence had not kept me from making the biggest blunder of my life. I cried because it was the only thing left in my power to do.

A person can only weep for themselves for so long, and then they have to rise and return to their situation. I fought my depression by staying busy. As I went about my days, seeing patients, caring for my son, I became painfully aware of the reality of my life. I was alone with a son. A solution to my predicament would only come from me. No one else could rescue me. My son needed me, so suicide was not an option, though some women did take that course of action. Practicing medicine helped my confidence return, so my focus was on my future alone. In Pakistani culture, the only safe option for divorced women is to return to their parents' house. But my father had been clear; I could never return. Even then, I was not like so many other women in my predicament. I didn't need a man to support me if I could free myself.

One day at work, I arrived at a solution. The next time I saw Erfun, I gave him an ultimatum.

"Erfun, I have decided what I am going to do."

He gave me an interested look for the first time in a while. "You will allow me to marry other women?"

"I can never do that. You already know that."

"I will not divorce you. If you don't agree to my demands, you can live alone here for the rest of your life."

I shook my head. "I'll give you three months to agree to live with me as a loving husband and father."

He had a silly smirk on his face, which was growing thicker around the jowls. He was not taking care of himself as he used to, and his drinking was catching up to him.

"Three months, and that's it. You must give them all up for me."

He laughed. "Then what?"

"You'll see. I will leave your house."

He laughed and left, slamming the door like usual.

Every time, I saw him, I asked. "Do you want to live with me as a loving husband and father?"

Every time, he answered no, that I must be the one who compromised.

I counted the days. During those three months, I began looking for a job that provided a residence. I didn't have any money to rent a house. Also, If I rented a place, I knew Erfun would find me and have me thrown out, forcing me to return to his house. But many hospitals provided residences for doctors on staff who had to work nights. These physicians would serve as the on-call physician after hours. I found such an opportunity at Naseerabad Hospital, a women's hospital, near the Nine Zero. At that time, I wasn't aware that it was the home turf of MQM; I would not ordinarily live in such a place, marked by violence and protests. But in those days I was just focusing on finding any place, which would be better than living with Erfun. Our situation at home was very dangerous. Whenever Erfun snatched my son for a few days, his physical and psychological health began deteriorating day by day; he looked scared all the time, especially when he saw Erfun.

After interviewing with Dr. Soofia, the hospital director, she hired me and offered me an apartment on the top floor of the residences. I looked over the place, and it was more than suitable. The hospital had childcare available, so everything I needed was right here. I set the date to begin work.

Now, I just had to tell Erfun I was leaving.

CHAPTER 8
Seeking Khula

I WAS A MARRIED WOMAN LEAVING my husband in a country that despised women who defied their men. Nevertheless, I had made up my mind: I was committed and focused on raising my son on my own and having a life full of love and peace. The turmoil roiling my mind and heart for the last four years had subsided once I made the decision and began packing. Erfun was rarely around, allowing me to work undisturbed. Even then, I couldn't shake the chronic depression I had fallen into.

The day I had set to leave, Erfun came home a transformed man. He was the charming, kind, sweet-talking man I thought I had married. He begged me not to go, making outlandish comments, complimenting my beauty and my intelligence, saying that I would meet a decent man to marry right away. He said he could never live without me.

Then he got down on his knees and touched my feet, and said, "I love you. Please don't leave me."

My heart was an iceberg, my body frozen with tension at the touch of his fingers on my feet. "Since we left Murree, except for two weeks at home, you have not lived with me one day in love and kindness. Not one day!"

He stood, leaning back on one foot, he narrowed his eyes at me, a pent-up fury gathering behind his large brown eyes, and then he leaned toward me. "I will never let you go. If you leave, I will see that you're never happily married."

"I am not going to marry anyone. I hate men after your abuse. I am going to work, and live alone, and raise my son. I don't need a man to live."

"I will not allow you to keep a job. I will defame you to management, so that they will fire you. No one will give you a place to live." He pointed a hostile finger at me. "You will come crawling back to me and beg for something to eat and a place to live."

"Over my dead body."

"You are like a child. You do not know the world is full of vultures. You are too innocent; you will not survive. At least let me arrange a house and a car so both of you can live comfortably. I will give you a good amount every month."

"Every word that comes out of your mouth is empty. You still haven't given my *Haqq Mehar* money, which as a Muslim husband, you have to give me at the time of *Nikah*. If I accept your offer, it will give you the satisfaction that you atoned. I want you to live with the guilt that you destroyed that woman whom you claim you loved, and she left you with empty hands."

I saw an expression of humiliation on his face.

He stepped forward, held out his hands to take Taimoor. "Give me the boy, and I will pay you what you want."

I held my son to me. "I will never allow you to take him to that woman. She will ruin him. I want him to be a confident and strong man. I will raise him myself."

I moved around him to the door. He didn't try to stop me. With Taimoor in my arms, I slammed the door behind me and made my way downstairs to a waiting cab.

Settling in the back seat, I felt as if I had just been released from prison. But was I clever enough to deal with the vultures?

I moved into an apartment on the top floor of the Naseerabad Hospital near Nine Zero. The district was named after the house of the leader of the MQM, Altaf Hussain, who lived here, and the area was the hub for terrorist activities. I worked in the Obstetrics and Pediatric Unit in the evening shift and on-call night duty. Despite my unresolved marital situation, I felt happy to be back at work, and safe inside the hospital.

Out the window of my apartment, I watched the party members of the local MQM as they gathered every night on the roof of the apartment building across the street. The roof was at the same level as my apartment, and I could see them meeting as they planned their night's raids. The men brandished their weapons and shouted slogans before riding off on their motorbikes to beat, rape, kidnap, rob, and kill those who opposed them in their own torture cells.

This neighborhood wasn't safe for us. I could not allow my son to run outside and play, but this job had saved my sanity, so I had to make do. The years I was caged in Erfun's house, I had been cut off from the world. I hadn't been aware of the havoc the MQM was sowing in the district, and across Karachi, and seeing it firsthand came as a bit of shock.

When Taimoor turned four, I organized a birthday party for him. He invited his friends from the neighborhood. I had never seen my son happier. I invited Erfun, but he didn't show up.

Neither did he wait long to act on his threats. Visiting Dr. Soofia, he tried to smear me, claiming I was a woman of bad character and should not have a job. She demanded that he leave her office immediately and never return. If he did, she would have him arrested. Her brother was the Deputy Superintendent of Police. She sought me out and told me about her meeting, that he was drunk when he came to see her. She was disgusted with the man's drunken behavior. She advised me that the best thing I could do for myself was to divorce him.

I told her Erfun would never grant me a divorce.

"Then you must seek a *khula*," she said. "He doesn't deserve you."

I agreed with her wholeheartedly.

In Islam, there is a concept of *khula* that allows a woman to initiate a divorce for any reason. On a phone call, I told Erfun what I was planning if he didn't grant me a divorce. He continued to threaten me, and he was adamant that he would never sign the *khula* papers. He even taunted me, "Where will you get the two witnesses to vouch for you?"

Before I could be granted a *khula*, two witnesses to my abuse must sign the documents.

I didn't know how I could get him to sign it, but I knew I could find two witnesses, and I was determined to pursue the process.

On a day off, I took Taimoor and visited my parents. They knew my situation well, and during the visit, I announced that I had decided to seek a divorce. My father's back stiffened; his square jaw seemed to become more pronounced.

"I need your help filing the papers." I looked right at him, with a confident voice, just the way I had since my childhood.

He shook his head slowly, "I can't allow you to defame the family honor by getting a divorce. No, Baby, I cannot help you."

My mother pleaded with him. "Please help her. Our daughter has a very strong personality, she can never compromise. You know she will eventually get what she wants. So why not help her?"

He was silent.

"Look at her," my mother said. "She doesn't cry. She never smiles anymore. Always she was the liveliest girl. Now she has constant head-aches and is always quiet and sad."

"Who knows her better than me?" my father said. "She is my beloved daughter. But she has to face the consequences of her decision to marry Erfun."

"Father, your daughter made a mistake. And now she's falling apart. Won't you hold her hand and help lift her out of her terrible situation. Will you leave me alone at the mercy of our culture that is cruel to women?"

"If you insist on a divorce, listen carefully, as I said earlier, the doors of this house are closed to you."

I took a gulp and held my tongue. I would never dispute with my father. His sense of honor was unassailable. I understood that.

"Yes. I know. That's why I am forced to live in Nine Zero, the most dangerous area in all of Pakistan. My son and I, our lives are in con-stant danger. But still, you refuse to allow me to live at home, which is traditional for a divorced woman."

He didn't say a word.

I left greatly disappointed, but even more determined to seek *khula*.

Divorce is a very serious business in Pakistan. Divorced women face pressure and humiliation from society and their family. That is why so many women cannot tolerate being divorced. It means more abuse from their family and society. Living alone is very difficult, even for an educated woman like myself. If I went through with the divorce, I would not have the protection of my father's house, an additional measure of risk that I had to weigh. My son would be stigmatized as coming from a broken home. While I feared that, I knew I could overcome many problems if I protected him and saw to his education.

I sought out Dr. Soofia for advice. She was surprised to hear my father's refusal to help. How could he abandon his daughter? Especially when he was a competent attorney and had expertise in these kinds of cases. She suggested I seek help through the Community Council. Each district has a Council that will help individuals with family matters. She offered to call the Council's office in the neighborhood for an appointment, since they knew her well. She assured me the process would be quick, that I didn't need to worry. She also offered to sign as a witness and support me in court if it became necessary.

Her encouragement gave me a new boost of hope. I visited the office and filed the paperwork.

My cousin and sister-in-law, Farah, who was my brother Rahat's wife, also signed the *khula* papers as a witness of Erfun's mistreatment. Once I had the approval of the Council and my two witnesses, I only had to have Erfun sign.

When I called him and told him the papers were ready for him to sign, he immediately asked me who had witnessed the papers. He grunted when I told him. He then stated emphatically he would never sign them because I was his property. No one else had the right to marry me.

"You will live your life alone." Then he hung up the phone.

This stalemate went on for weeks. I thought he would eventually tire of me pestering him. I knew for sure that he had another mistress in addition to Shesta, and who knew how many others. So why was he hanging on to me, causing me so much pain? Every day became a chore to get beyond the anguish of my heart. This ignorant man had stomped on my dream of doing postgraduate work and living a productive and happy life. He had no reason, other than his inflated ego, to think that he owned me. I would never accept that.

One day I called and asked him to come and sign the papers. I tried to convince him. "Islam expects husbands to treat their women with kindness. When a couple has a dispute and feel divorce is inevitable, then you must divorce your wife respectfully and promptly so she can remarry if she wishes."

"Who told you that?" he shouted.

"Read Sura Nisa in the Quran. You will learn that Islam gives women so many rights, too."

"I will come very soon to give you the rights you deserve." He slammed the phone down.

The next day, I was in a clinic with patients when Erfun walked in. He was bleary-eyed, and I knew he was drunk. Before I could run, he grabbed my hand and began pulling me to the outside gate.

"Come with me outside," he repeated with a slurred voice, forcing me out of the ward.

Even in his condition, he was so strong I could not escape. "What are you doing?" I screamed.

"You are asking for *khula* and talking about your rights. I am taking you to the street, and I will tear your dress off in front of everyone."

I felt a wave of anger, a burning fire race through me—I felt so much strength in me. I rescued my hand from his grip and I stared into his eyes and shouted in my rage. "Go and undress your sister and mother first in public. Both are women like me, then come to Taimoor's mother."

He stopped with a shocked look. He stared at me for some time, but didn't let me go. I had no idea what he was thinking. Was he going to kill me on the spot? After a while, he let me go and left.

I couldn't sleep after that episode. I kept turning over in my mind the same question: *How could he even think to do this to me?* I was his wife, and the mother of his child. He had no respect for anyone, not even the mother of his child. That feeling caused me extreme pain as if he had stuck a knife right through my heart, and blood drops were oozing from that wound. I didn't feel this would ever heal. I carried it with me every moment for so long.

I lived in a state of limbo, fearing to go outside because of Erfun's desire to harm me and the presence of the MQM across the way, which made even walking in the neighborhood treacherous.

In the face of this opposition, I turned to my faith. I had been reciting the Quran since I was a child. I said a verse every day, several times a day, with so much faith until it became a prayer in my heart.

After three weeks, Erfun came to the hospital and signed the papers. He was calm, quiet, and uncharacteristically sober. I already left my dowry when I left his house, and I never received *Haqq Mehar*, so I didn't have anything to return to him after the *khula* was completed.

I felt free from his prison.

Soon after that, Gezala came to the hospital and asked to meet with me. She apologized for her behavior. She sought my forgiveness. She had remarried and suffered a stillbirth. Her grief was so intense, she began to think of all the wrong she had done to me and regretted it. I forgave her readily. But the memory of her mistreatment of my newborn son and me is with me to this day. I told her, "You are one of the main reasons for my divorce. I never want to see you again."

Sequestered in the hospital and free from Erfun and his family, I was at peace for the first time in nearly five years. My life settled into a calm routine of seeing patients and caring for my son.

A few weeks later, I was in the back of a taxi on my way back to the hospital, when it stopped at a stoplight. I was lost in my thoughts; I spotted Erfun in the car next to us. My window was open, right across from his. His window was only a few feet away from me. He raised his hand, at first I thought he was waving at me, but I felt an instant alarm. My body tensed. Did he have a gun or a knife? He made a throwing motion toward me. At first, I couldn't imagine what he was doing. At the moment I realized his intention, I ducked, and a few drops of liquid glanced off my left arm. The acid sizzled on the back of the seat instead of my face. My left deltoid was on fire, but luckily, my face was saved.

I yelled at the driver to get me to the hospital—fast. The putrid chemical smell quickly permeated the car. I refused to weep over this man's actions, but instead I took deep breaths to stave off the burning. The taxi driver drove like a madman, up on the sidewalk, honking at bicyclists and jitney drivers, speeding to get me to the hospital. Eventually, my wounds healed, but to this day I still have a ragged scar on my arm. These type of attacks happen quite often in remote areas of Pakistan, mostly by uneducated men. I never imagined I would be the victim of an acid attack one day.

Erfun had warned me many times that he would kill me, or throw acid on me to disfigure me, so no one would ever love me. So I was prepared mentally for more torture. But when it came, I was still surprised. However, his abuse and threats wouldn't stop my struggle to live a dignified life. His injured ego was too fragile to watch me becoming stronger and independent. With this act Erfun showed his true self. He was jealous, angry, and violent, not the gentle and loving man he had pretended to be so convincingly for two years before we were married.

I enrolled my son in preschool at St. John's, a school not too far from the hospital. The challenge was getting back and forth to get him there safely, as the MQM terrorists were becoming more violent and brazen. The police were afraid of the MQM and allowed them to run the district the way they wanted. Rangers had to take over from time to time to protect innocent citizens from harm.

One day my nurse on the ward, Meher, informed me someone wanted to talk to me over the phone. When I took the call, someone said in an ominous sounding voice that he was calling from Nine Zero, and he would kidnap me very soon. I didn't want to show my fear. I replied, "No, you can't kidnap me. You don't have enough courage."

"How can you say that? Tell me, who is at your back?"

"The strongest and superior one is at my back," I said, confident that God would keep me strong.

"Oh, Altaf Bhai, okay. Okay." (He thought only MQM leader Altaf Hussain is the most superior one.)

He hung up. I thanked God.

The government had announced a curfew to control the terrorist activities of the MQM thugs. Their terror had become intolerable to everyone so that the Rangers had to take over. Taimoor became very sick during those days from jaundice and a high fever. He couldn't eat anything but liquids, but there was nothing for him. Everything, including the milk in the fridge, had spoiled because of load shedding that went on for most of the day. I promised him that I would find him some food. In the meanwhile, Taimoor became very weak and drowsy and I feared he would faint, or worse. I carried him on my shoulder and went outside.

On the empty streets, I walked up and down the dark, narrow boulevards with only the moonlight to show me the way. Not one shop or store was open. Gunshots echoed in the distance. I became tired and hungry, and fear began to set in. Out of nowhere, a boy on a bicycle stopped near me.

"Dr. Raana! Why are you outside? Don't you know there's a curfew? If the terrorists or the Rangers find you, they will shoot you." I recognized the voice right away. He was the son of my nurse, Meher.

I started crying. "It's Taimoor. I need medicine and milk for him. With the continuous curfew since yesterday, how else can I get him some food?"

"Please go home. I will try to arrange what you need." I gave him some money and trudged home. An hour or so later, he returned with milk, some food for me and Panadol syrup. Meanwhile, Taimoor had fainted. I feared the worst. All I could do was pray to God to preserve his life. When the milk arrived, I fed him with a spoon and he began to revive. His big eyelashes fluttered. "Mom," he said in a weak voice.

"Yes, my sweetheart, I am here."

One day, returning from picking Taimoor up after school, we strolled down the sidewalk. We weren't too far from the school, the sky was bright and clear, and we were enjoying taking some fresh air. We spent so much time inside; I wanted to soak up a few moments of sunshine.

In one instant, I felt safe, and in the next, I sensed activity behind me. I glanced around. A man clutching a Kalashnikov, his face and head wrapped in a scarf with only a slit for his eyes, rode on the hood of a car that slowly rolled down the street after me. I thought I recognized him despite his disguise. He was often on the roof of the apartment house across from me. Once the car came closer, he jumped off the hood. Someone said to him, "Yes, Bhai! That is her."

I scooped up Taimoor and suddenly changed my route, instead of

walking straight; I hid, mingled in with some people who were cross-
ing the street after picking up their children from school. I crossed over
without any panic.

"Where is she?" I heard the voice of the man with the scarf.

"She was just here a few seconds ago. Search for her!"

I ducked into a small restaurant, pushing past the curtain that
served as a door. I selected a small table at the rear. The electricity was
still off, so it was completely dark.

"It's time for a treat," I announced to Taimoor. "Order whatever
you like."

He started clapping. Men stomped into the restaurant.

"Where is she?"

"I don't know." They looked through the curtain, but didn't come
inside. They stood outside talking.

After a while, I could no longer hear them outside. I let Taimoor
finish his food. When he was full, I rose. "Let's go."

With Taimoor in my arms and his heavy school bag on my shoulder, I hustled toward the hospital's back gate. We were less than
twenty feet from the door when I spotted the same scarf man with
his Kalashnikov waiting near the gate. I was terrified. I turned and
started running toward the front gate. After rounding the building,
we reached the front door, but it was locked. The scarf man caught up
with me. He pointed his Kalashnikov at my head and said very calmly
through his scarf.

"Be ready to die."

It was useless to run. He would callously shoot us down. I held my
head high and stared into his eyes. "Give me one minute, please."

He nodded.

I patted my son on his head, and I spoke to him in a comforting
voice. "Close your eyes, sweet one, and lay your head on my shoulder
and sleep."

After he stilled, I said to the terrorist, "Okay, I am ready to die.
Now you can kill me."

I stood up as tall as I could, and looked right into his eyes. He
placed the barrel of the gun at my temple.

"I thought you'd cry and beg for your life."

"Never. I will never beg. Go ahead, shoot."

He closed one eye and pushed the barrel hard into my head.

I said in my heart, *God, please save my child.*

He then raised his gun over my head and fired into the air.

"I could kill you in a second. I tried to kidnap you a few times, but you always dodge me. I have never seen such a brave woman. Go."

I did not believe what he was saying. These men had no heart. They never showed mercy to anyone. I stood paralyzed in uncertainty.

"Go, before I change my mind." He stepped back.

I clutched Taimoor tightly, ran to the hospital back doors, and pushed my way inside. A few minutes later, we were upstairs in our apartment. I set Taimoor down, and he just stared up at me, a question already forming on his lips. He was on the verge of tears; he was so afraid.

"Why was he going to kill us? What did we do? Why were we running?"

I took both his hands in mine and swung him around once, trying my best to calm him. "No, no, he was not going to kill us. He just wanted to test us, to see how brave we are. And you are the bravest boy in the entire city." I touched his nose. "You didn't even cry. You are so brave. Let's dance."

I swung him around, singing an old ditty I learned as a child. We bounced on the carpet, kicking our feet, and swirling away our troubles. "You are the bravest boy ever. . ." I sang repeatedly. And so, we danced on, our fears passing from us like a black rain cloud blown away by a fresh wind, and we twirled and sang until the sunshine of my boy's smile returned.

CHAPTER 9
Who is at Your Back?

I LIVED AND WORKED FOR TWO years in Naseerabad Hospital before I began looking for another job in a safer neighborhood, and one opportunity stood out: the Gas Company, a semi-government-owned operation, needed a physician in one of their company clinics. The interview went well, but the interviewer was clear that they'd had over 350 applicants, and it would take a couple of months to make a proper decision.

Any job at a government-run or -affiliated organization usually was given to people with political ties, which I had none of. So I hoped that this time they would make a decision based on merit alone. I knew miracles still happened. After two months and no word from the Gas Company, I called one of the General Managers among the three who had interviewed me.

He was kind, but noncommittal. He assured me I was still being considered for the position since I had achieved high scores in the interview. He promised an answer in two weeks. When I didn't hear from him, I showed up at his office in person. He was surprised to see me, but invited me into his office.

"Sir, you said it would take two months to make a decision. I've been counting the days to hear your decision. We need this job."

"We?"

"Yes, my four-year-old son and I. I've been praying every day for this job."

"I am very sorry to disappoint you, but we have given this job to

Dr. Sheela, who has worked at a company clinic in Balochistan for many years. Now she wants a job in Karachi."

I couldn't believe they hadn't told me sooner. "Sir, I need this job. We have to leave the hospital where I'm living, because it's near Nine Zero and not safe for us."

He pursed his lips, reached into a drawer, pulled out a file folder, and opened it on his desk. He then perused my paperwork.

"You received the highest marks among all candidates in the interview and in medical college. You do deserve a position with us. We have one more opening in Unit C, where you will see our executive team and their families." He thought for a few moments. "Dr. Mrs. Moien will retire in one month. You can start then."

My heart lifted. "Thank you, sir. This makes me very happy."

"I will prepare an appointment letter. Please wait."

Within an hour, I had a letter appointing me to a staff medical doctor position in Unit C, to begin in one month. I was to report to Dr. Uqali, the medical director for Unit C, to introduce myself.

On the taxi ride back to the hospital, I felt some of the darkness of the past few years began to lift. It would be a new start for both of us. I would be entirely self-supporting and free of Erfun. I had one month to prepare for the move. My new office would be in one of the most beautiful neighborhoods in Karachi, near my parents' house.

I immediately turned in my resignation to Dr. Soofia. She was sad to see me move on, but she understood. It would be bittersweet to leave the hospital, but it was time. Taimoor would be starting first grade soon, and I wanted him to get the best education I could afford and to provide him a safer neighborhood.

In my free time, I began searching for a room to rent near my new workplace. One day I had Taimoor with me when a landlady told me that she could not rent to me since I was a young single woman. I told her I was not that young, and that I had a child and a job as a medical doctor. I could take care of myself.

Nevertheless, one door after another closed to me when I said I was not married. I had every right to rent an apartment in my name alone. I was divorced, a mother, and employed. The law was clearly in my favor. But the landlords I spoke with didn't care about that. All of them said the same thing: I would have to be married to rent an apartment.

I realized that unless I purchased my own home, I would never be truly independent. I was not able to return to my parent's home. I hated being excluded from decent housing just because of some archaic tradition.

When I was trying to figure out where to find housing, since I could not live in my hospital apartment after my employment ended, Taimoor, without prompting, mentioned to my mother that no one would rent to us. He had overheard a conversation with one of the property owners. Unbeknownst to me, she pleaded with my father to let us live at home for a time, so that I could save enough for a down payment on my own house. Owning my own home would be the only way I could be safe as a divorced woman in this society.

The Pakistani practice of treating single women like children who must be continuously chaperoned is one of the driving forces behind why married women in abusive marriages refuse to strike out on their own. It is also why divorced women seek out men to support them, even if those men are already married. Erfun used this fact in rationalizing taking Shesta as a second wife. If he didn't marry her, Shesta would be destitute, with nowhere to live. Since she couldn't rent a place on her own due to lack of education, and she had no skills to support herself, she had to find someone who would pose as her husband merely to be safely sheltered. She had even resorted to using black magic to get Erfun to break up our marriage. In one of her phone calls to me, pleading with me to let her marry Erfun, she had claimed she'd put a curse on me so Erfun would hate me. But I thought little of the power of black magic. Pakistanis used it to get what they wanted. But I never gave it any consideration as a reason for Erfun's behavior.

One day, my mother called me to say that my father had acquiesced to her requests. He would allow both of us to move into the family home for a set time. I knew my staunchly principled father had bent to the reality of my situation, and I was grateful. This arrangement would be the safest place for Taimoor and me. I set the date to move and my younger brothers Rehan and Rafhan helped me to move my belongings into my parent's house.

On the day set to meet Dr. Uqali in the Head Office, I waited outside his office seated across from his assistant, Razzak, as he flipped slowly through my file and scanned it with a sigh. He had a deep frown on his brow. I didn't understand why he appeared so troubled.

"You are Punjabi, correct?"

I nodded.

"Be careful, Dr. Raana, Dr. Uqali is Sindhi. He may not like you since you are Punjabi."

I took a breath. I had fought hard for this job. I had received the highest marks out of 350 applicants. I had earned this position, and I had no intention of giving in to fear at this moment. I smiled at Razzak confidently. "Thank you, but I am not worried."

A few moments later, he ushered me into the medical director's office. He was an imposing tall man, with thick white hair, well dressed, with a severe look on his face, as if he had made up his mind about me already. I handed him my appointment letter, and he motioned for me to be seated. He leaned back in his leather chair with a look of uncertainty and studied the document.

He spoke to me sharply. "How were you selected without my knowledge?"

Sir, I applied and appeared for an interview for Units A and B, but for some reason Mr. Khursheed transferred me here to Unit C."

He was watching me quietly.

"I scored the highest on all the interviews and exams. I was the most qualified for the position."

He rubbed his lips and set my letter down on the desk in front of him. He folded his arms. "Tell me, who is at your back? What is your political background?"

"I was selected based on my merits, Dr. Uqali. That is all I know."

"Who is at your back?" he asked.

After he asked the same question again, "Sir, God is at my back." I replied confidently.

He smiled for the first time. "Of course." His mood lightened. "There is no doubt; God must be at your back. But tell me truthfully: Who is at your back? What political party? What minister."

I remained quiet. That was the best I could do.

He called for my file. Razzak must have been at the door because he entered immediately and handed him the folder. Dr. Uqali perused it, page by page. "This is going to be difficult. You have no political affiliations. You are divorced, so you have no husband to protect you. You have no one at your back. That is a problem for you." He set the file down and leaned over his desk. "You are such a sweet little girl, how will you do your job here? You have no one to protect you."

"Sir, I am not afraid. You are here."

He smiled again, considering my words. Finally, he called Javed Khan, the manager of the medical department and had a conversation with him and Razzak. I was waiting outside, when Razzak came and told me to wait for about a half an hour, and that there would be a meeting in his office with the union leaders and some others.

When everyone gathered in his office, about ten or fifteen men, he spoke authoritatively to them.

He introduced me as the new physician that would work in Unit C, treating them and their families. "She is like my daughter. I don't want anyone bothering her or saying anything to her." Everyone nodded and greeted me kindly. I could not help smiling. God and Dr. Uqali, the medical director, were now at my back.

Later, after everyone left, and it was just the medical director and me, he asked about my divorce. I told him the sad tale of abuse, of Erfun's fixation on marrying Shesta; his threats and intimidation until I relented; and how I refused to give in to Erfun's demands and mistreatment.

"You are a child. You aren't even aware that in our culture it is common for women to use black magic on married women and then grab their husband."

This was the first time I had ever heard an educated and sophisticated person like Dr. Uqali speak of black magic as if it were true, a force to be reckoned with. I was still skeptical, but something or someone had turned my loving husband against me. Whether it was Gezala and her selfishness and ignorance, or Shesta and her wiles, I couldn't say. But Erfun had become a demon to me. But did that mean magic was real? I didn't know that for sure.

I began my career at the Gas Company working in three clinics. One day a week, I worked at the Head Office, three days at Karachi Terminal (KT), and one day at Rimpa Plaza, a modern office building in central Karachi. My clinic was on the tenth floor, and we had a small team of three: a male clerk, my male helper, and myself.

The clinic for the Units A and B was located on the first floor of Rimpa Plaza. It was a large and busy operation, with a sizable staff of doctors and helpers who treated the company's clerical and technical staff and their families, Dr. Sheela joined that office.

In the headquarters, I had an office where the Managing Director, Mr. Javeed ul Hasan, Dr. Uqali, and the other executives had their offices. During my three days job at KT, I examined and treated the female family members of the executives, who lived at the residential colony in the vicinity of the KT.

The work pace was leisurely, as I only treated executives and their families. Everyone was respectful and pleasant. I was excited about my new job.

When my son turned five, I took him to one of the finest schools in the city, St. Paul's School, which had an excellent reputation for providing a high-quality education. Before I could enroll Taimoor, he needed to take an entrance exam. Unfortunately, Taimoor did not pass the entrance exam. When I received the letter informing me, I was heartbroken, but determined to find a way to reverse that decision.

I met with the principal, Father Max, and explained to him that my son is very intelligent and that he didn't pass the exam because I didn't have time to prepare him adequately as I should have. I impressed on the principal of how important a quality education was to my son and myself, and that I would appreciate another opportunity to have him tested. He appreciated my enthusiasm and agreed to give me an additional two weeks to prepare him. This time, after receiving back the new test results, Taimoor passed, and he was enrolled in first grade.

When school began, I arranged a school bus for him. But I had to drop him off at the bus stop each morning before my scheduled shift, and my mother or one of my siblings picked him up each day from the bus stop while I was at work. My family's help enabled me to save my money. For one year, I scrimped every penny, saving for a down payment.

When I had enough saved, I searched and selected a new housing development project, that was under construction not far from my parent's home. I asked my father to accompany me for his blessings, and I signed the papers for a new home, similar to what is called a condominium in America. They had just begun building it so it would take a while to complete. The complex was called Chapal House.

I had to pay installments every three months. I wanted to pay it off quickly by myself, so I didn't take out a mortgage. Soon, I would be truly independent.

During the time I lived at my parent's home, Furqan visited my mother. He said he wanted to marry me. I told him I was in no mood to begin a new life. I had no feelings for him the first day I met him, and nothing had changed since then. I told him about my terrifying experience with Erfun, and I didn't know if I could ever trust a man again. No, I did not plan to marry again for a long time—if ever.

Before he left, Furqan told me he had used black magic to break up my marriage, and that was why I was so angry. If Furqan's magic had caused even a fraction of the pain I'd experienced the last six years, how could I love this man who would use evil to win my heart? I asked Furqan to leave. He was not to think I would ever marry him, so he should stop bothering me. We each needed to go live our own lives and hope for a peaceful future.

I still didn't believe that black magic had any effect on a person's life. I had studied the Quran diligently as a child, so I knew the scriptures forbade the practice of magic. There are many verses in the Quran to protect us from the magic and evil forces, but we must recite them with strong faith in God. Being a Muslim, we should not believe in magic, it was just another superstitious way of dealing with life's difficulties and to gain anything, it was practiced by ignorant people.

CHAPTER 10

Pretending to Smile

My LIFE AND MY WORK began to settle into a stable routine. The relaxed pace allowed me to regroup mentally. Finally, having respect as a physician, and living in peace and tranquility with my son and family, began to bring some comfort to my heart. The debilitating depression began to lift, but I still found it difficult to smile.

Erfun's parents came to meet me at my father's house; they were going to Mecca to perform Hajj. They were crying about my divorce and saying, God gave them such a wonderful daughter-in-law, and they've lost her. They were ashamed for their misbehavior, and asked forgiveness from me. I forgave them.

One day while working in my Rimpa office, a woman I had never met came in. She appeared older than me and was dressed casually in a *shalwar kameez* without the white lab coat the doctors and medical staff usually wore, so I didn't recognize her as part of the staff. My helper introduced her as Dr. Sheela, the physician who had transferred from Sui Gas in Balochistan, where she had worked for many years. She seemed interested in talking, so I invited her into my office.

She glanced around as if she were appraising everything. I offered her some coffee, but she demurred. We chatted a bit, and then she remarked that I appeared to be having an easy day. I sat, taking a break, and enjoying a cup of coffee at my desk, while my support staff handled the phone and the paperwork. I could relax between patients. For all she knew, I had been sitting here all day with nothing much to do, which hadn't been the case.

She made a point of noting that my office was a dream compared to hers. Downstairs, in Units A and B, where she treated the clerical and technical staff and their families, she had long lines with demanding patients and a lot of shouting and noise.

"Like a fish market," she said with a disgusted sneer.

I was surprised at her attitude. I thought she had preferred to work in the A and B Units. That's why I was sent to Unit C. Why was she now complaining?

She went on to tell me about how she had joined the company many years before in Balochistan, where she had treated many of the company's executives and staff. Many of them had become her friends. When she applied for a transfer to Karachi, the only opening they had offered was for Units A and B. Even the interview was set up for her, the understanding was that she would take a post in Units A and B regardless of the interview results.

Since she wanted to transfer to Karachi, she had resigned her position with the understanding she would take up a post to work in Units A and B on the first floor of the same building I worked in. Evidently, because she had resigned her position before taking her new assignment in Karachi, she had lost her seniority.

I, on the other hand, had earned the top marks in the exam and had persuaded management that I was the most qualified applicant. I also believed my son's prayers were not in vain. Now I understood that God must have been watching over me, because my position in Unit C had been a healing experience after the horrible years of my marriage.

Unit C was very orderly and organized. There were seventeen physicians, and I was the only female doctor amongst them. All the medical assistants were male. It was the custom of the party in power to appoint their own members, often without any interview process. All of the doctors I worked with had been selected during Prime Minister Zulfiqar Ali Bhutto's government through his People's Party, or subsequently during Benazir Bhutto's tenure as Prime Minister. They were all Sindhi because Dr. Uqali was Sindhi.

At the time, I was the only exception.

I knew that Dr. Sheela had lobbied hard for the approval for her transfer for the opportunity to work in Karachi instead of the backwaters of Balochistan. The position in Units A and B in Karachi must be better than Balochistan, but not better than Unit C.

After she left, I felt confused. Her visit hadn't been amiable. She didn't seem interested in getting to know me as a fellow doctor, but instead had tried to weasel information out of me. She seemed motivated more out of jealousy than any sense of collegial cooperation. My intuition told me that she harbored a growing resentment that she had to work so hard with difficult patients and trying surroundings, while I seemed at ease with patient care.

I didn't acknowledge any of her observations, even though I sympathized with her. If Unit C was quieter, I needed those quiet moments between patients to allow me to relax from the stress of what I had endured for the last six years. Overall, I thought her visit strange. She didn't strike me as sincere in her intentions, whatever they may have been. But after a while, I thought nothing of her visit.

Mother suddenly fell ill. She was diagnosed with cancer, and she began to deteriorate rapidly. I knew that with the right treatment, patients with her diagnosis could survive. There were always new therapies available, so I went to meet with her oncologists. When I spoke with her doctors about their treatment plan, they told me that in her case it was their opinion that there was very little they could do for her.

She had lost her will to survive, and no longer wished to fight the disease. I could see it in her eyes. She was not only sad, but disappointed in how my marriage had turned out. She had always told me she felt my pain, and she knew I was suffering. I was no longer joyful and outgoing as I had been as a child and as a student. All the happiness in my life had gone missing. I had become quiet and reserved. She would tell me the best thing I could do was to open up and talk about what Erfun had done, and what I had experienced. But it would be too painful to complain and whine about Erfun to her. She was the only one who always had my best interests at heart, and I didn't want to do anything that would cause her more grief than she already carried.

By the time she began her chemotherapy, one month after her diagnosis, she had become a shell of the vibrant, beautiful woman who had brought me into this world and nurtured all of my dreams and aspirations. She did not survive her first chemotherapy treatment.

The day before she died, as I sat by her bedside, she turned to me. "If you had shared with me what you had suffered in Erfun's house, I would have more hope to live."

I turned my face from her and tried to hide my tears. My heart felt ready to burst with the pain she must be feeling for me. I wanted to tell her the truth, but those days in Erfun's home had confused me emotionally, filling me with feelings of doubt—perhaps I had been wrong in the way I had responded to him. Maybe I was responsible for the collapse of my marriage, and so I had earned these consequences I was facing. As much as I tried to explain my feelings to her, I couldn't bring myself to talk about what Erfun had done to me. The hurt was so deep that merely thinking about all those chilling episodes made me weak inside. I knew my silence was slowly killing her, and I was helpless to take another path.

It was impossible for me to shake the evil words of Erfun, his wicked sister, shameless mistress, and callous parents. Those words had become part of me. Despite all the kindness from Dr. Soofia, who constantly told me that Erfun didn't deserve me and that I was an exceptional woman, I could not easily undo the four years of mental and physical torture.

After I pulled myself together, Mother held my hand and said she had something important she wanted to tell me. Her voice was low and breathless as she slowly articulated her words.

As I knew, when I was born and during my childhood, she had a series of horrible dreams. She believed God had given her portents of evil things that would happen to me as an adult. She was convinced I would face many difficulties in my life, and no one would help me. She wanted to protect me. But now she regretted allowing me to stay isolated during my childhood and teen years, when I should have learned to trust others. She allowed me to hide from the world behind my books and my intellectual efforts, and submerge myself in my own imaginary world, a world which would always be beautiful and peaceful. Instead, she should have prepared me to deal with the adversity of a practical life and to understand how to deal with people better.

Even now, after my divorce, she believed I was too innocent to deal effectively with the true intentions of a culture that favors hypocrites and exhibitionists. Even after all I had been through, I was naïve about the world. Grief over what had happened to me had become a drag on her life.

She pleaded with me to marry a good man, a man who would protect me, care for me, and bring me happiness. She did not want to die thinking that I would be unhappy living alone my entire life. Her soul would not be at rest if she died thinking I would never find happiness. Listening to her explain her fears, I could not control the tears running from my eyes.

She then went on to suggest a few men from our immediate and extended family who she thought would be good matches for me. She especially insisted I consider her brother's son, who was a doctor in Punjab and who had always wanted to marry me. We were the same age and had known each other since childhood. But I feared if I moved to Punjab, Taimoor's education would be compromised.

My heart was breaking during the entire conversation, to think that I had caused her so much grief on top of what I had experienced. I did not want her to pass with so many regrets.

I took her feeble hand. "Mother, I promise, when I am ready, I will marry a good man. But right now, I can't." The entire experience with Erfun was still too raw for me to think of loving another man again. Especially since my father's advice to me was that I should give up my son, so a new husband would not have the burden of raising another man's child. I could not bear to consider that option.

She smiled wanly. Cancer had emaciated her—her cheeks were sunken, and the glow of life in her eyes that had once been so bright flickered. She sighed, and she looked at peace.

She died the next day.

I went through the motions of the Islamic funeral rites in a state of disbelief. Though I was burying my mother, the only person who had loved me without any reservations, I could not accept her death. As her enshrouded body passed before me, a new sense of aloneness came over me. At the cemetery surrounded by my brothers and sisters, uncles and aunts who had traveled from Punjab, and my father, I stood among them, but alone. Mother had been my bulwark against the cruel world. She had tried her entire life to protect me, but as diligent as she had been, what she feared for my life had come to pass. What did my future hold if there was not one person who could at least try to protect me?

I stood rigid and unsmiling in the midst of my grieving family, fearing that if I moved, I would break open. But as long as I remained quiet, I was dry-eyed and stoic.

At the gravesite, my father, in a moment of tenderness, tried to hug me. I shrugged away from him. He had always helped me, but when I needed him most to deal with my evil husband, he refused me. And now he wanted me to give up Taimoor, the only good thing in my life. I could not hug him now.

I must have shocked my staid and steady father because when I moved away from him, my always composed father began to wail. But I could not comfort his cries.

On the third day of our grieving at Soyam, our maid came to me.

"Baji, your mother always cried for you, worried about you living with your in-laws. She was always waiting for you and watching the door, expecting your visit. She loved you."

Overcome by emotion, I fled to my room and closed the door. I could not hold back the tears. I threw myself on my bed, and my grief overwhelmed me. I was alone now, and I would have to make my way the best I could. And pray that God will watch over me.

Losing Mother only filled me with more regrets that I had not listened to my father. I should have told him about Erfun's threat to kidnap my sister if I didn't agree to marry him. Now I see that he would have protected me against Erfun. I should never have told my father I loved Erfun. I hadn't understood Erfun's true motivations for marrying me, and the truth of it was that I didn't even understand my own feelings. I sifted around in my mind for clues. Why couldn't I see Erfun for who he was—a womanizing alcoholic who didn't truly love me? How could I be so naïve? For my mother to blame herself for what had happened to me with Erfun troubled me. She was the only person who knew the depths of what I had suffered from him.

After a time of mourning, I realized I had taken off a full month from work to care for Mother during her illness. When the week was completed, I returned to work, carrying sadness with me.

One day, Dr. Uqali, who was always pleasant to me, called me into his office. He expressed condolences for the death of my mother.

"I know you are very sad over your mother's death. But, Dr. Raana, you need to begin to live again. You have always been very quiet since you joined the company, but now you look sad, too. You have to begin to smile again. You are like my daughter. It's very difficult to see you so sad."

He told me that patients were complaining about me, saying that I had been rude to them. They thought I was well-mannered and considerate, that I diagnosed them well, and treated them correctly, but I never smiled.

I listened to what he had to say. "I don't know how to smile anymore."

"If you practice smiling, it will be much easier for you."

"Practice?"

"Yes, then in time, you will feel better, and life will be easier. Force yourself to smile, and soon it will come easily."

I knew he was right, but it was very challenging to me because I had become very cynical about people and their intentions. In time, I did begin to smile again. I learned I could pretend to smile, but that didn't mean I was happy.

One day Javed Khan, the manager of the medical department called me into his office to tell me that Dr. Sheela, the doctor whom I had met a few months before, had requested to be transferred to Unit C. That would mean I would be moved to Units A and B. I had an excellent job with pleasant surroundings, and I didn't want to lose it. But Dr. Sheela was well-connected, and had started lobbying for the transfer as soon as she saw my clinic. She had lots of opportunities for lobbying during my one-month absence.

The sense that I was somehow being cheated out of something I truly loved came over me. I knew this new change would affect me, but I just didn't know how much.

CHAPTER 11
Second Wife

A FEW MONTHS AFTER I JOINED Sui Gas, when I was at work, Nashad, a colleague I had worked with at Fon Hospital two years prior, showed up on my parents' doorstep with all her luggage. When my mother answered the door, Nashad began to cry, claiming she had nowhere to turn. Her parents' home had become too difficult for her to live in. She was a Muslim, like her father. He was married, for a second time, to a Christian nurse, and she had remained a Christian with her husband's permission. With the second wife a Christian and the first wife a Muslim, Nashad's home had become a nightmare. She decided to move out, and I was the only one she could think of that would help, although we had only ever been colleagues, not friends.

My mother was too kind to turn her away. When I arrived home that day, Nashad had already moved into our house. She stayed for three months.

She wasn't interested in working; rather, she was on the hunt for a wealthy husband. When she moved in, she was separated from her Agha Khani husband, a very wealthy married businessman from Islamabad. She had carried on an affair with him and eventually had married him. When he visited Karachi from Islamabad, they would stay in a hotel. Her neighbors believed that she was more of a mistress than a second wife. Now the two of them were separated, and would likely divorce.

Because she refused to work and her husband wouldn't support her, her financial situation had become dire. She wanted to divorce him, and find a more suitable husband, one that would support the lifestyle she imagined she was entitled to. Because of her financial situation, she was constantly borrowing money with a promise she would pay me back.

One day my brother Rasikh told me that I had to make her move out. Her family was well-off and lived in a large home not far from ours. He was upset by her behavior, staying out late, arriving home in the early morning, and then sleeping all day.

I confronted her, but she cried that she had nowhere to go. She would leave once she found a husband. When her search became futile, she began pestering me to go with her to a magician.

In Pakistan, if a family doesn't make a match for a women, or if she doesn't meet a man through work or school, a single women can seek a religious solution. She can pray and recite certain verses in the Quran, in the belief the repetition will attract a nice partner. Many times very decent women spend all their lives patiently waiting for a man who never appears, and they end up living isolated and lonely lives.

For others, there is no other alternative but to use a magician to woo a man—either married or unmarried—into falling in love with you. It is a sordid superstition forbidden in Islam, but often practiced out of despair for the lack of alternatives.

I told Nashad that I didn't believe in magic, and refused to accompany her. The entire experience with Shesta was still fresh in my mind. But she persisted, threatening that if I didn't go with her, she would convert to Christianity. When she realized I didn't care if she became a Christian or not, she began crying. As distasteful as her conversion would be, I should have let her become a Christian and forced her to leave our home. I reluctantly agreed to accompany her.

At the magician's office, Nashad introduced me, but I refused to speak to him. I sat and waited in silence. Later Nashad told me that the magician asked her about me, why I wouldn't speak to him. I didn't think much of that visit after we left. I had done what she asked.

A few days later, she asked to borrow 25,000 rupees, a large sum for me. She knew I was saving money to make payments on my home, but she insisted she desperately needed the money. She promised to return the sum in one week. When she didn't repay me on time, I asked her to return the money. But she had already spent everything on designer dresses and couldn't pay me back. I was shocked at her cruelty and irresponsibility.

The next day when I returned from work, she was not there. She had moved out without saying anything.

I couldn't believe my dilemma. I had an installment payment due, and I needed the money. I stayed in my room that evening, skipping dinner. My mother came in and insisted I eat. I came to the table, but I was so depressed that I just stared at my food. I faced the loss of the home I had been making payments on. After dinner, Rasikh came to me. He told me not to worry about the money. He knew that Nashad had left without paying me. He lent me the funds to make the installment payment. I was so thankful for such a gracious and kind brother.

I saved every penny and paid him back, and that was the first and last time I ever borrowed money from anyone.

Shortly after that episode, my mother fell ill. As her condition worsened, I took off work to care for her. When my mother eventually passed and I returned to work, I spent many months grieving. A dark cloud followed me everywhere, and I could not shake the sense that I was responsible for her dying so young. Sometimes I heard her voice in the middle of the night: *Baby, my daughter, my soul cannot rest in peace until you fulfill your promise.* Her voice woke me, and I couldn't sleep the rest of the night.

My anger festered during those days. The Islam I had come to trust and believe, that I had studied so diligently as a child, had failed me. Erfun and his family, who said they followed Islam, were corrupt and self-centered. My dreams of a happy life, one of peace and fulfillment, were dashed forever. Now my only wish was to survive, to become an independent woman, and take care of my precious son. I was thankful that I had a good job, and I could save my money.

I'm convinced that the majority of people in Pakistan who claim to be Muslim have never read the Quran in their native tongue. I believe that they have only memorized verses in Arabic, the language of the Quran, and have never bothered to study the true meaning of the book. So these men treat women any way they like, and the depraved customs that older men hand down to them are nothing. But the treatment I had received at the hands of those who claimed to practice their religion—treatment that was entirely unethical and abhorrent to Islam—left me bitter. It was unjust and hateful. My life had become a struggle to get beyond this biting anger in my soul.

I had learned to smile as Dr. Uqali had asked of me.

As the days moved on, and the kindness of my colleagues began to work on me, I slowly changed. Once during a company sponsored medical seminar, I engaged my colleagues and even bantered with them as we ate our lunch. I noticed Dr. Uqali in the distance, watching and smiling at seeing me with my colleagues, enjoying their conversation. I knew how to be polite, to listen to others, and to seem interested, even if I had to force myself. On occasion, I even smiled.

Over time, my negative disposition evaporated. My colleagues, our medical director, and the staff were all so helpful, kind, and respectful. I believe they all were on a mission to bring me back from the dead.

I continued saving for my house, frugally wearing the same old dresses and shoes. One day my colleague, Dr. Qaze, laughed at me. "Dr. Raana, I am tired of seeing you wearing the same dresses. What do you do with your salary?"

He even offered to purchase some new dresses for me.

"These dresses are fine, Dr. Qaze. Thank you for the offer."

He laughed at me.

In a moment of pride, I said: "I'm saving every penny I make because I'm purchasing my own home. When my new house is paid for, I'll buy some new dresses."

He gave me an astonished, but respectful, smile, nodded his head, and returned to work.

One day, Taimoor's teacher called me. She was concerned about his behavior. He was very timid and hardly spoke in class, and never interacted with the other children. She thought maybe he was sick, or had trouble at home. I didn't tell her about my divorce, but insisted his father treated him well.

I thanked her for her concern, and told her I would address his behavior the best I knew how. I began consulting a child psychologist, who convinced me that Taimoor was depressed and suffered from anxiety, yet he possessed a high IQ. He suggested I find an outlet for his intelligence and to try to socialize him more.

I called his paternal grandfather and asked if he would send Erfun's younger brother to take him on Fridays and Saturdays to his house. Then he could meet his grandparents, uncles, and other family members. I requested that he never allow Erfun to leave the house with him. I feared he would take Taimoor, and leave him with Shesta, who abused him mentally and physically. He agreed, and that Saturday, instead of Erfun, his younger brother took him. He perked up immediately.

I recalled that during my childhood, my father would take all of us every Sunday for a picnic or to a hotel for brunch, a movie, or the circus. I bought a used Toyota, and every Sunday I took Taimoor to different places, to the seaside at Clifton, to the zoo, wherever he wanted to go. Sometimes I took his friends with us. He started laughing again and focused again on his studies.

One day I arrived home from work, and my younger brother, Rehan, who was a student at Textile Engineering University in Punjab, was visiting. I met him outside our home, and he asked me to come with him. He wanted to show me something very strange. He pointed to Taimoor.

My brother was shocked, pointing at six-year-old Taimoor, "Look at your boy, he is playing with girls!"

My son looked up at me, bewildered. He was with friends his own age, including my brother's four-year-old daughter. They all gathered around me, waiting for an explanation as what they had done wrong. My son looked especially worried. I shooed them off. "Go play."

They all ran away, laughing, jumping, and continued on with their games. I feared if I said one word to Taimoor about my brother's fears, it would destroy his personality and psyche.

I turned to my brother. "They are just kids having fun." I took my brother aside and told him. "Father never stopped me from playing with boys. All of my school years were coeducational. Please don't interfere with my son."

He didn't like what I told him, but he respected my request.

That night, I sat with Taimoor as usual and we read stories before bed. Before he fell asleep, I set the book down and spoke softly to him. "During your school years, you're going to meet girls. In college, on your job, everywhere you go. Treat them as sisters and friends. Always be respectful of them as human beings. Do not treat them as inferiors, as some men do, just because they're girls or women."

I know he listened carefully to me. I could see the thoughtfulness in his eyes as he tried to make sense of what I was saying. I knew as he grew my words would be very important to him.

Dr. Uqali, ever the considerate man, pointed me toward some potential husbands, but I was not mentally ready for marriage.

At one gathering, I met with a Pakistani International Airlines (PIA) pilot, Mr. Shah. He noticed I sat alone at the event, and came over and struck up a conversation. After a few minutes, he asked about my marital status. I told him I was married. He noted I wasn't wearing a ring. (I had developed the habit of warding off potential suitors by simply saying I was married.)

He wasn't put off by my closed-off attitude.

"I've traveled a lot and met many people," he said. "I can see in your face that you're not happy."

He then told me his story. He had suffered through a very painful divorce, and he had sat through many gatherings like this, just as I was doing, alone and not speaking with anyone. It took him a while to want to talk to people again.

Changing topics, he asked, "What do you do for recreation?"

I couldn't think of anything besides praying, working, and taking care of my son.

"But what do you do for yourself?"

I had no answer for him.

"Your hobbies. What are your hobbies?"

I still had no answer for him, as I hadn't painted in years.

"You must have friends?"

I shook my head. This man was truly trying to help me. What he was saying began to make sense.

"You are still suffering from the trauma of your divorce. Time is a good healer. You will die young if you don't do some fun things, go to the cinema, take a long drive, go swimming. You must do something for yourself."

He said many other things, but before leaving, he told me, "One day your pain will go away, then you will be ready for a loving marriage." With that, he rose and left me.

His words stayed with me. I wanted what he said to come true soon, but I knew I still had a long way to go before that happened.

After my mother passed away, I was introduced to a very nice man named Malik by a physician colleague during an event at a local hotel. He grew up in Pakistan, but he had been in New York for many years; however, he wanted to return to Pakistan to establish a business and settle down. He was well-educated, handsome, and very kind. For the first time in quite a while, I felt attracted to a man. But in my heart, I was hesitant to open myself up to a new life. I often remembered Mr. Shah's wise words: that when the trauma passed, I would be ready again for marriage.

Malik was interested in me and over the next month, he met my family, and I met his parents. Everyone was very nice and respectful, what I had expected a compatible match would be like all along. Still I felt a hesitancy in my heart.

He must have sensed my reluctance to commit, so one day he asked me what I thought about marriage. So I told him about my abusive ex-husband. I asked him how men can be so abusive and cruel to people they say they love?

He was very patient and understanding. I could tell that he was sympathetic to my feelings. Then he told me his story. He said that women were not the only victims of abuse. That his ex-wife had treated him so horribly, that for a time he had hated women, and thought he could never bring himself to marry again. But as time passed, his wounds began to heal, and he began to feel differently.

Now he wanted a fresh start. As I listened to him, his pain seemed genuine. His story allowed me to understand that men experienced abuse as well. We both had painful pasts.

When he proposed to me, I took his offer seriously. Now it was up to me. I told him I would think it over and give him an answer soon. I wanted to be certain in my heart that I was ready for new love.

Before I met him, I had already contracted for my new home in Chapal. Since it was under construction, I still lived at my parents' home. I took him to see the new building. He admired that I had done this on my own and liked the apartment. But he said, after we married he would prefer to provide us a larger home, where there would be space for Taimoor, as well as for us.

I did begin to smile more and began to think my life was about to take a turn for the better. My mother's soul would be at peace in heaven if I married. Malik was so gentle and kind that I decided I would marry him. He would be good for Taimoor, too.

I decided to tell him the very next day that I would marry him. The day I decided, Nashad visited our home.

I had not seen her in many months. She had married a police officer and had all the money she needed. She returned the 25,000 rupees she owed me. Her husband was already married, so she was a second wife. I asked her why she would marry a married man. She said that his first wife had enough time to be a wife and now it was her turn. (Her mother had said the same thing when she married her father.) I was so surprised to hear her explanation. It struck me that she was just manipulating what Islam allowed. Second marriages in Islam are a beautiful concept, if someone has a valid reason, can afford both wives, and treats them both the same, but ignorant Muslims misuse it. After Nashad married this man, he sent his first wife away to live alone with their small children.

Nashad offered her condolences for my mother, and she asked about my life. So I told her about Malik.

The next day she visited me again. She came directly from her magician with a message for me. Her magician advised me not to marry Malik, but to wait. Someone more suitable would come along soon.

How could he know such a thing? I dismissed her advice as the door closed behind her. I became more determined to marry Malik. I would not take counsel from a charlatan. Magic was a superstition of ignorant people, even if they were educated.

That day I phoned Malik's office, but he already gone for the day. I was very excited to speak with him about my decision. I waited two days for Malik to return my call. When I didn't hear from him, I called his office again. I was told he no longer worked for the company.

A little disturbed by the sudden changes, the next morning before work, I went directly to his apartment. As I stepped off the elevator to his floor, I found him standing on the landing with all of his luggage. He claimed he didn't have time to speak to me at that moment. He had an urgent matter in New York and had to leave immediately. He didn't know when, or if, he would return.

It was the strangest thing; for two months, he put time into our future life, meeting my family and getting to know one another, then to just fly away. All the talk of a future together, our mutual plans, and desires and then in a moment everything just evaporated into thin air. I watched him wordlessly load his luggage into the elevator and the door closed behind him, and on both of us.

I never heard from him again.

CHAPTER 12

The Devil

ONE SUNDAY, I RETURNED HOME with Taimoor from a weekend at the seaside, and I was surprised to see Mansoor Suhail outside my home, waiting for me. He said he had traveled from New York to visit me. I asked him why.

"Are you not going to invite me inside?" He smiled ruefully, as if he could make me fall for him so easily.

"I wasn't expecting visitors, so I can't receive you right now."

He began insisting that he had traveled far to see me, so I asked him, "Why are you creating a scene? Everyone is watching us."

He glanced around and suddenly became conscious of our surroundings.

"Can you meet me at a restaurant? I'd like to talk for a few minutes."

I agreed and took Taimoor inside and settled him. A little later I met Mansoor at Furqania, a nice restaurant not far from my home.

"I was sorry to hear about your divorce. I wanted to stop by and see how you were doing. You look very nice. You are so beautiful and attractive, you are just shining. You must be having a good time."

My anger began to rise as I listened to him trying to sweet talk me, as if what I had gone through in my marriage was nothing. My failed marriage had quickened the death of my mother, then my youngest brother Rafhan's terrible accident. I had endured four of the most horrible years of my life, and then two years of harassment at the hands of MQM terrorists. I was still heartbroken over the disappearance of Malik, I struggled to make the payments on my Chapal house, and my work had turned into a battle with Dr. Sheela. I was tolerating the selfishness and cruelty of society. And this man in front of me could only think that I was enjoying my single life. I wanted to slap him.

I suddenly burst out, "You came here all the way from New York to ask me if I was having a good time? You shouldn't have bothered." I stood to leave.

He apologized and asked me to sit for a moment. I shouldn't have, but I sat back down. He then told me his story. He had been appointed to the United Nations Pakistan Mission as the press attaché. He was happily married and doing very well, but he had never been able to get me off his mind.

"Years ago," I said, glaring at him, "when I went to Islamabad to meet President Zia-ul-Haq, and I met you the first time, I was only nineteen. I fell in love with you because you played with my feelings, and I thought you were single. You gave me the impression you were single then. Why didn't you tell me back then you were engaged? I was so attracted to you; I couldn't focus on my studies. I wouldn't have fallen in love with you if I knew you were engaged."

"I didn't say anything because I didn't want to lose such a nice girl."

He might have thought that was flattering to me, but those were the exact same words Erfun used as an excuse for not telling me the truth about his relationship with Shesta. I stood, this time determined to leave.

"I came all this way because I want to marry you."

"You are happily married, right?"

"Yes."

"Then go away. Don't ever come back here or send me a birthday card again."

"But Islam gives me permission to—"

I cut him off. "Stop!" I shouted. "Do not manipulate Islam! I will never marry a married man. Particularly a happily married man." I turned away from him to leave.

"You've become so aggressive, bitter, and rude," he said to my back.

Yes, I had, I told myself. Pain had made me that way, and I felt no shame in anything I had said to him.

Despite my troubles with Dr. Sheela, my job was very satisfying, and I began working every day with new enthusiasm. I was assigned to work in Karachi Terminal clinic (KT) three days a week, and one day a week in Rimpa Plaza clinic. The KT clinic was surrounded by Sui Gas Co. guard checkpoints, and it was one of the safest places to work. I wouldn't have to worry about Furqan or Erfun barging in and disrupting my work.

At school, Taimoor began to thrive, studying hard, playing with other children, and otherwise developing into a well-adjusted young man. He wouldn't let me kiss him any longer in front of other boys, telling me one day, "No, Mom, I am a big boy now."

It made me feel good that he was growing and maturing, becoming independent. One day he proved how independent and brave he could be. He had been asking me to take him to the Sunday Bazaar. I hesitated to shop at this place, as it was crowded, noisy, and there are always unruly people there. But he insisted. So one Sunday we went shopping there, strolling among the stalls, perusing the variety of goods. It didn't take long before a group of vulgar young men began following me, whistling and making crude remarks. This, unfortunately, is typical of the bazaar, and the police were nowhere in sight. I sped us up to try and escape this bunch of rowdy boys, but they chased me.

We couldn't escape them, so in an inspired moment of bravado, Taimoor jumped up on one of the stalls so that he was the same height as the boys, and shouted directly at the leader, the most obnoxious one, "Uncle, go home and bother your mother. Don't bother my mom."

The lead boy was so ashamed, his face turned red, he stopped harassing me, and they all left.

My little Taimoor was growing up. We stayed in the bazaar, and I purchased a few things for him. It was rewarding to not have to be chased away from a day of shopping because of the boorish behavior of a pack of wolves.

Things were going well. When our Chapal apartment was completed, Taimoor and I finally moved in. After settling in, we arranged a housewarming party for my family and neighbors. It was a cordial event, and it was nice to meet all the neighbors.

At work in the KT clinic, I began seeing female patients in a small exam room they had built for me. As my reputation for helping women spread, my caseload increased, and management arranged for a nurse to help me. One day Dr. Uqali asked me about my work. I told him I was happy working in the clinic seeing female patients, and that more and more women were coming to see me. He was glad to hear of my progress and assigned me to work five days at the clinic.

On another occasion, a junior officer came into my office and asked me for a letter of referral for his wife to allow a medical procedure. The particular procedure wasn't allowed by our company policy, and I thought it unusual that the woman didn't come herself. I told him to have his wife make an appointment, and I would examine her and prescribe the appropriate treatment.

He began arguing with me that the procedure only cost 500 rupees, ($4) and that I should just approve it. When I refused without seeing his wife, he threatened to inform the union leaders. I knew that if I allowed him to intimidate me, men would be breaking down my door to get procedures for their wives. So I refused the pressure to give in.

Soon the officer came back to me, pleading for the procedure. There is a custom in Pakistan when a man wants to humble himself to supplicate a superior, he will kneel at the person's feet and hold them. This is what he did, right in my office. I stood in panic.

"What are you doing? Please don't insult yourself like this for such a little bit of money." I opened my handbag, took out 500 rupees, and handed it to him. He took the money and left.

I just couldn't bear him humiliating himself like that. I felt a sudden surge of hatred for men—they were so manipulative. When the man grabbed my feet it reminded me of Erfun when he took my feet before I left his house. He had also done that to my father to convince him to allow me to marry him.

Despite all of these experiences, I began to realize that I worked with some very decent men. Slowly, my hatred for all men vanished from my heart. There were men around me who not only treated their wives well, but treated every woman with great respect. I began to see the kindness in many men's hearts. It was a liberating experience.

Rumors were spreading amongst the staff that Dr. Uqali was ready to retire. Instead, he was promoted to General Manager of the medical department. He had the strong endorsement of the Pakistan People's Party (PPP). Everyone in the medical department was happy, including me.

Javed Khan, manager of the medical department, called to tip me off. "Dr. Raana. The lady doctor from Units A and B is pushing her friends to get her transferred to your department, and for you to get reassigned."

I knew it was Dr. Sheela. She was up to her old tricks. She wanted to send me back to work in the abhorrent Units A and B. I had worked hard to carve out a place for myself, and I was pleased with my office, the staff, and my patients. And now the old shadow of Dr. Sheela cast a pall over my happiness.

A few weeks later, I received a letter from Dr. Uqali. Effective immediately, I was to begin working in Units A and B on the first floor of Rimpa Plaza. Dr. Sheela would take my place in Unit C, and take over my practice.

That news hit me as if I had been caught in a bomb blast. I had worked hard to make my office a calm and attractive place to work, and now I had to give it up. I feared I wouldn't be able to take the pressure in my new assignment. I called Javed to see if there was anything that could be done for me. He again said, "I've been warning you for a while now that it will happen. She is too well-connected for her not to get her way. While you were working hard at your job, she was over here at headquarters working on her connections."

I had made the honest mistake of thinking job performance counted more than connections. But this was the way the system worked, and I had to resign myself to it. The next morning I reported to Dr. Iqbal at the clinic in Rimpa Plaza. It was situated in the heart of the Saddar district, which was filled with blaring traffic noise and pollution from trucks, buses, and cars. The clinic itself was chaotic. The workers were unruly, shouting and carrying on. Workers and union leaders were in the habit of always asking for favors, and they often refused to follow well-established policies. Most of the employees, it turned out, were the most egregious abusers of the company medical system. They not only brought their entire extended families to be treated, but also demanded expensive medicines and referral letters to specialist doctors and for surgeries. When I refused to go against company policy, I spent half my day arguing with employees, their families, and others. It was exhausting.

I tried to keep up with the pace, but it became impossible, and I began to suffer from severe headaches. I came home exhausted not only physically, but emotionally, and I was of no use to Taimoor. I couldn't help him with his homework or spend time with him without thinking about the horrible conditions of my job.

After a few months, Taimoor and I had suffered enough. I called Dr. Uqali and asked him kindly to return to my former clinic. He said that it was beyond his powers.

I was surprised to hear that. Sitting in my apartment, considering what to do, I decided to talk to God. I started a series of special prayers. I prayed a whole night for God to do something for the sake of my son. I believed He had the power to do anything.

After a few days, Javed Khan, who had always been sincere and kind, called and suggested I come to the head office and meet with the Managing Director, Mr. Javeed ul Hassan. On my first day, I had visited Mr. Hassan in his office on the fifth floor. He told me that his doors were always open to me to discuss any issues or concerns I might have. I decided to take him up on his offer.

That day, I left work early and went to his office. His secretary said he was in a meeting, and then he had to leave directly afterward. I should return another day. I decided to wait for him. When his meeting was over, a line of executives streamed out of his office. I stood when I saw Mr. Hassan in his office doorway holding his briefcase. He stopped to see me.

"Sir, I came here to speak to you if you can give me a few minutes."

He smiled. "Of course."

His secretary Ms. Dsouza also stood. "Sir, I told her you were leaving soon."

He offered me a seat, and he asked how he could help me. I

reminded him that when I first came to work I was appointed to work in Unit C. Only later did Dr. Sheela come to work in Units A and B. I told him everything, how she came and looked over my office, and then began lobbying the head office staff for a transfer, and how I had developed an all-female practice in Unit C. And now she had changed everything.

After I finished my story, I said to him. "I have a small son, and I have some personal issues. The noise and pollution in my workplace and traffic in that area are intolerable. I need my office back."

The next day I was transferred back to Unit C. I was thrilled to work in my own office again. No doubt, Mr. Hassan was the most decent man I had ever met.

My work routine quickly returned to normal, and the clinic operated smoothly. Soon, Javed Khan called me to tell me I was being considered for promotion to chief medical officer, along with Dr. Sheela, and a newly arrived male doctor who had transferred in from Hyderabad, Sindh. The new physician had powerful political connections to PPP, but I had the most seniority and the best job performance reviews.

Not giving up, Dr. Sheela kept manipulating head office staff to find a way to take my job in Unit C. I knew another transfer was coming, and I decided I wanted to see if I could make the best of it by changing the work culture in Units A and B. I had meetings with all the doctors and the staff and tried to boost employee morale, but none of the other doctors cooperated. They wanted to maintain the status quo, get what they could, and be done with it. After several months of effort, I gave up.

Since Dr. Uqali, Mr. Hassan, and few other good executives had retired, I visited the head office of Units A and B, and met with Mr. Khursheed, the same general manager who had hired me. I knew he preferred Dr. Sheela, but I decided to take a chance that he would listen to me. I prayed hard that day and visited him full of hope. He listened carefully, and afterward, he transferred me back to Unit C. I had found a kind man with an open heart. But I knew in my heart that my battle with Dr. Sheela had only just begun.

After Dr. Uqali retired, there was a panic in the medical department. He was such a kind man, and no one knew what to expect from our next Chief Medical Officer Dr. Iqbal. The General Manager of the Medical Dept., Mr. Waheed, had always behaved well in the presence of the previous management. But as soon as they were gone, he began harassing the doctors and medical staff. After a few months Mr. Waheed was transferred to another department, and Captain Arif was appointed general manager of the medical department. Javed called to reassure me that Arif was a decent and religious man who had been working elsewhere in the head office. He said everything will be alright now.

In his first meeting with the medical staff, Captain Arif said he was aware of all the issues we were facing, and that he intended to resolve them. Everyone left the meeting buoyed by his positive attitude and willingness to support the physicians and staff.

Not too long afterward, Javed called me from the head office. Evidently, he'd seen Dr. Sheela visiting Captain Arif's office. They had met for several hours, but Javed didn't know what they discussed. He assumed I was about to get transferred again, and wanted me to prepare myself. I was transferred the next day. This time I met with a new GM, Dr. Fiyaz. He also belonged to PPP. He listened to everything I said, and promised to resolve my issues once and for all. He appointed both of us to the same office in Unit C. Now Dr. Sheela sat in my office with me, and she tried very hard to gain my trust. The next week, Dr. Sheela told me she was going to meet with Captain Arif, to give him some suggestions.

After her meeting, Arif began visiting Karachi Terminal. He ordered me to vacate my room and give it to Dr. Sheela. I started seeing patients in the waiting room just opposite the office. They had converted the waiting room to my office with doors and chairs. I continued to use the restroom in my previous office during breaks.

Captain Arif began visiting her office every day at lunch. They ate together in her room, or at least that's what I thought. Once I entered the room to use the restroom, and they were embracing. Embarrassed at being caught, he quickly let her go. I was told that I could no longer use the restroom inside that office. Instead, Arif wanted me to go to the other side of the building to use the restroom for male doctors.

I understood why. He did not want any interruption during their sexual activity. I refused to use that restroom and started using the one for the female patients, which was adjacent to Sheela's office. I could hear them. I ignored them since what they were doing was their business.

Once I glimpsed their tryst, but I did not intend to bother them or inform anyone of their behavior. Arif stopped me from using that bathroom, too.

I began going home at lunchtime, to pray, to eat lunch, and to use the bathroom in my Chapal apartment, which was a five-minute drive away. After I came back from lunch break one day, a few employees were gathered outside the office in the parking area. The two lovers had neglected to close the window coverings all the way, and staff had spotted Dr. Sheela and Captain Arif having sex. Word spread, and reached the union leaders, who began to protest that those two should not be doing that at work on the table used for examining patients.

Management didn't do anything about their behavior. So the protests continued.

I received a letter from Captain Arif that I can no longer leave the premises during lunch.

I went back to using the restroom for the female patients. After a few days, someone put a padlock on the door so no one could use it. Still, the protests continued, so Captain Arif invited all the union leaders and employees who witnessed their tryst into his office. He offered them favors if they would stop protesting. Instead, they should start a campaign against me.

I only heard about this later.

The next day, I heard a knock at my door during lunchtime. Arif stood at my door. "From now on," he said, "I will sit in your room during lunchtime." I refused to allow him into my office.

"Listen, you can't sit in my room. I am not Dr. Sheela. Go to her room. She welcomes you. I am Dr. Raana, and always remember, I am a different person."

"Why are you so proud?"

"I think it is self-respect and the morals that my parents taught me."

"If you don't let me in, you will find out what I can do."

I closed and locked the door before we could say anything else to each other. I just wanted him to go away and leave me to do my job, but I feared he would not do that. All the peace and harmony that Dr. Uqali had brought to our department had disappeared. Now a sense of foreboding came over everyone in the office: something terrible was about to happen.

Soon after I refused Arif's advances, his entire demeanor and attitude toward me changed. He began pressuring me to go along with the usual practices in Units A and B of writing prescriptions for expensive medications for patients and their families that weren't needed. The labor leaders complained to the head offices about my refusal to give in to their demands, despite the fact they knew I wasn't allowed to order the expensive medications they demanded.

Warning letters from Captain Arif began arriving soon after. The letters threatened me with disciplinary action for not prescribing the proper medications and for not having my office available to see patients during my scheduled hours. Because of these false letters in my file, I was denied raises and promotions that I had earned.

Dr. Sheela would not stop trying to thwart me. New people came to see me as patients, people whom I knew were friends of Dr. Sheela, and they made loud, emotional scenes when I prescribed medicine for them or gave a diagnosis. One in particular, Nasrin Naz, a telephone operator, made a despicable scene. She usually saw male doctors, but she came to me that day. I was busy examining a patient and the waiting area was full. She opened my office door without knocking and began shouting nonstop until spittle oozed from her lips. She claimed I was incompetent, stupid, ignorant, and a worthless doctor.

I was so humiliated and too shocked to speak. I decided the best thing for me to do was to remain calm. After she left, I had to sit alone for some time to regain my composure. After that episode, I decided that I wasn't going to tolerate this behavior anymore.

I checked the directory for the GM of the Telecommunications Department and was very glad to discover it was someone I knew, Mr. Naeem Akhond. I had met him several times and knew him as a decent and fair-minded man.

I called him and told him about his employee's behavior. He was shocked and promised to investigate my complaint. Not long after, he called me back and said Nasrin Naz had admitted to her ugly behavior. She confessed that Dr. Sheela had put her up to it. She was crying, promised not to do it again, and asked for my forgiveness. Mr. Akhond was certain she would never bother me again. Her family would suffer if she was fired, so he was certain she would behave.

Of course, I forgave her. She was just a pawn in someone else's game. It gave me some satisfaction that he would reprimand her. But I knew that wouldn't put a stop to the efforts to discredit me.

CHAPTER 13
Unseen Forces

ONE DAY AT A FAMILY gathering, I overheard my father asking my cousin to help him find a match for me. He said it would be painful for him to see me stay unmarried my entire life. When I heard him talking, I took him aside and said, "Yes, I am ready to consider marrying again, if you have a nice person to introduce me to."

One day he introduced me to a man from my cousin's circle. His name was Osman.

He was young, good-looking, divorced, and a well-educated civil engineer. He worked for the Civil Aviation Authority. Over the next few weeks I met his mother and married sister. I also visited his office at the Civil Aviation Authority.

We spent time together talking. I wanted to go into a new relationship with my eyes open. I asked him many questions directly: Did he drink? Did he have a girlfriend? Would he allow me to continue working as a doctor? What did he think of having children? I refused to allow a man's inflated ego to box me in again.

He was adamant that he didn't drink, didn't have a girlfriend, and wouldn't even consider making me quit my job as a doctor. He admired the fact that I had made my own way in the world. He seemed eager and asked me to marry him.

I had no reason to rush into another marriage. But he began asking me for a decision every time I saw him.

"You must give me time."

"I can touch your feet if that pleases you. Marry me next month."

The foot touching ritual as a form of respect and humility was nothing more to me than a broken promise. I could never erase the image of Erfun bowing low and holding my feet, intimating that he would respect me forever. The entire ceremony was fraudulent. For me, there was no honor, no principle, and no integrity in the touching of one's feet. I needed more than good intentions in a husband. I needed to see more of Osman's behavior and character.

"I must have two months to think over my decision."

"If we wait too long, you will change your mind."

He had a point. If I waited, would I take the quiet moments to nurse my hurts, to rehearse in my mind the many reasons I should never marry again? Maybe I would never be able to love another man again. Then there was this earnest man, Osman, who was someone my family knew. He seemed to be a man of good intentions. I slowly realized we probably could never know another person's real character. But my sense of who he was, made me think that Osman would be good for me.

In June 1996, we were married in a simple gathering. I invited Dr. Uqali, who was happy to see me happy. I knew he was about to retire, and he wanted me to have a strong man at my back, a good husband to see me safely through the troubled waters of Pakistani life.

After we married, Osman moved to my Chapal apartment, and I was ready for a new life together, with more children, and much love and happiness.

After our *Nikah*, Osman told me he was impotent, and we would most likely not have any children together. I stared at him—shocked, then confused, then angry. Why hadn't he told me this before we were married?

What disturbed me most was that I had shown him everything about me—my medical records, my financial situation, my ID card, my home. I was explicit that I wanted more children. I asked him why he hadn't been up front with me about his condition. He said he hadn't wanted to lose me.

I had heard that excuse before. Did all men use this excuse to get what they wanted?

"This destroys a dream I've had of having a large family."

He was sheepish, but he had little to say.

What could I do? I did not want another divorce. I did love him and wanted us to be together, so I decided to forgive him and make the best of it.

After that, he left for a few days to travel to Hyderabad for his civil aviation duties.

That night, I received a call from a woman who introduced herself as Faryal. She claimed to be Osman's girlfriend. She told me a tale that made my heart sink right down into my shoes. As she talked my knees became weak, and I had to sit down. She claimed she was Osman's longtime girlfriend. She had four children, and two of them were Osman's children.

"But you were never married to him, were you?"

"No, we were only girlfriend and boyfriend."

"Why didn't you marry him, instead of allowing him to carry on with me?"

"I am already married. My husband is Dr. Anjum. I didn't want Osman to marry you, but he did anyway. Now I'm very hurt. I hate that he's married to you."

"Why didn't you divorce your husband and marry Osman?"

"My husband won't divorce me. He's okay with Osman."

The entire conversation puzzled me. How could Osman have children if he was impotent? How could this woman's husband be happy with such a situation?

"He told me he is impotent. How can he have children with you?"

"He wasn't always this way, but when he decided to marry you, I performed magic on him. He will never have children with you."

I hung up the phone, dazed. I stumbled around my apartment. Osman was still away so I couldn't talk to him. I paced the floor of my apartment almost the entire night.

Faryal called the next day and the day after that. I told her to leave me alone. I didn't want to believe her. Finally, the last time she called, she pushed me hard to accept the fact that she had Osman's children.

"I will come over to your apartment with the children and show them to you. I will make a scene in your building."

"If you do that, people will not like what you've done, destroying your marriage and mine." According to Islam, what she and Osman had done was a sin, but she didn't seem to care at all.

The next day after work, I went to Osman's mother's house and confronted her. She confirmed that it was true. "Yes, he has two children with that woman. But what could I say to you? I wanted to tell you, but if I had, Osman would have been furious at me."

"Better for him to be angry at you than to destroy my life." I rose and left. She was as weak and as much a liar as her son.

When Osman returned from Hyderabad, I confronted him about his girlfriend's calls, his children, and his lying. He slumped down into a chair.

"I wanted to get away from her, that's why I married you. I was able to have children with her, so I thought I would with you. But she's done something to me."

The next time Faryal called, I asked her what she had done to Osman that he couldn't have any more children.

"I performed powerful magic on him."

I scoffed at her. "This is a medical problem, not a magic problem."

"You'll see. In fifteen days, he will leave you forever, and there is nothing you can do to stop him."

Each day following that call seemed normal. Osman and I arrived home from work about the same time. The evenings moved along as I expected. Suspecting Faryal might be right, but not thoroughly believing her prediction, I kept alert for any signs of trouble. We never argued. We were still in the beginning stages of easing into our married life. Then one day, Osman came home looking haggard and upset. He said he'd suddenly started having heart palpitations and feelings of dread, as if something terrible was about to happen. His episodes got worse and worse until he thought he might have a heart attack. I told him to see a doctor immediately.

On the fifteenth day, he did not come home at all. When I returned home from work, there was a letter on the table. He couldn't escape the fear of dread, and he wanted to live apart for a while and see if the panic would subside. He said he was going to live with his mother for a while. Then, if he felt better, he would return. I searched the apartment, and it seemed more like a robbery than fear that had driven him to leave. He had taken my money, my jewelry, and anything valuable in the house.

I crashed onto the sofa in tears. We were married for less than one month, and the man had stripped me of everything—my valuables, my dignity, and the tiny bit of faith that remained that I could ever trust a man.

In the next few weeks, I discovered that he had taken out a loan against my apartment. Now I was deeply in debt and on the verge of another divorce.

The night he left, I cried into the early morning. I feared I was destined to live alone my entire life. The next morning, I woke up with my face on fire and painful to touch. When I looked in the mirror, my face had turned darker, with patches of skin darker than my normal skin tone. My body had become bloated, and I was hot all over. I had a high fever and feelings of lethargy. How had all of this happened in one night?

Those symptoms and fever continued for two years. I visited several specialists who gave me a variety of reasons why this would happen, but all the tests came back normal, so they had no definitive answer. I was horrified by my appearance, and no amount of makeup could cover up the story on my face.

I never talked about my personal life at work with anyone, but it must have been evident from my appearance that something had happened. When people asked me if I was okay, I told them I am fine. Soon the news spread, because Osman began sending letters to my job and family that my marriage had turned tragic. This turn of events shattered me emotionally.

The general manager, Mr. Waheed, called me into the head office to talk. Once in his office, he asked me directly. "I proposed to you so many times. Why would you marry someone you hardly knew?"

"But you're already married." I had it in my mind that my married life would look like my parents, two spouses in love with each other. I had come too far to change that idea. Why was that dream so far out of reach for me? Mr. Waheed didn't laugh, but he did smile ruefully. Did he pity me that I didn't understand the nature of marriage in Pakistan?

That I didn't understand it was a man's world, and men did what they wanted when they wanted. Or that I was just plain ignorant of how things operated in a country saturated with superstition and corruption to the point no one could ever sort out right from wrong, good from bad, true faith from the demons lurking in the shadows.

I left the general manager's office confused but more determined than ever to sort out my life. I had a right to a happy marriage, just like any other woman, and I had to have a better grasp of what was going on around me.

Faryal continued calling, taunting me. She said Osman would send me the divorce papers soon, and she would leave Pakistan with her husband and children. But before that happened she wanted to take Osman from me. I couldn't believe this woman. Was there no justice in the world? Why was I deprived of happiness?

I went to Osman's employer at the Civil Aviation Authority (CAA). I spilled out the entire story—how Osman had left with everything, stealing my money and jewelry, and taking out a loan on my apartment without my knowledge. The general manager Sadiq appeared very concerned. He said he would get justice for me very quickly, and get the return of all my property—if I slept with him for a night.

I stood in shock. He could have plunged a dagger through my heart, and I wouldn't have felt more pain that I experienced at that moment. Without answering him, I left. I was so angry I went directly to the office of Director General of CAA, Mr. Amir Sharif, and made a written complaint against him. The next day I received a call from the Assistant DG, Air Vice Marshall Mr. Zulfiqar Shah, thanking me for my written complaint. He complimented me on my bravery. He said they heard many rumors about the man, but none of the women would come forward with official complaints. This time I had and they ended up firing the general manager. At least there is some justice in the world.

At home, in the quiet when Taimoor was asleep, I began to piece all of the bizarre events together. Why was I experiencing strange incidents—my failed marriage with Erfun because of Shesta, the disappearance of Malik as that magician had predicted, and now Osman's mistress's claim of using black magic to steal him away from me? Had Malik been pressured by some unseen forces to leave without even saying a word to me? Had Osman left the house on the exact day that Faryal said he would? His leaving me without explanation shook me so hard that it took me weeks to regain my composure. I scrutinized every detail I could remember from when I first met him up until the last time I saw him. I tried to figure out what had happened between us. Was it something I had said or done?

And what about Furqan? This man wouldn't let me go. It didn't matter how many times I married, the marriages would never work. How could someone be so cruel to wish that on me? All the magic in the world would never make me have feelings for that man. It didn't seem to matter how many times I told him, he would still show up in my life at unexpected moments.

All of this left me with an eerie sense that I was under surveillance, that an unseen force was observing me keenly from the shadows. And this observer or supernatural power was not my friend. As much as I tried to rationalize what was happening to me, I couldn't get my second marriage out of my head. I wanted a happily married life, so I could fulfill my promise to my mother, and not disappoint my father. As soon as a very nice man like Osman showed up, one whom I could trust, this force came and spoiled everything.

Still, despite everything that happened to me, I wasn't confident that magic had any power over me. Since my childhood study of the Quran, I believed that God was my friend, that he was the most potent force in the universe. He didn't want me to live alone, did he? Didn't I deserve happiness and a peaceful life?

I kept thinking about this supposed supernatural force. If such a force did exist, I had to find a way to escape it. I tried hiding my plans from people. I learned that those who practiced magic had to know something personal about the person they are targeting. I tried playing hide-and-seek with the mysterious force. But it seemed to turn the tables on me.

I decided there was still a chance to pray. Maybe Osman would return. Maybe Faryal would leave Osman. I went to Molvi Sahib and asked him to pray for my marriage. I prayed every day for two months.

Then Osman returned from London. Soon afterward, I received divorce papers in the mail. Dr. Sheela found out about the papers and laughed at me, but my father was very hurt. Hurt and despondent, I asked Molvi Sahib, "Why didn't your prayers work?"

"I prayed and I requested Imam e Kaaba through my friend to pray for you during Hajj e Akbar. He prayed for you over the loudspeaker and every pilgrim was saying, Amin. But your divorce was inevitable. It appears many people must be performing black magic on you. The forces against you are too strong. You must go to a magician to remove the black magic."

This was the most surprising conversation I'd ever had with a religious person, especially one who had memorized the Quran and who understood its meaning and message. He would know about the prohibitions against consulting and practicing magic. I feared either he didn't have thorough knowledge of Islam or God is angry with me for some reason.

With the divorce in the process of becoming legal, I had to protect my rights under the law. At the time of marriage, the *Nikah* contract spells out the *haq mehar*, or amount of money to be paid by the husband to the wife. The *haq mehar* becomes her property if the marriage contract is broken by the husband. So, I filed in court my right to obtain the *haq mehar*, the funds promised to me, along with an accounting of all the possessions and funds that Osman had taken from me. The court awarded me almost three quarters of what I asked for, so at least I wouldn't be penniless. I was able to pay off the loan that Osman took out on my home and purchase a small car.

After the divorce was final, I visited my father at Eid. He was shocked that I was again divorced. "What's wrong with you?" he asked. His voice was full of emotions and pain. He didn't want to hear about what Osman had done. He just could not believe I would be divorced after not even a half a year.

He must have seen the hurt on my face. "Why you are asking me that?"

"I'm asking because I'm your father. You are my beloved daughter, and my heart cries for you."

We both were silent. Tears welled in his eyes. I knew what he said was true. His heart was crying for me. I knew he loved me very much. But I had no good answers for him. I was still angry at the entire catastrophe of my life.

"Don't ask me why I got divorced. Ask God. I have no answers to your question."

I was shattered. I wanted to just sit and weep, but couldn't do that in front of my father.

During that period, whenever I needed something important, it vanished. I was supposed to travel, and one night I put my passport on the table ready to take it with me in a day or two. It just disappeared. After searching the whole house repeatedly, I was forced to apply for a new one. My jewelry and clothes vanished from in front of me. When I needed a document, I couldn't find it. Much later, I would see it on a side table in another room. How could I have missed it?

The disappearing and reappearing of items exhausted me. It came to the point I was searching for my things all the time. Was someone trying to keep me busy with useless activities? I decided I needed to search out the root cause of these mysterious incidents.

Were all of these incidences mere coincidences, or something more? Was someone using black magic on me, trying to drive me crazy? I began to suspect there existed a power I didn't understand, and knew that I needed to learn more.

I started my research by reaching out to experts, those who could give me the right answers. I visited so many places and met so many different kinds of magicians: those who claimed they were simple magicians, those who were called black magicians. Practitioners of Siffle knowledge, numerologists, and experts of Jafar knowledge, those who purported to control *djinns*. I even visited a magician who claimed to have control over Satan. I learned more than I ever expected about the deep roots of magic used in our culture. My conclusions were simple— most of those I met were charlatans. They used simple tricks to defraud innocent people of their money and honor by raping women.

There was one thing that was common among all of them: they spread fear and terror among people. If they could get someone to believe that their entire family, friends, and colleagues were performing magic on them, then the magicians would earn big money to provide protection against the powers of evil. It's a fraudulent scheme that many in Pakistan fall for.

In the course of my research, I spoke with a very nice man, a Roohani expert, Khawaja Shamsuddin Azimi, who taught me to meditate to find God, but my mind was so agitated, I found it very difficult to practice. I also met Shah Sahib, expert on Jafar and numerology, who answered some of my questions. At the time I visited, a group of executives from one of the most prominent newspapers in Pakistan was seeking help to open a private TV channel. They wanted Shah Sahib to destroy the business of a competing channel. I was surprised that reputable business people sought help from magicians, too.

Shah Sahib calculated my horoscope. He informed me that my birth was during an alignment of stars that produced a deep attraction to my personality. But because I had a strong character and strong faith in God I resisted people's intentions, so that they resorted to more nefarious ways to try and influence me. He was surprised I hadn't gone insane or wasn't dead.

I wondered the same things some days.

I asked him a question that burned in me: if Islam prohibited magic, why did it exist?

"Magic exists," he replied. "Our Prophet also suffered from magic spells, which were only removed by the last four *surahs* of the Quran."

"I recite them regularly, but I'm still not free. What do I do now?"

"You are exceptional. You have suffered continuously since you were a child. But you are not willing to surrender yet. God lives in your heart."

I told him about my severe headaches and pains.

"Your case is very difficult." After I told him about all the disappearing items, he said someone in my circle wants to keep me so distracted so that I won't pay attention to my priorities. He offered to visit my Chapal apartment to help me get rid of the *djinns*.

I told him that I would handle it myself.

"That is your strong personality. You will not surrender, that is good. But it is very dangerous."

I recited *Surah Baqarah* for twenty-one days. Then I recited *Surah Jinn* in a loud voice every day. I demanded that *djinns* go away from my house and let me live peacefully: "This is my house and I have the right to live here. I am not bothering you. So please don't bother me." Whoever they were, they left my house and all the mysterious incidents stopped.

I found no way to be free of the black magic. But I kept reciting verses from the Quran that were specific to protect me from magic.

One day the gardener at Chapal found a *Tavez* at the root of an old tree wrapped with plastic. My name was written in the center. On the outside of the rectangular paper at every corner were the names of Satan, Ferron, Namrood, and Iblis. Then the words: Death, Defamation, Destruction, Divorce, and Disease. When I read it, I fainted. After I regained my composure, I drove to the ocean, and threw it into the sea. After two years of suffering, within two hours my fever, hyperpigmentation, and bloating disappeared.

CHAPTER 14
Fighting for Taimoor

ONE DAY IN MY OFFICE, a staff member handed me a legal document that had been delivered for me. She said it looked like a court order. My heart started sinking as I held it. After reading the letter, I became dizzy. It was a notice from the court that Erfun was suing me for custody of Taimoor, who was eleven years old. The court order stated that from now on Erfun would have full custody of my son, because I had remarried, although I had again divorced. Taking Taimoor would be stripping my last hope from me. How could I live without my son? I tried my best not to cry, but I couldn't stand. I fainted in my office.

My nurse rushed in, calling my name, "Dr. Raana, Dr. Raana." She put a glass of glucose water to my lips, and then gave me a vitamin injection. After a few minutes, I regained consciousness, but everything was a blur. She wanted me to see one of the doctors, but I declined. Except for this new threat to take away Taimoor, I was in perfect health. She helped me to my feet, and I resumed seeing patients.

At home that night, I decided to make it my priority to fight Erfun in court. I hired an excellent advocate, who prepared the case. I visited my doctor, who was surprised to see my new blood report. My cholesterol and sugar, in just one week, had risen dangerously. And my eyesight had become very weak. She asked me if I was under any stress. I didn't tell her about my battle for my son. She said I needed to change my lifestyle; it should be stress free. I smiled. "Yes, of course. I will do that."

I started wearing glasses and taking medicine for cholesterol, and made an effort to control my blood sugar through diet and exercise.

When we had our day in court, Taimoor informed the judge that he wanted to live with me. He respected his father and stepmother, but he didn't like the movies they watched while he was at their home. He also told the judge his father and stepmother offered him beer and other alcohol every time he was in their home. He described how at night after they thought he was asleep, he could hear his stepmother cursing and swearing. It made him afraid, and he didn't know what to do.

The judge asked him more questions about his experiences at his father's home, and at home with me. He told the judge how I made him do his homework and attend school, and how I took care of him. After deliberation, the judge granted full custody to me. I was elated.

Every week, I sent Taimoor to spend time at his grandparents and with his father. I felt he needed to have good relationships with his paternal uncles and aunties. Their love would create good memories for him that would last a lifetime. I knew Erfun had a right to see his son, even though he hadn't done anything to deserve a relationship with Taimoor. So I let Taimoor visit him. He needed to know his father. Shesta, however, was another matter. She proved herself to be completely untrustworthy.

Taimoor told me that Erfun and Shesta were planning to move abroad. Shesta had said to him that his stepbrother, Khizer, would study in the US. Taimoor was sad because she had also said he would never have any success with an education in Pakistan. I encouraged him, saying that studying abroad was not a guarantee of success, that he could get a good education here at home. I promised that someday I would find a way for him to attend college in America. That seemed to appease his fears.

Life settled into a remarkably calm routine, until one day Taimoor did not come home.

My habit was to wait at the bus stop for him to arrive home from school. When he didn't step off the bus, as usual, I approached his friends and asked for his whereabouts. They told me that his father and aunty picked him up, and asked him to get in the car instead of the bus. They said they would drop him at home later. When Taimoor refused, they took him by force. The kids shouted at the bus driver to do something, but he refused to intervene, saying it was a family matter.

I immediately sped to the police station and filed a report. The police sent a team to search at Erfun's parents' and grandparents' houses. Erfun's own house was vacant. The neighbors didn't know where they were. His grandparents informed the police they weren't aware of Erfun's plans and whereabouts.

I feared that Erfun and Shesta had taken Taimoor abroad with them. I went to the police station again that night and spoke to the Superintendent of Police. He assured me they were searching every- where to find Taimoor. I started crying. I couldn't help fearing I would never see him again. I couldn't eat or drink. The chief tried to comfort me by reassuring me he would do everything he could to find my son. I sat in the station, with my hands in my face, and prayed for strength.

I wanted to stay at the station overnight, but the chief said, "No, please go home and rest. You have to eat and take care of yourself. We will keep searching."

He gave me the direct number to his office, as well as his cell phone number. He allowed me to contact him anytime. He would supervise my son's search himself. I left the police station with a heavy heart.

All the way home, I kept telling myself to have faith in God that he would be found. I just kept repeating in my heart, "Have faith in God."

But a black wedge of doubt began to creep into my thinking. Did God care about me anymore? Was he listening to my prayers?

The next day, as usual, I went to my office. I attended to my duties even with my heavy heart. I went through my daily routine with patients the best I could and kept to myself.

On the weekends, my apartment was horribly lonely without Taimoor. The silence nearly killed me. I called the station many times, but they had no news. My brother Rahat, by this time a Navy Commander, was abroad on his ship. His wife Farah called and invited me to spend the weekend at her house. My mind wouldn't stop thinking of the disaster of missing Taimoor, and in time I felt it would be better for me to visit her. Driving to her house, I absentmindedly didn't brake for a stop sign in time, and rear-ended the car in front of me.

The woman was furious, rushing out of her car to my window. She claimed the car belonged to the American Embassy, and I needed to follow her to the police station. She was the wife of an officer at the US Embassy.

I apologized for the accident, which caused only a minor scratch on her bumper. I insisted I was willing to pay for the loss. I offered her my contact information, but she wouldn't take it. She insisted we go to the station. One of the nearby street hawkers waved at me. "Just go," he said. "What can she do?"

I knew the woman was a foreigner and she would then think that not all Pakistanis are trustworthy. I followed her to the police station, and we waited for her husband. I was very scared and couldn't help worrying. About an hour later, an older, soft-spoken American man entered. He told her the car had only been scratched and that it was insured. There was no need for me to be detained. The police officer told me, "Dr. Raana, you can go." I offered my contact information again, but he said it was fine. I was allowed to leave.

On the following Monday, I returned to work. The weekend at my brother's house had been restful, but as soon as I came home to my apartment in Chapal, all the loneliness returned. There was still no news from the police regarding Taimoor. My thoughts turned obsessive: *Was Taimoor being treated well? Was Taimoor eating enough? Were they taking care of him?*

During the day at work, I used the phone in the office to contact the police station for news. This was before cell phones became commonplace, and the doctors had no phones in their small offices. News of my son's abduction spread through the entire building, even though I had not said a word to anyone.

Weeks passed, and I had not heard a word about Taimoor's whereabouts. I kept in touch with Erfun's parents, but they claimed they had not heard from Erfun either. One day a man whom I did not know called me at the office. He said my son was in Peshawar. My heart stopped. "Peshawar!" I had never been to Peshawar, but the city was in the news constantly, with terrorist bombings and shootings all the time. It was a city of death. The terrorists were very active in the district surrounding the city.

I asked the caller how he knew for sure my son was in Peshawar. Did he know the address of where he was staying? He told me that he was Erfun's friend, and had met me once when I was still married to him. When he heard that Erfun was taking Taimoor to Peshawar, he thought that the man didn't care about his son, so he called me. Shesta's parents lived in the city, and they were most likely staying with them. I began pleading with him to get me an address so I can rescue my son, but he had already hung up the phone.

I paced my office. I had to go to Peshawar, even if it meant great danger to me. I called the police station and spoke again to the superintendent. They promised to arrange a team to send to the city to search for Taimoor. However, the next day I called back, and they still had not organized a plan of action.

I decided right then that I would go myself and search, and told the superintendent so. He was shocked, insisting that the city was too dangerous, especially for a single woman alone. But what did these men know of danger for a single woman? All of Pakistan is a dangerous place for a single woman with no man to protect her.

That evening I packed a small bag to take with me and began planning a trip to Peshawar when my house phone rang. It was late evening. Who would call this late? I answered tentatively.

"Mother," a small voice whispered on the other end.

I recognized him immediately. "Taimoor." Tears of joy streaked my cheeks. "Where are you?" It had been two months since I heard his voice.

"Listen, Mom, quickly. If someone comes, I will have to hang up. I was in Peshawar, but now I'm in Karachi. We've been here only a few hours, and we are leaving early in the morning. You must come get me now."

"Where, where? I'll come now."

He explained they were staying in an apartment on Tariq Road. I knew the area well.

"Come right now. I will come outside."

We made a plan to meet in one hour outside the building. Before he hung up, he told me that he had been enrolled in a cadet college in Peshawar and they would be taking him back there in the morning. His father and Shesta planned to emigrate to America very soon.

If I didn't get there on time, they would scuttle him away, back to Peshawar. They had only returned to Karachi for a brief time to collect some belongings before they planned to leave the country. Taimoor would be left at the cadet college by himself, and it would be even harder to rescue him there. He was crying when we hung up.

I fumbled for my keys and dashed out the door. I tried calling the police station, but the phone was busy. The direct number to the superintendent went to a recording machine. Cell phones were also busy. I wanted a police officer to meet me outside the apartment in case Erfun resisted me. I had to choose to wait for the police, or to go right now and rescue him myself.

I chose not to wait. I rushed to my car and sped toward the address on Tariq Road. Running red lights, dodging cars and taxis, I reached that address in no time. It was a huge, five-story residential complex. The gatekeeper stopped me. I didn't know the apartment number, only the street address of the complex, so he wouldn't allow me to enter.

I stood outside on the sidewalk, and shouted, "Taimoor, Taimoor," repeatedly. Lights flashed on in windows. I kept shouting, "Taimooooorrr!" The guard came and tried to hush me, but I kept shouting.

Suddenly I saw a boy running across the parking lot. It was Taimoor, running madly, arms flying, his shirttails trailing in the wind. Before he reached the gate, Erfun and Shesta appeared from between two buildings, running swiftly toward him.

It had been almost eight years since I had last seen Erfun. If he had still been that handsome, physically fit man that he had been when we met, he would have easily run down Taimoor, but now he was a red-faced, bloated, disheveled creature, huffing and puffing across the lot, wearing a dirty *salwar kameez*.

Just as Taimoor reached me, Erfun grabbed him. A bedraggled Shesta came up behind, out of breath and panting. I latched onto Taimoor's arm, but Erfun grabbed my hand and twisted it so hard I thought he broke it. I swung and hit him in the stomach, and Erfun stopped struggling. Taimoor came to me, hugging me with all his might.

Erfun let up, holding his stomach.

"I'd leave now if I were you," I said. "The police will be here any moment. I've filed a report for your arrest."

Shesta backed off, staring at me defiantly. "Look at this shameless woman, shouting for Taimoor."

I didn't answer her. There was no use talking to an idiot. She was the most brazen woman I'd ever encountered. I would never give her the satisfaction of getting a rise from me. I smiled at her and held Taimoor close to me. I guided him to my car, and we both drove away. Erfun watched us as we left. I hoped this would be the loneliest moment of his life.

At home, Taimoor told me that every day with them in Peshawar for two months, he had been depressed. He even thought of suicide. I shuddered to think of the horror those two selfish people put my son through. I reminded him that Islam forbids suicide. We have to be hopeful, always. I held him close, and pleaded with him in gentle tones, "Please, Taimoor, promise me today, never ever think of suicide again."

He promised me.

In the morning, I called the police station and told them I had rescued my son myself, and I didn't need their help any longer.

The next day I took Taimoor with me and went to the hospital to get treatment for my arm. My right arm, especially my thumb, was swollen and painful. The medicolegal doctor asked me what happened. I told him my ex-husband had attacked me. He offered to help me by making a very strong case against Erfun and see him put in jail, if I performed a sexual favor for him. I became very angry, "I'm also a doctor. I don't need your help, but I must file a complaint against you first, in the police station, for what you have just said to me." He looked ashamed, and he apologized to me.

He set to work. The x-rays showed I had a fractured thumb. The doctor wrapped it, gave me some medication, and Taimoor and I went home.

After that, I decided it was too dangerous to allow Taimoor to go to regular school where he would learn to be independent, disciplined, and confident. I didn't believe Erfun would stop trying to make my life miserable. After talking it over with Taimoor, I enrolled him in Cadet College Petaro, one of the finest boarding schools in the country. It meant I would only see him during vacations, but I would be assured he would be safe at all times. I informed his school that Taimoor's father was not allowed to see him. Then, and only then, was I able to resume my full schedule of seeing patients.

In time, my thumb healed, and my fears over Taimoor's safety subsided, but the scars of the treachery and betrayal from a man I once loved would be etched forever across my heart. I could only hope that in time, they would fade from my memory.

CHAPTER 15
The Final Injustice

In the clinic, Dr. Sheela continued to pry into every aspect of my life. She knew about Osman and the terrible divorce I'd just suffered. My skin was still blotched with the hyperpigmentation, and I must have stood out as walking testimony to misfortune. Everything had gone sour in my life, and I just wanted to work and be left alone. But that wasn't in Captain Arif's plans. I had defied him once, and now he refused to give up, even though he was sleeping with Dr. Sheela.

Captain Arif continued to come to Karachi Terminal, where both Dr. Sheela and I worked. During my lunch, either he would come into my office and proposition me, and I would ask him to leave, or he would go directly to Dr. Sheela's office and close the door. He played a dark game. He appeared to get immense pleasure out of making my life miserable.

I was so disgusted I wanted to quit. As badly as I needed the job, the harassment was beyond what I could bear. But in speaking to several of my physician colleagues, they encouraged me to struggle through it. Jobs like this were difficult, if not impossible, to come by unless one had very high connections in the ruling party. The consensus was that with the management changes that took place so often, the men who were harassing me would one day get tired of their games, and move on or get fired. I felt confident that if I just maintained my excellent job performance, my position would be safe, and someday justice would be served on these persecutors.

So I decided to stay and persevere. If I gave up, men like Arif would gloat and think every woman in the company was his plaything. One day Captain Arif would be gone, Dr. Sheela would get what she wanted, and things would settle down. It wasn't fair, but then I had learned the hard way that fairness had little to do with my life.

Dr. Sheela knew everything about my mistreatment by Arif and about my divorce, and she gloated regularly at my expense. In between seeing patients, she would make snide remarks about why I had such difficult times with men, often giving me suggestive advice for pleasing men. I did my best to keep from exploding at her. I stayed calm, thanked her, and moved away as quickly as I could.

Ignoring her only deepened the crisis as far as she was concerned. She would go out of her way to find me in the clinic and ask me how I was doing. She knew I was grieving, but her concern wasn't genuine. I took her words as a way of mocking me. I tried a fake smile, but sometimes when I pushed myself to smile, tears rolled down my cheeks instead. I hated crying in front of her, but my heartbreak was profound. She laughed and turned away.

The only relief from her was when Captain Arif arrived, and the two of them disappeared into her room and shut the door. I didn't care what they did together, but I still did not understand why they felt compelled to drag me into their dirty game.

One morning news spread like wildfire about Captain Arif and Dr. Sheela's affair. It became such a public scandal that the local newspapers even published a story about their infidelity. The affair became known after the fire broke out in the gas plant premises of Karachi Terminal. The large blaze erupted in the early morning. It was quite a sight, and journalists, firemen, and police officers from all over the city converged on the scene. Just as the fireman arrived, Dr. Sheela and Captain Arif arrived together at the same time. With the doctor and the General Manager standing together, appearing every bit a couple, those around them began to ask questions.

One journalist sensed a salacious story and began to question the two. The reporter dug into the details about their affair and published a damning story about the two of them. The story reported that when the fire broke out sometime after midnight, the two of them had been sleeping together inside the building. This embarrassed them both, and they became the objects of ridicule throughout the company. But even in their shame, they would not stop harassing me.

The furor died down after a couple of months, but not Dr. Sheela's contempt for me. One day she came into my office and asked me to come into hers.

"Someone is here to see you," she said.

I refused to follow her. "Please leave me alone. I have a patient to see."

She kept insisting, implying she was doing me a favor. I finally relented, thinking maybe she's had a change of heart, and wanted to be nice to me.

I opened the door to her office, and Furqan, the man I had met many years before in art school, sat in her office, a sheepish grin on his face.

"What are you doing here?"

He stammered, "I was invited. Your friend told me you wanted to speak to me."

"I didn't ask you to come here."

"Listen to me please." He stood pleading with hands. "Come in and let's talk."

"I have nothing to say to you."

He pulled out an envelope. "I have a gift for you. It is five crore." (In Pakistan, 1 crore equals 10 million rupees; 5 crore equals about USD $350,000). "Have you ever seen five crores?"

He was quiet. It was absurd that he was offering it to me, and in Dr. Sheela's office. I feared this was all a setup of some sort. Besides, what was this man doing here with all this money?

"Where did you get money like that?"

"I inherited it from my father. I want to give it to you."

I felt reluctant to carry on this conversation any longer. While I didn't want his money—his offer stank of desperation—I knew this entire meeting was a trap of some sort. Dr. Sheela stood behind me, her arms crossed, watching. Others from the office stood behind her.

"Furqan, I didn't ask you to come here. If Dr. Sheela invited you, that is wrong. You can only come here on business. You'll need to leave. Thank you anyway, but I have a house and money. Please go."

I returned to my office, out of breath. I closed my door and slumped into my chair to compose myself. I could not believe how low this woman would stoop to embarrass me. I calmed my breathing and straightened my hair. Patients were at my door. It was time to get back to work. I opened my door and greeted a woman with a smile and ushered her into my office. I refused to let Dr. Sheela and her tricks overwhelm me.

I received a formal reprimand the next day for conducting personal business in my office and distracting the entire staff. I was indignant but not surprised. Furqan had just become another pawn in her game of intimidation. Since I already had several other letters of reprimand in my file, I had to answer this letter. Arif had gone to great effort to collect several letters that were included in my file. Though it was difficult to fire a doctor who had been through the interview process, I knew he was setting me up. If I couldn't explain what happened convincingly to satisfy the head office managers, I knew that one day it would be easy for him to fire me by showing all the complaint letters in my file.

I sat down to write. In my letter, I tried to explain my background with Furqan, how he regularly has chased me from place to place, and how I didn't invite him to the office. I realized once I sent it off, it was a weak letter. I feared losing my job, but then I discovered that one of the senior executives of Unit C stood up for me. Evidently, when Dr. Sheela made a big production in the office about my visitor, he was outside my office waiting for treatment for his mother. He heard me ask why Furqan had come and who had invited him. He stated that I made it very clear that I had not invited him, and instructed him to leave at once. An investigation ensued, and it was discovered that when Furqan reached the checkpoints and showed his ID, the guards called Dr. Sheela to confirm his invitation. It was clear that she had created the office drama to humiliate me.

Despite all of this drama, I refused to quit. I believed this harassment would pass.

During that time, my son needed dental treatment. When I

submitted my request for approval of his treatment, it was denied. I discovered that Arif said he wasn't eligible. I called him and objected that the very same procedure had been allowed for Dr. Sheela's children. He said that I couldn't compare myself with her. She granted favors, and in return, she got what she wanted.

"It's an insult to compare me to that characterless woman. I just expected access to the benefits I'd earned from being an employee." I hung up the phone and took Taimoor to a private dentist.

Soon after, I heard from other doctors that Dr. Sheela had enrolled in a post-graduate course at one of the hospitals. These courses were essential for a promotion, but they required full-time attendance. So she began showing up each morning at 9 a.m. to sign in on the attendance roster and then disappeared for the rest of the day. She got her special favors, and she made the most of them.

Dr. Sheela started visiting the head office to meet the new executives. At Dr. Sheela's insistence, the new Managing Director merged Units A and B, and Unit C, into one. Now the flow of patients increased exponentially at the clinic in the Karachi Terminal. The calm, orderly clinic that I had come to enjoy became an unruly, loud, crowded clinic. Dr. Sheela's office was across from mine, and a completely new group of faces, people I had never seen before, crowded into her room. The clinic became so crowded and noisy that employees and union leaders began to complain openly in the clinic that they weren't being treated correctly, or being prescribed the correct medications. My workplace had been turned into a zoo, Dr. Sheela was absent most of the time, and I was examining the patients nonstop.

I began getting more letters from Captain Arif, stating that my attendance was poor. In those days we didn't have time clocks, but we would just put a mark by our names in a ledger when we arrived. After receiving letters about my attendance, I checked the ledgers in the office, and Dr. Sheela showed perfect attendance, although on most days she was at the hospital for her post-graduate work or visiting the head office. My marks showed I had been absent for several days each week. Someone had tampered with our attendance records. After seeing that, I knew I wasn't long for this job, and began to think about what I would do next to support my son and myself.

In 1997, in a surprise change of events, Captain Arif showed up at Karachi Terminal and announced that from now on I was the doctor in charge of the clinic. Dr. Sheela had been promoted to work in the head office. I moved into my original office again, and the next nine months were my most rewarding time at Sui Gas. I supervised the staff, reorganized the patient flow to make it less chaotic, and worked toward making it easier for the doctors to treat patients. During my brief tenure managing the unit, I was able to keep the unit on budget and running smoothly. I wasn't fully able to stop the aggressive behavior of some of the patients and union leaders who wanted special treatment and favors for their family and themselves, but the unethical activities diminished over time when they realized I wouldn't bend easily to their threats.

What surprised Captain Arif the most was that I was able to cut costs by controlling expenses, and subsequently not have everyone angry with me. He assumed that I would fail miserably under the pressure of the union leaders and crush of patient requests. He was looking for the final and most significant cause for firing me, non-performance. In this case, I was a great disappointment to him.

After the calm period, chaos returned. Without warning, Captain Arif removed me from managing the Karachi Terminal clinic and rescinded my promotion to manager. In my place, he promoted Dr. Sheela and the other doctor who was in the running for the chief medical officer.

When I objected, Captain Arif called me to his office.

"Dr. Sheela gives me sexual favors. She deserved a promotion. Soon she will be the CMO. If you want a promotion, you will have to do the same."

I looked directly at him, with as firm a gaze as I could muster. "I deserved a promotion based on my performance. I'm the hardest working doctor here. I'm the only doctor who was hired based on merit and not political affiliations." I went on, reminding him of what I'd accomplished in the Karachi Terminal as manager, how many patients I treated, how I controlled the budget and managed everyone fairly.

He shook his head. "None of that matters."

"You have Dr. Sheela. Why can't you be happy with her? You have a beautiful wife and children, as well. Why isn't your family enough for you?"

He said, "Dr. Sheela is married and has four children. If she is willing to be involved with me, why won't you?"

"Dr. Sheela is willing to do what you want. Why do you bother me? She's going to get what she wants; I'm okay with that."

"You must do what I want."

I stood, my anger burning so hot that I became injudicious with my words. "If you so much as look at me with those dirty eyes of yours, I'll snatch them out of your head. If you threaten me, I will kill you. That's my answer to you."

He looked startled that I had stood up to him. I knew he was propositioning many of the secretaries and phone operators in the company. He wasn't used to being turned down. My words had shocked him, set him back for a moment. How could I fear such a mean man, so shriveled in his soul that he had to corrupt everyone around him? I despised everything about him, and I sensed he could feel that I loathed him. As I strode out of his office, I was gripped with a moment of elation, but under it was the knowledge that this man would find a way to strike back.

A few days later, Dr. Sheela, showed up at my door. Her expression was rather grim. She stood in the doorway as if she didn't want to come too close. She had a message for me from the head office. "Arif wants me to tell you that he will crush your ego soon."

Ah, the game these two played. "No one can crush me as long as I'm alive. And I have no intention of dying soon."

She shook her head as if to suggest I was too stubborn for my own good. She left without flashing me her usual know-it-all smirk. She didn't know how this would play out, and neither did I, but I meant every word of what I had said to Arif in his office. He would die before me if he ever forced himself on me.

One day Dr. Sheela came to the clinic and said, "Dr. Raana, please stop seeing patients. I want to talk to you."

She closed the door to my office, and put her face on my shoulder and started crying.

"What happened?"

"Doctors suspect I have cancer in one breast." She had a swelling in her left breast with a greenish discharge. Her tone was so soft, apologetic. She asked me for forgiveness. She knew she had bothered me, harassed me. She promised not to do it anymore.

I didn't respond. I couldn't get the thought out of my mind that this was another of her tricks.

My silence must have made her fear I wouldn't forgive her.

"I swear to God, I will not bother you again." Then she began weeping.

It didn't surprise me that this woman could so easily crumble under the threat of disease and death. She had no faith, and what religion she did have, she had made a mockery of it with her behavior.

I spoke quietly to her. "Yes, I will forgive you."

Before she left that day, she pleaded with me to pray for her. I assured her I would. She knew I prayed every day at lunchtime. Maybe I was the only person she knew that prayed. She called me from the head office every day, asking for a prayer for her health.

This went on for about a month while she was under investigation. I prayed for her, asking God to heal her. One day she called me, ecstatic; she was cancer-free. The lump was benign. My days of calm were over. After that, it didn't take her long to forget her promises.

I sent a complaint letter to Dr. Iqbal, the CMO, detailing all the threats I had received from Captain Arif. When I didn't hear from him, I visited his office. He saw me, listened, and with a straight face, he looked at me and said, "I'm sorry, but there is no way I can help you. I'm powerless in this situation."

I left his office in disgust, but not despair. It was weak men like Dr. Iqbal that held places of power in Pakistan. They were in their positions not because they deserved it, but because they had friends in high political positions. They feared power as much as they refused to use it for good, to help those who worked for them. Pakistan rots from the inside out because of weak men like Dr. Iqbal.

Many other females in the company faced the same sexual harassment as me. Dr. Sheela had opened up a Pandora's Box of extortion and compromise. Captain Arif became emboldened to pressure secretaries, telephone operators, and other women in the company. If a woman sought opportunities to move up, promotions they could not earn otherwise, they secretly became involved in Captain Arif's activities. He and other managers had turned the company into a brothel. And because the new managing director didn't take action on any of the complaints pouring into his office, everyone was convinced he was also involved in the sexual corruption.

Everyone knew about how I had openly resisted Captain Arif's advances. Soon, other women began visiting my office. Their stories were horrible, but similar to mine. I became a symbol of resistance against the corruption and comprise required of women in Sui Gas. I began to believe that my presence in the company had a purpose. I could help the other women who were enduring the same treatment as me.

One day, several women were in my office, and as we discussed what to do, one said to me, "Dr. Raana, why don't you inform Prime Minister Nawaz Sharif about what's taking place in our company."

"I don't have any access to him."

"I've heard he is nice and listens to people. If you call or write a letter, he will definitely listen and do something about these people."

Another woman said, "I've heard he has extramarital affairs, too." There were rumors that he had an affair with a married woman who worked in the media.

"It doesn't matter. He's the prime minister. This is a semi-government company. He should know what's happening here." I promised them I would follow up on the suggestion.

I began calling his Islamabad office. Over the next two weeks, no one, not even his assistant, would get on the phone with me. So, I decided to write a letter detailing the suffering and persecution women were experiencing everyday at Sui Gas. After I mailed it, I began counting the days until he, or someone in his office, answered me. My naivety surfaced again: I truly believed that once the prime minister became involved, the culture at Sui Gas would change.

Captain Arif called me and said he needed to speak with me in his office. I refused to go. He responded with a warning letter. I informed him that I had sent a letter detailing his abuses to the prime minister in Islamabad and that I was expecting his reply soon, and then he will put an end to all this nonsense, and probably his job.

When I went to his office, it was almost as if Captain Arif had become a different person overnight. He began treating me kindly. He even gave me a promotion, one I surely had earned months before. I was now a senior doctor. While my colleagues and I were waiting for an answer from the prime minister, Captain Arif and his circle acted very scared.

My hopes rose. There was a chance now at some real reform. I knew the prime minister would answer soon. Javed Khan, my friend in the head office, called me every few days, wondering if I had heard from the prime minister. As the days dragged on into weeks, reality dawned. Either the prime minister didn't read his mail, or he did, and didn't care. That last thought sank my heart to the lowest it had been in a long time.

Captain Arif at last figured out the truth; in the blink of an eye, he turned from an angel of kindness back to his true nature—a perverted devil. Some of the women in the group could not afford to lose their jobs. Once Captain Arif and his circle began to pressure them for sexual favors, they had little choice. The lack of response from the head of government emboldened Arif. There was little secrecy about his dirty game and everyone now knew the rules of that game. If these women wanted to feed their families, they would have to comply with whatever perverse requests Arif and his friends made.

Javed Khan called me one day. He knew we had not heard from the prime minister, and understood what a disappointment that was to so many women in the company. He tried to encourage me.

"Dr. Raana, whatever happens, please don't change. This world exists because of people like you. You are rare."

"Don't worry, Javed. I will never change. I will bear the consequences."

That weekend, I drove out to visit my brother Rahat. He was always a good listener and a great friend. After I told him the entire story of Captain Arif and Dr. Sheela, and the pressure people are under to be part of their corrupt practices, he gave me some wise advice.

"The one who is best friends with the decision-makers will get the CMO position. It doesn't matter who the candidates are, or how many there are, or what their qualifications are."

Then he said something very profound, something I hadn't wanted to accept, but now I understood to be true: "If you don't want to participate in their corruption, then you must leave the competition to become CMO. You'll never be able to compete with Dr. Sheela since you don't use her methods."

A short time after speaking with my brother, and the next time when Capt. Arif called me to repeat the same favor, I told him I wanted to withdraw from consideration as the next CMO. I would rather perform my duties as a senior doctor.

He listened for a moment than shot back at me, "You can't continue working in the company unless you accept my offer."

"Why do you need me? You have Dr. Sheela and the others."

He dismissed me with an arrogant wave of his hand. As I left his office, he said to my back, "Your time will come, Dr. Raana. You'll see."

Captain Arif's wife, Sanobe, found out about her husband's behavior from the wives of other executives. She became furious and left his house. She went to her parents, and in her absence, Dr. Sheela began coming home with him. When Sanobe returned, her neighbors told her everything. Captain Arif pressured her to accept his relationship with Dr. Sheela, or he would divorce her. But she didn't want a divorce. Her parents were old, and she wasn't educated and had no way of supporting her parents, her children, and herself. With divorce, she'd also lose her status in society as the wife of the general manager of Sui Gas. She had to accept Dr. Sheela's intrusion into their marriage.

Captain Arif began holding meetings in the evenings in the head office after the clinics closed. Attendance was mandatory for all doctors. During one of the meetings, one of Arif's assistants handed me a note. It stated that I needed to stay after to meet with Arif. I crumpled the note up, and dropped it on the floor. I had no intention of staying. When the meeting adjourned, I mingled with the other doctors and headed for my car.

The next day, another disciplinary letter was delivered to my office. I immediately sat down and wrote a reply. Since I had already worked the entire day, and the meeting ran until 7 p.m., I wasn't able to stay any later. I further admonished Captain Arif to not hold meetings so late, and not to expect staff to stay even later when they have family responsibilities. I didn't think this was the time to be delicate. The man was an oaf, and he needed to be taken down.

After finishing the letter and sending it off, I felt a new level of fatigue, my emotional strength drained out of me. It was time I left this useless drama. I told my friends at work that I had reached my breaking point. It was time for me to move on to a position where I would be appreciated. My friends were disturbed. If I gave up, what would happen to them? I was the bold voice of resistance.

Then Dr. Uqali called me from his home. He had heard from friends that I was considering resigning. He encouraged me to fight on as if I were some grand gladiator, and I could bring an end to all this with a swipe of my sword. I didn't think ending the corrupt practices was possible. It was very much a part of Pakistani culture and society. Soon after, I received a note from former Managing Director Mr. Javed ul Hassan, extolling me not to give up and to keep fighting.

These messages were like a cold drink on a parched tongue. I felt revived. With new energy to fight on, I was called into another after-hours meeting. Captain Arif made it clear that he needed to talk with me after the group meeting. After he finished his presentation, I stayed, despite the concerns of all my colleagues. He had staff present, so I figured he wouldn't force himself on me with others around.

I entered his office. He offered me a seat. I refused, preferring to stand. He closed the door, and we stood facing each other. In his tailored blue suit, he looked important, but the heavy, haggard circles under his dark bulging eyes, told a different story. A glint of desperation filled his gaze, as if my resistance to his sexual advances, which were as clumsy as a street vendor's, had wounded him so deeply he couldn't sleep. The thought that I had caused him a twinge of agony made me smile inside. He got right to the point.

"Why are you struggling so much? You've complained everywhere, and no one will lift a finger to help you. To continue working here, you must do as I ask."

"My struggle will never be over."

He raised his voice. "It's over. Your file is so full of complaints against you from all over the company, if you make any more accusations against me, I will ask management to begin an investigation. When they review your file, it will be over for you."

"All those are false accusations. You know it. My job performance is excellent."

His voice went suddenly soft. "I could force you if I wanted to."

"I told you already that if you try to touch me, I will kill you." I held my chin up. A bit of defiance goes a long way in murdering a man's ego.

He touched his lips with his fingers and stared at me, weighing my words. This struggle was no longer about sex—if it had ever been. It was about his power over me. The thought that I didn't quiver at his threats shook his most profound sense of identity as a man. It was so sad to see such a mean person in such a big job.

I opened the door and strode out, past his three assistants at his desk, waiting by the intercom. Would they have listened in on Arif's perversions? Was that part of their game?

I gave one of the assistants a defiant glare. He stood at my passing.

"You three are as shameless as he is."

The next morning, I sent a fax to the Ministry of Petroleum in Islamabad. I asked for an appointment with the Secretary of Petroleum, Gul Faraz, and the Minister of Petroleum, Ch. Nisar Ali Khan. I received a quick and positive reply from their Joint Secretary of Petroleum, Mr. Abbas. He had faxed me back that both of the men had agreed to meet with me. He even included appointment times and dates.

I visited Islamabad and went to Gul Faraz's office. He was sitting in his chair behind a table; he saw me at the door of his office, but didn't invite me inside.

"I'm sorry, Dr. Raana, but I can't talk to you," he said very rudely.

"Why not? I'm here, and I've come all the way from Karachi. I only need a few minutes."

"I'm sorry, but I can't meet with you. You must leave." He continued reading a file. I was extremely disheartened and disappointed. I went to his secretary's office.

"What happened? Why did he agree to meet with me and then refuse?"

"I'm sorry, Dr. Raana," the man said. "Shortly before you arrived, he received few calls from a high executive at Sui Gas instructing him not to listen to you."

I tamped down my disgust with Sui Gas executives. I knew who the other secretary was.

Dr. Sheela was very proudly telling everyone that her husband's big brother was appointed to the ministry. I stomped over to Mr. Nisar's office. Conveniently, he was not in. I left my name and contact information, and asked for a response from him directly.

In Karachi a week later, I received a call from the petroleum minister's secretary. He was in town, and he wanted to meet me in his guesthouse in Clifton at 10:30 that evening. Clifton was a resort suburb of Karachi by the coast.

"The meeting time is very late."

"Don't worry. We are sending a car for you."

I didn't like this at all. Clifton was a beach resort. The time was late. And since I was being driven there, I wouldn't be able to leave when I wanted to. This didn't sound like a meeting arranged to help me, but rather one to entrap me in a compromising position.

"I have my own car, and I can drive at night. But that time is too late for me. I need a more appropriate appointment. Can I see him in his office during business hours?"

His secretary claimed he was leaving for the US in the morning, and didn't have time the next day to meet.

"When he returns, we can meet then."

The voice on the other line became angry. "Do you want to meet the minister or not?"

"Yes, I do. I have issues in my workplace that need resolving."

"But you refuse to meet with him tonight."

"I'm not refusing. I came to his office in Islamabad to meet him. Why can't we meet in an office to discuss the issues, and not in his guest house?"

The voice took on an exasperated tone. "How can he help you if you don't come down tonight?"

"I'm not coming to his place at 10:30 at night."

"Then forget it." The line clicked dead.

After a few days, Mr. Abbas called me from Islamabad. He wanted to convey a personal message from the petroleum minister.

I had a moment of excitement that he changed his mind about our meeting.

"The minister wants to marry you."

I was too stunned to speak, and I almost lost my grip on the phone. What was this man thinking? Did he think I was stupid? He didn't have business on his agenda when he invited me to his guesthouse. Justice was not on this man's mind. I held the phone silently, unable to answer Mr. Abbas's questions. The last thing I heard was the dial tone.

Later that year, Captain Arif announced that all the doctors would have computers installed in their offices, and they would need training. I was told an IT expert assigned by the head office would visit my office to teach me to use it. Shabbir, an IT technician, showed up at my office a few days later. He was not only ugly and unkempt, but his entire face was blotched with acne that appeared to ooze. We sat in front of the terminal, and he began his tutorial by inserting a CD, evidently for us to watch. Only when the video began it wasn't about computer training, but a recording of explicit pornography. I looked at him, shocked. I opened the door and left the room. He took his CD and slunk out without a word. I went back inside and slammed the door behind him.

I was so disturbed, but was confused as to whom I could complain to. Captain Arif would just laugh at me. I called my friend Javed. He suggested I just let it pass since no one would listen to me. Other women were experiencing the same thing. He advised me that I should lay low at this time. With all of the political turmoil in the country, the end of the PPP and Benazir Bhutto's government, and the rise of the PML and the Nawaz Sharif government, followers of the PPP were being pushed out everywhere, so there was room for the friends of the new government. I had voted for Nawaz Sharif with the hope he would bring an end to the rampant political corruption. But it was business as usual.

My life at Sui Gas had come to a head. I would be forced out one way or the other. I didn't want to go without a fight. I decided to take my struggle heard at the very top. I went to see the new Managing Director (MD), Mr. Moien. Three times, I stood at his secretary's desk and asked for an appointment about an important matter. Three times, she went into his office to announce me, and three times, she returned saying he didn't want to speak with me. The fourth time, I saw him sitting in his office, and his secretary tried to stop me from entering. I warned her to get out of my way, and I brushed past her, opened his door, and entered. Mr. Moien, a short thin man with neatly parted hair, sat behind his large desk. I said I needed to speak to him about an urgent matter. He invited me to sit. I spilled out the entire story, from the beginning to the end, not leaving out any salacious details.

He listened very calmly. When I finished, he asked. "Do you have any proof of these allegations against Captain Arif?"

"What good would proof do me? If you did a simple investigation, you would have all the proof you need."

"I understand."

When he didn't say anything more, I added, "I will give you proof. But I expect action."

"Dr. Raana, if you can't prove your allegations, you will have to resign."

"Yes, Sir."

"You must promise."

"Yes, Sir. I will keep my word."

He nodded his agreement. By the time I reached my office, I had already conceived a plan to flood his office with witnesses to the pervasive sexual harassment in the company.

I gathered many of the women I was in contact with in my office. None of them were willing to speak to the MD out of fear of losing their jobs. I argued with them that the MD would take immediate action if had more witnesses and more evidence.

One of the women at the meeting laughed. She insisted that the

MD Moien was as corrupt as Captain Arif. She emphasized that Dr. Sheela spent a lot of time with him in his office, behind closed doors.

I did remember once seeing Dr. Sheela enter his office and close the door. I could understand their fears. I next asked if they would sign a petition with me detailing the sexual pressure they were under from managers. That was the moment of truth for many of them, and they refused to sign. They all were providing for spouses, children, and parents in some way, and could not risk losing a job that would be nearly impossible to replace.

Before they left, one woman said to me, "Your hope is in the wrong man. Moien knows everything that goes on, and he's part of it. He won't do anything."

Possibly it was true, but I refused to give up. If I went down, I wanted to go down fighting.

I started planning. I bought a small tape recorder. I knew I would eventually have another encounter with Captain Arif. When he called and asked me to stay after the next meeting, I agreed. Before I went to the meeting, I tested the recorder to make sure I could get a clean recording. I practiced turning it on and off as unobtrusively as possible.

In his office after the meeting, we went through the same routine. He propositioned me, and then he said something that both bewildered and amazed me. The man's capacity for duplicity and treacherousness was unparalleled.

"After we spend time together, I will make you the next CMO. You are far more qualified than Dr. Sheela. Besides, you are more beautiful and younger than her."

"But you have been with her all this time!"

"I was just passing the time with her, having some fun. I have always had my eyes on you."

I tried to smile to set him at ease. "I will think about it. Give me a few days. It's a very generous offer."

He gave me two days to think it over, before I had to get back to him. At home when I heard his conversation, it was very clear. I was enthusiastic that everything would work out fine. When I didn't call him for two weeks, he called my office and demanded I come to see him.

With my recorder in my purse, I went to his office. He asked me about my decision. I told him I needed more time to think it over.

"I need your answer now," he said, impatience in his voice. "There is no more time left. Let's go tonight. I'll book a room, and we'll stay together. Then you'll be the CMO."

He went to his desk, picked up his phone to call the hotel. When he saw I was headed to the door, he jumped and quickly blocked my way, and locked the door.

"Enough," he shouted. "You have wasted my time. No more excuses. We will do it now in my office and get it over with."

It was Friday, and he wore a *shalwar kameez*, for the afternoon prayers, the *Namaz e Juma*. Standing by the table, he started to open his *shalwar* (pants).

Outrage at this man's perverseness overtook me. I leaned close and slapped him so hard across his face that his head flew to the side. A big red welt formed on his cheek.

"I've told you so many times, I am not Dr. Sheela. I don't want to be CMO."

I walked to the door confidently, unlocked it, and swung it open. He didn't move to stop me. He stood by the table holding his palm to his cheek, with the other hand he was trying to hold his *shalwar*, but it fell down, and now he was naked, staring at me wide-eyed. I smiled at him tauntingly. His male staff, who had strict instructions not to open the door when a woman was inside, looked confused when I hustled by them.

"I think Captain Arif needs you. He looks like he's hurt."

I nearly ran to the elevator. I took it to the fifth floor, where the managing director had an office. When the elevator door opened, Moien stood on the landing with some other men. I took him aside. I was still burning. "You didn't do anything, and just now Arif called me into his office, he said he would fire me." I opened my purse and showed him the small tape recorder. "I have it all on tape."

"This is the proof I needed." He asked for the recorder and said he would present it to an investigative committee of executives. "I will call you in a week."

I gave him the tape recorder.

After one week, I received a call from the MD's office, asking me to attend a meeting at the head office. We were to meet in the big conference room. I was excited as I entered the room. Seven executives sat at a round table facing me, as if it were a panel interview. I was asked to take a seat at a huge table in front of them. I had never seen these men before. After I was seated, one of them told me that they had conducted their investigation and they couldn't find any evidence of sexual harassment.

My shock turned quickly to anger, but I forced myself to keep calm. "Everything on the tape was very clear."

"We can't find any evidence to back up your accusations. There was nothing on the tape that substantiates your claims, so based on the records in your file, we are asking you to resign, effective immediately. This will put an end to all of your troubles."

"I want justice for all that I've been through. The proof is in the tape."

One of the men laid a piece of paper and a pen in front of me. I stared at them. Not one of them said a word. I was alone, with no one to defend me.

"Just sign the paper in front of you," one of them demanded.

They all watched me. All these well-dressed men, going to such lengths to maintain their power and to cover each other's weaknesses. So this is the Islamic Republic of Pakistan these men are so proud of, where the innocent are punished for the corruption of others.

"Dr. Raana, as a good Muslim you must sign the document. You promised to resign; keep your word."

The paper in front of me was blank. A pen lay across it. Someone forced my hand to take up the pen and write, "I, Dr. Raana, am resigning because of the corruption of Dr. Sheela and Captain Arif." Then I signed my name at the bottom.

When I completed my signature, I put my head down on the table. I must have passed out because everything after that is hazy. I don't know how long I sat hunched over like that before someone roused me.

I went to the elevator in a trance. The next thing I knew, I was on the doorstep of my father's house. He took me in, and I laid in my childhood bed for several days, hardly speaking. I don't remember eating, or drinking, or washing. I was in the middle of a nervous breakdown.

My father asked me why I wasn't going to my job. All I remember saying was, "What job?" I lost track of time, surrounded by a deep silence. I'd been cut off from the world around me, and I gradually sunk down into my soul.

I don't remember when, but a letter came for me from the company. It confirmed my resignation and termination of my job, with a payout of three lac rupees. My father was surprised that I had resigned, and that after ten years of service, they would pay me so little.

"Why did you resign such a good job?"

I said nothing.

He asked again. "Baby, why did you resign?"

"I didn't."

"You're playing with your life. You need to take this seriously."

I rose and went to my room. I slept in the same dress for the next week, hardly moving from the bed. The maid brought food to the room, but I told her I wasn't hungry. One day my father came to my room, took me by the hand and led me to the dining room table where I took a seat. He gently encouraged me to eat.

"Tell me, what happened?"

I looked at him, his earnest eyes pleading with me to speak. The only words that came out of my mouth were, "Is this the Islamic Republic of Pakistan?"

He said with sympathy, "What has happened to you?"

He left me alone, only to come and tell me my colleagues from work were calling and wanted to speak to me. I refused to come to the phone.

One day my father answered the phone, and the person insisted on talking to me. My father made me come to the phone. He put it on speaker. A man was laughing. "Dr. Raana is dead. She is no more," he said in a taunting voice.

That roused me. I shouted, "No, I am still alive. Dr. Raana is not dead."

CHAPTER 16

A New Direction

WITH TAIMOOR AT PETARO CADET College, I stayed at my father's house for several months. I spent my days in a disoriented funk. Some days I couldn't remember why I was at my father's, and not at my own home. Then I would have flashbacks to the horrible moment in the conference room, the details of the meeting melting into a foggy cacophony of angry voices. I remember the blank piece of paper in front of me, and the men shouting at me to sign it. A nerve-wracking weakness came over me every time I thought about working, seeing patients, dealing with overbearing men intent on only getting what they wanted. This went on until I blacked out. When I tried to imagine the outside world, I could only see darkness.

Perhaps that was a blessing. I needed to decompress from the years of emotional abuse I'd experienced. It isn't unusual for trauma patients to lose their memories of the events surrounding their injury. The details of my ordeal faded in and out. When I tried to remember facts and names, I came down with a debilitating headache. I had to lay down and sleep, or just close my eyes. I found I didn't have any strength to read a book, to learn new facts, or to explore ideas, which had been the driving passions of my life.

I spent many hours watching fashion shows on TV, one after the other, all day if I could find them. The pretty women seemed so content in their new dresses, slacks, blouses, coats, and sweaters. The beauty of the pageantry was a palliative to my brain. I thought of buying a new dress, but I couldn't figure out how I would do that, where I would go, or how I would pay for it.

One day my father came to me. "Baby, why don't you find something useful to do? You can still help people. You could work at a hospital or do social work. There are so many things you could be doing."

Of course, he was right. After he left for his office, I went to the front door, opened it, and looked out onto the stoop, the same steps that I had played on as a child. The familiar street, one I knew well since I was a child, seemed odd to me. I could not bring myself to put my foot across the threshold and stand under the morning sky, alone. A fear possessed me that I could never go outside. I didn't know how to communicate with whatever existed out there, beyond the gate. It was too strange, too mysterious, and I didn't know why. I slammed the door and went back inside.

On a bright summer morning, my father knocked on my bedroom door and asked me to dress for work. He wanted to take me with him to his office. That would be exciting. I had happy memories of doing that as a child, strolling with my father down the street, him in his snappy business suit, and me in a colorful new frock and shoes.

At the door of the house, I hesitated to follow him outside. Halfway down the walk, he turned to me. He returned, and with his convincing smile, he held out his hand. "Let's go, Baby." I took his warm firm palm, and he led me down the stoop, through the gate, and to his car on the street. It was noisy, with cars flashing by and people on the go. It all gave me a shot of adrenaline. But the feelings didn't overwhelm me.

I spent all day at his office. He had me greeting clients, retrieving client files, filing papers. I felt stronger as the day went on. I chatted with his clients after they came out of his office, or talked with them while they waited. I felt again what it was like for me as a little girl, to be my father's daughter, talking with his friends, and conversing on important issues of the day.

At lunchtime, I strolled outside in the sunshine, my father beside me.

"Baby, do you see any enemies?"

"No, I don't." I felt comfortable.

We walked on that day to a favorite restaurant. I didn't see any enemies, only longtime friends of my father who greeted us both with great respect. After that day, at home, laying on my bed, I realized there were good people around, men like my father, his friends, and there must be others. And most of all there was hope in the world.

On the days I didn't go with him to his office, he began bringing me sweet *Jalebi* from a sweet shop near his office.

"Do you remember what your friends used to call you?"

"Baby Jalebi." I laughed. He laughed with me. Those days were such happy times. Such a simple thing, *Jalebi* candy. Tasting that candy while laughing was a magic tonic. It was as if I awoke from a deep sleep.

One night soon after, at the dining table, I said, "I need a job."

"It shouldn't be hard for you to find one." My father smiled, and we talked like old times. I could suddenly see better days ahead. I began to laugh, read, and take an interest in my appearance. After my father left for his office each morning, I sat at the dining room table thinking about the next step. I needed a job, but where could I begin? I would spend the day reading and looking through the newspaper.

At dinner, my father said to me, "Your money won't last forever. You have to be strong to face the world, Baby."

I had the severance from Sui Gas, three lac rupees (about USD $5,000). But that wouldn't last long with Taimoor's schooling and his future needs for college. When my father saw my hesitation to get started, he nudged me forward.

"I would start my search with the hospitals," he said. I don't know why that hadn't occurred to me. I decided that the next day I would begin my search. I called several hospitals, and it was easy to get appointments to meet. I went for interviews, but I was told they could never hire me. They all agreed I had a fantastic resume, but I didn't receive any offers of employment. I didn't understand why.

Finally, an honest hiring officer told me about calls he had received from Sui Gas suggesting I would not be a good employee. For some reason, it wasn't enough that Captain Arif ruined my career at Sui Gas, now he wanted to put a permanent blot on my reputation. Sui Gas was an influential company with rich resources, and it referred many patients to local hospitals. None of them wanted to get on Sui Gas's bad side.

After two months, I received a call from Sui Gas in Karachi. The person on the phone told me about an opening for a doctor in Sui Balochistan. It was a sister firm to Sui Gas. Dr. Sheela had served there before transferring to Karachi. The hiring officer offered me the job and said that I would be very well paid, and I'd be pleased with the many perks. I could fly back and forth from Balochistan to Karachi in a company plane. It also came with special housing privileges, including a spacious home, and recreational facilities with a swimming pool.

After thinking it over, I turned it down. I knew they had tried to entice me with the salary and the benefits of the job, but that had never been my motivation for taking a particular job. I didn't have a good feeling about the offer. Why would they call me and make it so attractive?

The position was given to Dr. Shazia Khalid. Her husband also worked for Sui Gas as a petroleum engineer. He had been sent to Libya to oversee the construction of oil facilities. Dr. Khalid went to Balochistan by herself, with the understanding that her husband would join her within the year.

Not too many months after she took the position, I read in the newspapers that she'd had been attacked in her home late one night, brutally raped, and beaten. She claimed she had been attacked by an influential army officer. The more adamant she was that it was a certain officer, the more her mental and emotional state was questioned—the military regime would not betray one of their own. Under orders from the government, she was confined to a psychiatric hospital as a mental patient. As part of her agreement for release, she and her husband were both forced to flee the country. They received asylum in England.

There is little justice for women in my country.

I kept up my job search, and I went to the Aga Khan Hospital and met Dr. Riaz Qureshi, the head of the family medicine department. When he checked my resume, a look of surprise came over his face: "Oh, you are Dr. Raana."

I immediately feared another rejection. "Yes, I am Dr. Raana."

"We've been hearing stories about what's taking place over at Sui Gas." He explained that his practice received many referrals from Sui Gas for specialist treatment. One patient had recently told him about a doctor who was going through terrible struggles over there until she finally quit.

"So it's you!"

"I didn't quit. They forced me to resign."

He retrieved a box of tissues and handed it to me. Just mentioning my ordeal had brought a stream of tears down my face. He was a very kind man, who allowed me to talk about what I had been through, and how I was doing since my termination.

"Dr. Raana, you must leave your suffering to God. He watches over you, and someday He will give you justice. He knows everything. You will have a big reward someday. You must now work on recuperating."

Besides being a medical doctor, Dr. Riaz was also a renowned psychologist. He treated me for my nervous breakdown, and gave me a prescription that would help with my depression, stress, and anxiety.

"Please rest and take the medication. When you feel ready, you can begin working here anytime. We would enjoy having you on staff, Dr. Raana."

Leaving his office, I realized that not all men were weak managers and out for themselves. Dr. Riaz was a kind man and so supportive. He knew about my struggles at Sui Gas and admired me for taking a stand. I felt better already. Each day from then on, my strength returned, my fears of going outside diminished, and I could walk alone again.

My new life had begun.

After I started feeling better, I called Mr. Zia Awan, president of the human rights organization Lawyers for Human Rights and Legal Aid (LHRLA). I volunteered to work with children in juvenile jail. I enjoyed the work so much, I asked Mr. Awan about joining his organization full-time. He asked about my previous work experience, and I told him everything.

He was surprised I hadn't come to him earlier. He informed me that he would have filed a human rights case. He was confident he would have gotten my job back, or at least better compensation. I didn't want to work at Sui Gas again, but I did want justice.

Real justice would be to change the way women were treated in the workplace. I didn't want to force changes through a media campaign. The best way to effect change would be to work to transform the permissive culture that allowed such abuse to persist. I believed the best place to begin was through laws that protected all women in the workplace. Effective workplace laws could one day even transform the broader culture outside the workplace.

That's why I eventually decided to join Action Aid (a London-based NGO) as a volunteer. The organization worked to raise awareness of sexual harassment in the workplace. Through their efforts, we were able to get the attention of influential legislators. We proposed laws that would prohibit sexual harassment, procedures for investigating claims, and for punishing harassers. These laws were quite controversial in the beginning and received a lot of media attention.

As stories about my struggle became more widely known, friends still at Sui Gas began to contact me. Evidently, company management was taking my story and the legislation winding its way through the government channels seriously, and they had begun implementing new rules.

As the bill came closer to becoming a reality, one by one, executives started leaving the company, including Captain Arif and Managing Director Moien. By that time, Dr. Sheela had successfully pushed the weak Dr. Iqbal out of the company and took over as CMO. She also gave my former position to her sister-in-law, which had always been her plan. Many of Dr. Sheela's family and friends were given jobs within the company, and all gynecology cases were referred to her sister, who practiced at a nearby hospital. She got everything she wanted. Despite her nefarious methods, she was a very determined and competent person.

In addition to volunteering, I began working at Aga Khan Hospital with Dr. Riaz in family medicine. I worked there for six months, regaining my strength and confidence. While I enjoyed the work, I wanted to do more to help the poor and powerless in our country. It was something I'd dreamed of doing since I first began thinking about becoming a doctor as a child. As my confidence grew working with Dr. Riaz, I realized this was the time to act on that dream.

Back in the year 2001, soon after I resigned from Sui Gas, I began looking into different organizations that served the poor and needy. I noticed that the many different NGOs served specific segments of the population, but not one of them helped the elderly. An NGO to serve the growing elderly population in Pakistan was urgently needed because of the changing demographics of the country. Couples were having fewer children, and their children were becoming educated, thus seeking better economic opportunities and moving away from traditional family structures, which included the responsibility of caring for their elderly parents. Increasingly, the elderly were neglected and impoverished, with no retirement benefits and no family to care for them. There was a great need for an NGO that met this burgeoning need.

During my time at Agha Khan Hospital, I felt it was time to put my desires to help the elderly into action. I left my position with the hospital and founded my own NGO, focused on aiding the elderly. I called it the Geriatric Care Foundation. Using my severance money, I hired an advocate to draft the bylaws and legal documents and to process the government registration with the Sindh Social Welfare Department.

I created a whole structure, including a board of directors. I invited Mr. Qutubuddin Aziz, former ambassador to the UK, to be a chief patron. I also invited Dr. Riaz Qureshi, Head of Family Medicine at Agha Khan Hospital; Dr. Rashid, an eye specialist; Hamadan Ali, a journalist; and Dr. Javari, Director of Fon Hospital. All of them accepted my invitation to become the board of directors for the Geriatric Care Foundation. Later, others joined the board: Mr. Abrar Hussain, a successful and influential high-court advocate; and my eldest brother Rashid's wife, Iffat, a school principal.

I also invited my father, but he didn't want to be involved. His objections were difficult for me to understand. He would have been an excellent role model for my organization, and as much as he didn't want to accept it, he had just turned seventy-one, meaning that he would understand many of the NGO's needs. I knew that a person's age was not always relative to his physical condition. He was very active and he looked much younger than his years. He was also very disciplined, rising early to pray; he always walked and exercised regularly, and ate a simple diet. He still worked every day in his office as a patent and trademark attorney. I believed he would be an inspiration to so many older people on how to age gracefully. When I insisted that he would be a great asset to my organization, he finally agreed to join the board.

I rented an office on Tariq Road, Karachi, where I set up a clinic and day care center for senior citizens. It was a small beginning, but I had grand ambitions. I had a lot of work ahead of me to make this project successful.

On Parents' Day at Cadet College, I spent the day with Taimoor. I met his friends and viewed his progress. His success in school gave me a great sense of relief and joy. With the Eid celebration coming soon, I made arrangements for him to visit in Karachi.

I prepared for the holiday carefully. I bought him a new set of white silk *kurta* pajamas for the prayers.

Taimoor attended the mosque with my father and brothers. My brother Rafhan later related to me something that made my heart sing.

After prayers that day, one of our neighbors asked my father, "Ch. Sahib, who is this young prince? I have never seen him before."

My father turned to Taimoor, beaming. "He is my grandson. My daughter's son." Taimoor looked so handsome in his white silk outfit, tall and athletic, with a full head of black hair neatly combed. He carried himself like a cadet. My son stood a bit taller after his well-respected grandfather acknowledged him.

Later that evening at the Eid reception, we were all gathered—neighbors, friends, and extended family—to eat a communal meal. My father arrived late, and everyone had already begun eating. He sat beside us and glanced over at Taimoor, who sat in front of a full plate of food.

"Taimoor, you aren't eating tonight?"

"I'm waiting for you, grandfather. How can I start without you?"

My father looked very pleased. I had not seen him glow like that since my mother died. He was delighted.

After the meal, he turned to my son and said loud enough for all of us to hear: "Taimoor, you don't have to return to Patero. You can continue your schooling here in Karachi."

Taimoor had found a way into his heart, and I couldn't be happier.

To spread the news of the Geriatric Care Foundation, I arranged a press conference in the Karachi Press Club. I sent out invitations to journalists and interested parties. I announced that I was starting an NGO to provide healthcare for the elderly, to look after their medical care, and to help them obtain government benefits. The press meeting was well attended, and I presented my plans to meet the needs of a growing population.

As soon as I opened the doors, seniors began arriving at my clinic. Many of them attended the day care center, which provided books, indoor games, information about illnesses, and information on how to obtain services for their various health issues. As more clients arrived at the doors of the clinic and day care center, I began to understand the depth and variety of the needs, and the stigma of the myths surrounding aging, particularly for anyone over fifty, and especially for widows and divorcees. Once they turned fifty, these women were considered too old to have productive lives or remarry. Their family, including their own children, expected them to sit in the corner of the house, quietly waiting for death.

I began to meet seniors from every walk of life. I met the poor, the working class, those from middle-class families and many of the elite. Some were too embarrassed to discuss their needs in person, so they called me. Many of these elderly women were expected to simply accept their situation and live their lives in meaningless boredom, stuck in a relative's home, waiting for death. It was such a waste of potential when they could live full, productive lives.

One of my observations was that the elderly were more likely to die from flu and pneumonia, so I set up a health program of inoculations, exercise, and a simple diet that would boost their immune systems. I spent my free time researching geriatrics in the Agha Khan Library. From there I began writing articles and submitting them to the local newspapers.

My first published article was about the fall risk of the elderly and its prevention. Fractures and injuries from falling and accidents were a major reason that the aged lose their independence. At the *Naway e Waqat* newspaper I met a reporter, Miss Fasih, who gladly published my work. Based on the successes of my first few articles, I was soon asked to contribute a regular column for *Ummat*, a large Karachi paper. I wrote a question-and-answer column for seniors. The topics were wide-ranging, covering health, social, and financial issues. My articles began appearing in both Urdu and English newspapers and magazines.

With the news of the Geriatric Care Foundation spreading, I needed more funding to provide services for the increased patient load. I began meeting with pharmaceutical companies executives, government-funding agencies, and other NGO executives. In the office of one such executive, I was also ushered into the office of the CEO. He was tall, handsome, and smartly dressed, and surrounded by bodyguards who were stationed in his office. He waved them away, and we were left alone. He invited me to sit. He began by saying his secretary had briefed him on my struggle at Sui Gas, and he admired my courage. After a few minutes, he got down to business. He made a proposal of marriage. While that may seem abrupt by Western standards, in Pakistan men often do this. They know what they want, and what do they have to lose? If I accepted, he offered to arrange a house apart from his current wife, and make provisions for Taimoor to be educated abroad. For the first time, I began to think this might be the best for me, to be under the protection of such an accomplished and handsome man. But I doubted there was much between us except for a mutual and immediate attraction. While I considered, the failure of my two marriages lurked in the back of my mind. What if Furqan had been correct all along, and the powerful magic he had performed on me had doomed my relationships? What if my happiness was being manipulated by a mysterious power beyond my control? This man wanted my answer. At that moment all that occurred to me was to say, "No, thank you."

Later, I wondered if I had made the wrong decision. I had read about him, and I knew of his reputation. He was a strong and influential man.

My proposal to his organization to collaborate never went anywhere

after that, but unlike many of the other men who had made a sponta-
neous marriage proposal, he never bothered me again.

Radio Pakistan approached me to create a weekly, hour-long program
to address the concerns of the elderly. Over the six months of my contract, the program became very successful. I discussed health, social,
and financial issues, and gave advice to seniors who called in. I specifically advised then to save money for their old age and for rainy
days. And to protect themselves from cheaters and fraudsters. Many
seniors wrote and called to tell me their stories—of isolation, of living by themselves apart from their families, and of the lack of services for their chronic diseases. When my contract with that station
expired, I moved my program to two local radio stations, FM 101
and FM 100, and to ARY Digital TV, where I presented the program,
"My advice for your health," became very popular. I was invited to
appear on many programs, particularly political talk shows, which I
often refused. After many invitations, I finally agreed to appear on a
political talk show. I was asked what I thought of MQM leader, Altaf
Hussain. Remembering my experiences working near their headquarters, the violence I witnessed, and the personal harassment and death
threats from their followers, I said, "He is responsible for thousands of
deaths."

The host, Agha Masood, immediately went to a break and turned
to me. "Dr. Raana, don't say that. Just say he is a nice person and a
great leader."

"I will not say that. Why can't we speak the truth in this country?
Wrong is wrong." I had witnessed the terror the movement's followers
had perpetuated firsthand.

"If you talk like that on the air, they will kidnap you, or worse."

"I'm not afraid of them."

We finished the interview without bringing up the MQM or their
leader. I had no idea how my brief comment on TV would come back
to haunt me.

I spent the next year traveling and meeting influential people who
could help me promote and fund my work. I knew there were many

resources out there, and I began to research experts in the field of geriatrics. I began corresponding with Dr. Larry Gell, director of an international agency for economic development in New York City. He had organized a conference on aging in Iran, and once I explained to him about the work I'd undertaken, he proposed I host a similar meeting in Pakistan. He was impressed with my pioneering work.

In my mind, the most significant resource of aid and recognition was the United Nations in New York. Since my childhood, after listening to my mother speak highly of the United Nations, I wanted to visit. My wish came true, when the next year—2002—I traveled to New York with Taimoor. My purpose was to register my NGO with the United Nations, but also to network with program leaders who were also providing geriatric services. I wanted to learn what different countries were doing to address the needs of the elderly and bring the best practices back to Pakistan.

Before I left Pakistan, I had researched how the UN operated, and I found I needed to speak to with Ms. Hanifa Mezoui. She headed up all the NGO registrations in the United Nations. I called ahead and was able to book an appointment with her. I had a strict budget for the trip, so Taimoor and I stayed at the YMCA in Brooklyn.

The day of my meeting, I strode down 46th Street, and the sight of the iconic United Nations building next to the river thrilled me. I had dreamed of making this trip as a child, and now I was here. I found the reception center and called up the receptionist to let her know I was here for my appointment. After waiting briefly, I was escorted to Ms. Hanifa Mazoui's office. We had a wonderfully productive meeting. I explained the ongoing work of GCF in Pakistan, and that we were the only organization in the country working exclusively with seniors. When I described the extent of the problems, and how hard it was to meet all of these needs, I could tell she understood. She explained that her department was inundated with requests from NGOs from all over the world, and that it typically took many years to complete the process. But in my case, she would see to it that GCF's registration was completed within a year. She was equally impressed I had made a special trip to see her. It was a very productive meeting.

While I was in New York, I wanted to make the most of my time, so I also went to see Valerie Levy from the New York State Department of Aging. I wanted to take advantage of her expertise and learn how the elderly were cared for in the United States. My meeting with her also went well. I set up several other meetings: with Helen Hamlin of International Federation of Aging; Nora O'Brien and other senior doctors from the Research Institute for Aging, and Beth K. Lamont from The Humanist Society. All my meetings were productive and informative. I visited a few senior housing projects, including Fordham House for Seniors.

I also met Professor Nizam Uddin, Chief of the Aging Program at the UN. He was surprised that I had come to New York alone. September 11th was still fresh in everyone's mind. Many people from Pakistan were too fearful to come to America. I took advantage of our meeting and made a presentation of the work for GCF I was spearheading. When he saw the brochures and newsletter, he was amazed. He appreciated my efforts, and he invited me to a conference for the elderly commencing that week. At the conference, I gave a presentation on my work. This was an exciting opportunity, and I was honored to be asked to participate.

Upon returning to Pakistan, I visited Islamabad and called on the Ministry of Women's Development and Special Education, where I met Mrs. Agha, the secretary of that ministry. After I explained my mission and trip to New York, she invited me to become an executive member of the Committee on Aging. The committee met every few months, and she would make certain I had an invitation to attend the next meeting.

Before leaving Islamabad, I went to the office of the European Union. I met with the chief of their funding department, Rashid Khan. He liked my project. He understood the real need and thought I was doing good work. He said he would come to Karachi soon, and he would meet with me again.

True to his word, we met again in Karachi, but the meeting wasn't what I was expecting. He was pleasant, but bold. He made it clear that he wouldn't help me unless I gave him sexual favors. When he saw I was quiet, he repeated, "We only provide funding to those women who give us sexual favors."

For him to admit his corruption so openly, as if it were an ordinary transaction between us, shocked me. I even didn't pick up my presentation materials from the table as I abruptly stood up.

"Please continue to give funding to those women who will sleep with you. I don't need your funding." I stared at him indignantly.

He looked shocked, as if he was not used to being turned down. "This feels like you just kicked my ass," he said to me, possibly expecting me to feel bad for what I'd said.

"I hope for the rest of your life you feel I have kicked your ass." I turned and strode out the door. I never spoke or heard from him again.

The meeting reaffirmed for me what women must endure in my country to simply conduct everyday business. Men somehow think that this kind of appalling behavior is normal. In my heart, I will never believe trading sex with a man so he will perform a job he is paid to do is normal.

CHAPTER 17

Meeting an Old Acquaintance

In WESTERN COUNTRIES, WHEN CULTURAL or social problems arise, they are usually addressed openly. Once an issue is identified as vital to a significant sector of the population, planning and research is implemented to find solutions to the pressing needs of the population. This happened in the West with the AIDS crisis. There are so many additional examples. In developing nations, such as Pakistan, officials tend to deny that such issues exist until the problems spin out of control and threaten to destroy civil society. Only then does the government take action. This was the situation in Pakistan regarding geriatric issues. The elderly had become the forgotten, the neglected, the quiet ones who had no voice in a society gripped by political and economic corruption, sectarianism, extremism, and violence. Who had time or interest in caring for the most vulnerable in our country?

That was the case when I established my Day Care Center for the elderly and Geriatric Clinic. The press, the government, and powerful sources who could influence change in Pakistan denied there was a problem with the way the elderly were treated. When I began my program, as popular as my media programs were with the elderly, I heard from many detractors, who denied that the elderly were being neglected. But when I met with the elderly and heard their stories, and began relating their stories on the radio and TV programs, I noticed a change in many attitudes. The press picked up on the issue, and human interest stories were being published. Awareness produced changes.

One TV station broadcast a documentary on the daily lives of the neglected elderly citizens. The UN established October 1 as the International Day of the Elderly. Walks, seminars, and programs were created to raise awareness of the issue. It was an overwhelming response to my continuous efforts and dedication. Within a few years, the government began taking the issue seriously.

I believe during this time, one of my most effective achievements was increasing the awareness of the necessity of flu and pneumonia shots, of daily exercise, and a renewed culture of respect for the elderly as a whole. I began seeing forty to sixty clients a day in the Geriatric Clinic. The need was overwhelming, and I needed greater resources to operate.

Professor Frederick Fenech from Malta contacted me. He had read about my work and invited me to the International Conference on Aging in Malta, which he had organized. It was a great honor to receive that invitation, but I had minimal funds for travel. What funds I did have, I needed to operate the clinic. It was still an incredible honor to be invited.

At a local conference in Karachi, I met a government minister, Aftab Sheikh from MQM, a political party that had shared power in Karachi. After my speech, he told me that he appreciated my approach to addressing geriatric issues. He was elderly himself and said I could come to him any time if I needed anything. I immediately thought of the Malta conference. I told him that I needed airfare and expenses. He told me to bring him a letter from the Social Welfare Ministry, and he would help me fund the trip. I took an application to Dr. Saeeda Malik in the Ministry of Social Welfare, and she immediately signed it. Then Mr. Sheikh signed it, but then he laughed. "You are only asking for 48 thousand rupees [about USD $500]," he said slowly. "You should have asked for a few crores [one crore about USD $70,000], and we would divide it between us."

I was shocked at his suggestion, and I shouted, "No!"

"Dr. Raana, I was just joking, but this amount is so little. It won't cover all your expenses. What will you eat? How will you do any shopping?"

"Sir, this is all I need for travel. But when I return, I will come to you for more funding for some important projects."

He smiled and agreed. Since the conference was set to take place soon, he suggested I use my own funds to travel, and seek reimbursement when I return. This was because it usually took a few weeks to process a request through the finance department.

I arrived in Malta, and the arrangements went smoothly. On the first day of the conference, Dr. Fenech visited each of the delegations, and then gave a welcome speech. Malta was one of the first countries to recognize early on the problems of the aged. Their work resulted in the International Institute of Aging by the UN. I learned about the international efforts to address the common issues of the elderly. It was an exciting and inspiring time, and overall, it was a wonderful experience.

Upon my return, I went to the finance department three times to be reimbursed. Every time I was told that the secretary of finance, Fazal-ur-Rehman, was busy. On my fourth visit, I was told to wait. After an hour, I protested. I could hear the secretary in his office laughing and talking. I peeked in the door. He was with a group of men, drinking tea and eating cake. When his friends began to say goodbye, his assistant announced the secretary was leaving, and I needed to return another day.

I wasn't returning. I brushed past the startled man and confronted the secretary with my signed expense report.

He took the paper, scanned it briefly, and shoved it back to me, rudely. "Pakistan's treasury is empty. We can't give you this amount."

I thought of Mr. Sheikh laughing at me for asking for such a small amount. All the other participants had extra money that had been provided by their government and allowed them to shop and eat expensive meals, activities I couldn't afford. I was enraged. "Corrupt political leaders and bureaucrats like you are responsible for emptying the treasury. I was told I would be reimbursed for this small amount, and you drink tea and eat cake and have nothing to pay me."

He was so insulted he began shaking. His friends stood silently by.

"I need you to sign this now," I demanded. "This is my fourth visit here. I don't have time to come again."

He took it from me and signed it. In the next week, I received my check from the Social Welfare Department.

When I returned to seek additional funding for the Geriatric

Clinic, I was turned down. I was told that someone had submitted a request for funds using my name, and the NGO and had taken the funds set aside for geriatric care. I pursued an investigation and found out that some corrupt individuals had conspired with the staff in the Social Welfare Office to receive a grant of funds by using my name and documents to impersonate me. Like so many other stories of misuse of social welfare funds, it was disgusting and sad to hear this.

I began to seek other sources of funding and remuneration. At a gathering in Karachi, I met Mr. Abdul Sattar Edhi, a renowned social activist. He was aware of my work, and was kind enough to sit and talk with me. I told him about my work, and the tremendous financial pressures on me to keep the doors open.

"Do you have the courage to beg for funding?" he asked.

I must have had a tortured expression on my face.

"I see it in your face that begging is very hard for you. Most of the time it is the only option to continue operating your programs."

"Begging is difficult for me."

"Sometimes it gets down to standing on the street pleading for money."

I couldn't imagine this man having to stoop to standing on a street corner, but he was serious. I knew that I would have to do everything in my power to expand my network of contacts. There had to alternatives to becoming as desperate as Mr. Edhi had described.

In June 2003, I attended a two-week conference on the elderly hosted by Dr. Grace Clark at Catholic University in Washington, DC. Shaukat Tahir, joint secretary of Ministry of Women's Development and Special Education, included me in the official Pakistani delegation. I had initially decided not to go, but then he repeatedly called me from Islamabad, inquiring why I didn't want to attend. I told him I didn't want to take funds from the operation of the clinic to travel. He didn't offer to pay my way through government funds. Instead, he said I should sell my jewels, and fund it that way because it would be a great learning experience. I agreed and sold some valuables.

We stayed at the university. In between sessions, he asked me several times to go sightseeing with him. He offered to purchase some lovely gifts and meals. I told him that I had come here to learn, not to shop. He was disappointed, but I didn't see much of him after that. He took his shopping and having fun very seriously.

On the last day of the conference, senior government officials from the international delegations were scheduled to deliver speeches as closing remarks. Each government official was to announce what policies they were adopting in their country. The social welfare minister from India had arrived specifically to hear the last day of speeches. Joint Secretary Tahir was scheduled to give the closing remarks for the conference from the Pakistani delegation but chose to go shopping instead.

Early the next morning, I woke up to Dr. Clark knocking on my door in a panic. The joint secretary was nowhere to be found. Did I know where he was? I smirked, but didn't say anything. She asked if I could prepare a speech and deliver it that morning. I immediately said yes, and quickly pulled my notes together. I had been close to this topic for years now, and I had paid close attention to the conference, and I had a lot to address. Dr. Clark was relieved at my willingness to help, especially because I was the first speaker that morning. In my talk, I laid out the measures Pakistani society and government would need to adopt and the lack of a government support system for them. Then I injected some hope, speaking of the changes that were taking place because of the ongoing work by others and myself. My talk was very well received.

During my stay in Washington, DC, I received an email from Dr. Nizam, inviting me to attend a conference at Columbia University, which would be held later that month. I decided since I was already in the US, that I would stay and attend. I contacted Beth Lamont, whom I had met the year before on my first trip to New York, and told her that I was coming again to the city. She invited me to stay at her beautiful apartment in Battery Park. When the conference began, I moved into quarters provided by Columbia University.

Since I had time in New York, I visited all the offices I had gone to the year before to renew friendships and to learn. I returned to the NGO resource center at the UN to follow up on my NGO registration application. No one could find my file, and that caused me great disappointment. Then I met with Meena Suie, a very helpful Indian officer. She searched for my paperwork, but it evidently had vanished. I protested that it wasn't right for me to travel all this way at my own expense, and not be taken seriously. I set an appointment up with Ms. Hanifa Mazoui, and I told her everything. She suggested I go to the Pakistan Mission to the United Nations, and obtain a signature from a Pakistani representative. With a signature from a mission official, it would get more attention. But it would still take a year to complete the process.

I went to the Pakistan Mission, and I was ushered into the office of a man whom I immediately recognized: Mansoor Suhail. He invited me to sit. We had met nearly nineteen years before in Islamabad when I was in medical school, and again when he had come to Karachi seven years ago, and I had asked him not to contact me again. Those were dark days for me, but many good things had taken place since then. He remembered me instantly and didn't bring up our conversation in Karachi. I asked him to follow up on my application for recognition by the UN. He gladly agreed to do that for me.

Then he asked me a personal question. He wanted to know why I looked so sad. I smiled; I didn't think I was sad or quiet.

"When we first met, you smiled and laughed. Now you hardly smile at all."

I did smile, but most of the time I had to fake appearing calm and happy. The crush of trying to make my NGO work, and of navigating the bureaucracies of organizations that didn't seem intent on helping people, wore on me. And then there was the constant harassment and reluctance of my own countrymen to look beyond their own pleasures and appetites. All of those realizations made me aware that every day was a battle against the ineptitude and carelessness of people in responsible positions.

I did talk less, laugh less, and even smile less than I used to as a carefree student.

Then he asked, "I've often wondered, what do you think of me?"

My feelings regarding him had changed over the years, from infatuation when I first met him, to disappointment when I found out he was engaged, to utter disregard when he showed up on my doorstep. What could I say without causing injury or insult?

"You are a good human being."

He laughed. "That's what you are thinking, seriously? I was expecting more."

"This is a great compliment coming from me."

He had liked me since we first met years ago in Islamabad. He had wanted to marry me. I knew this already, but my trauma from Sui Gas had not entirely passed. My memory was still foggy and I had all the symptoms of post-traumatic stress. If he had shown up with a sincere heart earlier in my life, things might have been different between us.

Now his situation has changed. His wife was not mentally well, and they had filed for divorce. He opened a drawer and showed me several birthday cards that he had written to me, but had never mailed. He kept them in his drawer for the past seven years.

"I hoped one day you might change your mind. So every year I wrote to you and kept them in the drawer."

We reminisced for a while. When I needed to leave, he signed the papers I had brought, and he handed them to me. Mixed in with the returned UN paperwork were two envelopes addressed to Mansoor. The return addresses were from two different American women, but there were no letters inside. I returned both to him. He seemed embarrassed, saying that I didn't want to know about those women. They were no longer his girlfriends. His drawer was probably full of letters to and from women. He eyed me as if trying to figure out my reaction.

"It is your life," I said.

"You're different, you know that?"

"Oh!"

"Most Pakistani women would get hysterical at this point, crying and making a fuss. But you are so calm."

"I'm not the one who should be crying. Your wife should be the one crying."

When I handed in the paperwork to the appropriate staffer back at the UN, I asked her please to not lose it this time. She smiled at me, as she laid the folder on a stack of similar manila folders. All I could do was hope for the best, and keep following up.

After our meeting, Mansoor began calling me. He made marriage proposal after marriage proposal. I put him off; he was already married, and I didn't have any interest in a married man. He insisted his divorce would be finalized soon. He wanted me to rush into a decision, suggesting we could go to a nearby mosque for *Nikah* as soon as his divorce was finalized.

I told him to call me back when he has the divorce papers in hand so I could see them. But I would not consider a marriage proposal as serious until he traveled to Pakistan and spoke with my father. If we did marry, I told him, we will do so in Pakistan in front of both of our families. He frowned and became silent. I could tell he had not expected that answer.

One day we met for coffee, and he wanted to know why I had left my job. I told him the entire story, and he thought it was unfortunate I was forced to resign. He was employed in a bureaucracy, and he was familiar with how management can make false allegations to target someone they didn't want. He claimed to know about my situation, and who the people were in Islamabad who didn't help me when I went to them. They all wanted Dr. Sheela to be successful. He recited names and ministries, and seemed to be aware of details I hadn't mentioned.

Out of nowhere, he asked, "Did the oil minister, Ch. Nisar, propose to you?"

I held my peace.

"I know everything."

How did he know all of this? He said he had called his contacts in Islamabad and they told him the entire story.

"I can help you get your job back."

"I'm not interested. They've turned the place into a brothel. I'm much happier running my own clinic."

"If I help you return, the situation will be different. No one could say anything to you."

I didn't need his help, except to get my NGO recognized by the UN.

"Help me with the recognition for my NGO. That is what I need most."

"Yes, anything."

I also applied for the registration with the Department of Economic and Social Council at the UN. During my stay, I attended the UN general sessions and various meetings with other organizations. I was thrilled to be here in the building, watching and learning how everything worked. I also attended a reception for the World Love and Peace Society. I delivered a small speech on peace during the reception.

Mansoor called me afterward. He complimented me on the dress I wore to the reception. He said I looked glamorous. I'd worn an ordinary dress, one I'd worn many times in Karachi. But how did he know what I wore? Did he have someone spying on me? Or just a lot of friends?

He said he had a friend looking out for me, for my own protection, and that I shouldn't worry. That bothered me. I had traveled internationally alone several times. I knew how to take care of myself. I asked him to stop following me and spying on me.

Finally, the time came for the conference at Columbia University hosted by Dr. Nizamuddin, Chief of the Aging Program at the UN. I also met Professor Steve Albert, Chairman of the Public Health program at Columbia University. He was extremely knowledgeable about geriatric issues and the current trends in program development to address the problems. The conference expanded my understanding of what could be accomplished with the people I served. My presentation at the conference was well received. Dr. Larry Gell, Director of the International Agency for Economic Development had taken my interview and it was aired on a local New York TV channel. I didn't see it, but I was told that it was quite popular. Dr. Gell also wanted to collaborate with me to organize an international conference on aging in Pakistan, an event we'd never had before. I agreed, as it would be a great opportunity to highlight the geriatric needs in Pakistan.

Before I left, Dr. Nizam told me he would soon be settled at a university in Pakistan and would begin a research and education project on aging.

One day during the session, a mild rain started. An American colleague noticed I didn't have an umbrella, and I told her that I'd never used one. In Karachi, we never needed one. She insisted I take her umbrella because she had an extra. I thanked her and took it. As I began walking, the rain was light, but then suddenly it turned into a severe thunderstorm, breaking right over my head. I struggled with the umbrella, trying to figure out how to open it. The device was foreign to me. A well-dressed African American man watched me for a moment, then stepped in. I asked him to help me open the umbrella. He unbuttoned it, and flopped it open and said, "Like this," and we both laughed.

That evening Mansoor called me. We chatted, and then he said, "I know you were laughing on the street with an African American."

I thought it strange. Was he following me again? "Do you have someone following me?"

He brushed off my questions. "Why do you laugh with a stranger, but not with me?"

"Try just talking normally, instead of always prying into my personal life." I was beginning to distrust him for so many reasons.

Upon returning to Pakistan, I received a harsh email from Shaukat Tahir, the Joint Secretary, who didn't show up for his speech. He accused me of disrespecting Pakistan. This made me very angry. The audacity of the man, shirking his duty, trying to entice me into playing hooky, was astounding. I dashed off a very terse email, setting him straight on who did the defaming. I reminded him I attended the conference at my own cost, and that he went as the representative of the Pakistani government, at the government's expense. Instead of speaking as scheduled, he went shopping. I threatened to complain about him to the ministry. "You are the one who defamed Pakistan." After that, he left me alone.

The next year, Mansoor came to Karachi for a few days and visited my father. He never spoke to my father about marriage. Yet every time I spoke to Mansoor, he wanted to marry me. His behavior seemed odd, as if he had other things in mind besides a happy married life.

I continued to run my Geriatric Clinic, seeing dozens of patients a day who had little money to spend on their care. I had so many plans to reach more of the nation's elderly but little funds, and seeking funding from the nation's social welfare ministries, even the European Union, would require significant compromise on my part. I knew I lived in a corrupt society whose leaders were concerned about themselves, and not the welfare of the people they claimed to serve, but there were some true-hearted people. I had met so many who did care and were supportive of what I was attempting to accomplish. But raising funds had become like begging, and I despised that. So I came up with some alternatives.

A producer of ARY Digital TV channel contacted me, asking if I would be interested in hosting a regular health program focused on the elderly. I agreed, and I scripted and hosted a weekly show centered on offering advice on staying healthy, avoiding and treating common diseases, and other health topics. I started different programs on other TV channels, in which I interviewed guests—experts, patients, and others—who could speak on issues surrounding aging. They became quite popular, and attracted some significant sponsors, including pharmaceutical companies, banks, and prominent medical groups. I used the fees I earned to operate my clinic and support myself.

I was invited to write articles for *Global Watch* magazine, a periodical published by the United Nations, and *Geriatrics,* published in Malta. I believed I was making a difference and that my NGO was producing positive results for the seniors.

In 2004, I received an Ashoka Fellowship. They recognized me for social entrepreneurship advocating for the elderly. Ashoka International searches out activists all over the world who are engaged in pioneering work and awards them fellowships to meet their personal needs. Ashoka supplied an ongoing scholarship that met my personal needs for several years. With those funds, I had the peace of mind that I didn't have to worry about how I was going to eat. I was very excited and honored by this accolade, and I attended the induction ceremony in Mumbai, and Kolkata, India.

One of the Ashoka Fellows I met at the awards ceremony was Abdul Waheed Khan. He had started an organization that worked to reform the Madrassas, the religious schools for teaching Islam. He developed resources to modernize their curricula to include more subjects, such as math, reading, English language, and computers. Opposition to his work was intense, and when he returned to Pakistan after the award, he was brutally murdered on the streets of Karachi. It was a sad moment for all those children of Pakistan who deserved a better education.

CHAPTER 18
Forced Underground

MANSOOR SEEMED INTERESTED IN MY passion for the elderly. One day he called me from New York to tell me about Dr. Amna Buttar, a Pakistani social activist, geriatrician, and physician living in the US. She was protesting the treatment of Mukhtar Mai (a village girl, who was raped by a group of men at the command of the village council in retaliation for an accusation against her brother). The Pakistani prime minister was in New York at the mission, and Dr. Buttar and her fellow protesters rallied in front of Pakistan mission office. He offered to go outside and speak to her about my situation. I was surprised, but I said no to the opportunity. Mukhtar Mai's case was widely known because she forced the police to prosecute the men who raped her, a rare occurrence in Pakistan.

Mansoor sounded sympathetic to what I'd been through at Sui Gas, yet I had come out unscathed. Many women like Mukhtar had horrible experiences. He thought I was courageous, and I shouldn't have been forced to resign. He offered again to help me get my job back. He boasted of all the things he would do for me.

I listened, but in my mind, the past was past. But I did want him to speak to Dr. Amna Buttar since she an activist, physician and geriatrician like myself. It would be useful to compare notes and learn from her. When nothing came of his offer to reach out to her, I realized he was just trying to impress me. Did he even care about my work with the elderly? I couldn't say at this point. My problem, looking back, was that I often did want to believe the best of people.

Mansoor had met my son during his visit to my father in 2003. He often spoke of Taimoor, how handsome and intelligent he was. He wanted to match up my son with his daughter, who was much older than my son, who was only a teenager at the time.

Mansoor kept insisting that I talk to Taimoor about the opportunity. His daughter was a US citizen, and Taimoor could become one also. Then I could become a citizen too. I had no inclination to move away from Pakistan, and the age difference was too much for me to consider such a match appropriate. Taimoor was young, a happy student, and just on the verge of his adult life. He had no interest in marriage.

Mansoor became increasingly demanding. He expected me to be at home to answer his phone calls. I told him that was impossible. I had a clinic to run. He kept telling me since we were going to get married, that he would take care of me, and I didn't need to work. I listened, but I didn't like to expect and accept anything from him before we were married. So how was I to live if I quit everything? He didn't say anything. Besides, I had worked hard to be independent, and I didn't plan to give it up for another man's whims. The clinic, my TV program, article writing, organizing seminars and workshops, and raising Taimoor kept me very busy. I had no intention of just dropping it all because he wanted me to.

On one call, he said that other women listened to him, and did what he wanted.

"What other women?"

"I have a few women, one in Lahore and another in Islamabad. They quit their jobs for me and sit home and wait."

"Are you joking?"

"Why would I joke about what I want?"

I couldn't believe what he was saying. He was utterly shameless about what he was putting these women through. "How long have they been waiting?"

"I haven't lived in Pakistan for almost ten years, so at least that long."

"Do you intend to marry them?"

"No, I don't really care for them. I want to marry you."

He wasn't the caring and thoughtful person I imagined. I had built up this romantic picture of him when I was a young student, and I had kept that image of him in my mind. But in reality, he just used women. I asked why he hadn't told them not to wait any longer so they could find suitable husbands, have children, and enjoy a happy home.

"I've trapped them. They can never leave. I enjoy having them wait."

My God, what a cruel man. Did I truly know this man whom I was so attracted to?

Once he called from New York and asked me for permission.

"For what?"

"Tonight I'm going to a friend's house, and there will be several couples and single women there." He started explaining and elaborating what will be going on. It would be some kind of orgy.

I stopped him short. "You need to ask your wife, not me."

"She is too conservative. She will never allow me."

"I am more conservative. I don't even want to hear about what you're doing."

Something was not right with this man. I didn't know if he was testing me, to see what I would agree to, or if he was actually going to attend this party. He was sweet talker, but he had an immoral agenda that I wouldn't have anything to do with. He was handsome, charming, brilliant, and utterly perverse.

The next few phone calls were cryptic conversations about journalists pursuing an investigation into his sexual activities with women. He seemed afraid, as if he feared that if a scandal broke, then his fun would come to an end. He talked about returning soon to Pakistan, and then he could find a good man for his daughter. And we would get married.

I must have been crazy because I did have feelings for this man, but he was another womanizer. He was married. He had mistresses in different cities, and he engaged in group sex parties. What did I see in him?

I continued on with my busy schedule. Mansoor began to get very specific in his telephone conversations. He wanted me to sell my apartment and move to the US. He kept insisting I come to New York so we could marry. I asked him about his plans for Taimoor. He had no answer. I refused to leave my son in Pakistan.

In 2006, Mansoor returned to Islamabad as the Director General, External Publicity, Government of Pakistan, Ministry of Information & Broadcasting. He called me from Islamabad and said he was coming to Karachi, and that it was time for our marriage. I was happy, but still unsure of what his true intentions were. He invited me to join him at a fashion show held in Mohatta Palace in Karachi, an elaborate historical building and elegant venue for a fashion show.

The show was fabulous. Mansoor was popular amongst the attendees, and senior officials and celebrities greeted him respectfully. A talkative man, he had charming things to say to everyone he met.

Many of the local TV channels had crews at the show and interviewed the guests. Every time the camera panned to him, and I was next to him, he turned his face away. His behavior was odd in that instance, as he normally was someone so openly gregarious and popular. Appearing on TV was something he expected and usually did not shy away from. It seemed to me he didn't want to be seen publicly either with me or in Karachi or both. If we married, would he behave in the same way, afraid to be seen openly with me? Or would I be one of his many secrets? I knew his family lived in Lahore and Islamabad, and it would also be difficult to live openly there, even after his divorce was final.

After watching his act, I felt a dread in my heart. I could not go forward with this man. I had to have a frank conversation with him. I had to find a way to bring his secretive ways to light.

He must have noticed that I grew suddenly serious.

"What happened? Aren't you enjoying the show?"

"Yes, very much. I was just thinking about us. How we could make it work?"

"Don't worry about those things. Everything will be fine. I'm coming tomorrow to meet your father, and we'll settle our marriage."

"No, tomorrow I want to go meet your brother, Amin." Mansoor was staying at his brother's home in Defense District. He looked confused, but then his face brightened. "Come for lunch. We have others coming over. It will be a nice time."

The next day, I met his brother. Mansoor introduced me as his special guest. I showed Amin the ring Mansoor gave me at the show.

"We are going to marry in few days," I said directly to him. "We will marry in front of you and my father."

He didn't reply. I repeated my request that he attend. Still, he was quiet, pretending he wasn't listening.

Mansoor was busy in conversation with others, but when he saw me speaking to Amin, he came over.

"What were you talking about?"

"Your brother isn't too interested in our marriage."

"You shouldn't have told him."

"Why not?" I was growing angry, but I controlled my voice.

"It's complicated. We can marry in front of your father."

I wanted the truth. "Is your divorce finalized?"

He had a pained expression on his face. "When I told Lubna I was going to marry you, and I wanted a divorce, she cried so hard I thought she would die. She is old now, and she would live the rest of her life alone."

"So your wife is not a mental patient. You are not divorced. You don't intend to get divorced." That explained his brother's reaction to me. "That's why yesterday you were trying to stay away from me when the camera was around us. You have continuously lied to me for the last four years." I was so angry, all of my shock poured out on him.

"Please, please." He tried to calm me and led me to a sofa. After the guests left he sat beside me. I rested my head in my hands, shaking.

"I have loved you for since we first met. I want to marry you. I didn't want to lose you. You know that in Islam I can marry you because I can afford two wives."

"You know that according to Islam, lying is forbidden. In Islam, you are to treat both wives equally. Where am I to live? What home have you arranged for me?"

"Where you live now. I will live both places, Punjab and Karachi."

"I will never be able to visit Punjab, and we couldn't live openly there because of your relatives and circle of friends." I was certain now he had no intention of openly declaring me his second wife. "As a second wife, I would be in a weak position. If she cried to get what she wanted from you, you would do it."

He was furious, but controlled himself. "Your analysis is true, but I will take care of you, don't worry. I will be at your side. I will not allow anyone to violate your rights."

He then said something that put me off. "You know, you are in a weak and vulnerable position. You don't have a well-paying job. Financially you are weak and unstable. You live alone, which is dangerous for a woman. Still, you dare to say what you think is wrong. You have convictions. You are altogether different from other Pakistani women. You don't complain, you aren't materialistic, and you always thank God. You don't shout, curse, or cry. I gave everything to my wife—children, money, good care, but she always complained, and cried every time something didn't go her way. That's the reason I'm in love with you."

Of course, his words made me feel good. But that was the power of his flattery; he could talk his way out of almost anything. I was fighting a civil war inside—my head said to run from this man. But in my heart, I wanted to marry. I had wanted to marry him since the first time I met him.

"I always have tried to live up to what I believe a good Muslim does, to be true to our duties and responsibilities. But I have made many mistakes in my life because I'm human, like everyone else. But I have great fears."

"What do you fear? I will take care of you."

I didn't want to laugh in his face, nor did I want to cry. I would never let a man put me through the torture that Erfrun did. I could never live in a relationship where I was in competition for the love of my husband.

"I'm sorry, but I have to think this over."

"Look, I will divorce her in the future. But right now I'm searching for a husband for my daughter. Divorced parents make it harder to find a good family."

"If I married you without her knowing it, without her permission, it will create nothing but more lies in our marriage. It will end up torturing me. And I can't do that."

Now that I knew the truth, that his wife was not mentally ill, I wouldn't consider marrying him without her written permission. Mansoor's true intentions now were clear to me: he wanted me as a secret second wife. I would never be able to live openly with him. Even though it was permitted by Islam and it was legal in Pakistan, I would never agree to play that game. I would have few rights, and I refused to set myself up for more emotional anguish. When I told him my feelings, he was openly hostile, rising to his feet and yelling at me that I was unreasonable.

The next day, Mansoor met with my father and they talked for some time. But he never mentioned a marriage proposal. He left for Islamabad the next day. He kept calling, demanding that I curtail my social work, close my organization office, and geriatric clinic and day care center. His demands that I stay home and be a regular wife confused me. Who would pay for my son and me? He claimed he could use his influence to get me a well-paid medical job. But nothing ever came of his offers.

Mansoor kept calling me, but I refused his proposals. Once he started shouting at me, so I hung up the phone. He called back and spoke calmly. I told him I wasn't his wife. He couldn't treat me that way. But the more I pushed him away, the more he made promises. I knew now that he did not intend to keep any of them. He wanted me as a wife on his terms alone. He couldn't believe that I refused to marry him.

Around the same time, I began receiving calls from the contacts I'd made during my travels to the US. I began a new round of collaborations on articles, planning conferences, and my future travel plans. Several of the doctors I had met with called and informed me that they had received letters on official government letterhead saying that they shouldn't be involved with me, that I wasn't trustworthy. The letters stated I had been fired from a government job as a doctor and wasn't competent to work in the field. My colleagues asked if I was safe, expressing concern that some high official would try to slander me like this. None of them believed the accusations, but what could they do? They had officially been asked not to collaborate with me.

Slander and intimidation are not unheard of from the men in my country who feel they are going to be exposed because of their inflated egos.

Mansoor would not give up. He called constantly, using every charming phrase in his well-worn playboy book of tricks. He now became bolder, inviting me to join him in his group sex sessions. He gave me an address in Lahore where I could meet him. I thought he was just trying to shock me. But after a while, I realized this was a common practice with him. When he became graphic, I hung up. He always called back quickly, shouting that I was disrespectful to hang up on him.

"You must remember, you live alone. It's very dangerous in your neighborhood for a single woman. You need powerful friends now more than ever."

I didn't say anything. At this point, he could be capable of anything. He knew people in high places, and he was used to getting what he wanted. I tried to be pleasant, but I couldn't let this go on. I didn't want to answer the phone anymore, but I feared not doing so. Would he show up at my door? Would he send a spy to watch me, or worse?

After many calls inviting me to Lahore, I suggested, as kindly as I could, that he take his wife. I tried to reason with him. I thought he would react to my comment, but instead, he was somewhat truthful.

"She's boring. No one would like her."

He was an absolutely shameless man.

"Listen, Mansoor, I don't want to shout or get angry. I don't want to argue. I am not that kind of woman. I would never attend these parties. Please stop telling me about them."

Instead of honoring my dislike for the subject, he went on to tell me that the group has arranged to have some little girls there. My heart dropped at his words. I had heard of men who lured little girls, even small children, and exploited them sexually. It was one of the sickest parts of our culture, and here was a man openly admitting his depravity.

I took a breath. I wanted to know what parents would allow this. Mansoor went on to tell me that men recruit these girls from poor families in the countryside. Sometimes they are the children of their servants. They give the parents small gifts as incentives to provide their children. If any of the children die, he pays off the parents with 100 or 200 rupees (200 rupees is less than $3).

I realized I was on the phone with Satan.

This man and his friends placed no value on human life. No religion endorsed or allowed this behavior. The pain those little girls must feel at being abused swirled through my heart. I had to get away from this man without putting myself in further danger.

I demanded he stop calling me. His obnoxious talk gave me headaches, and I began feeling depressed. Memories of my days in Erfun's house flashed through my mind. When I insisted that he stop his filthy conversations, he became threatening.

My breath froze in my chest. He could pull strings. He could make anything happen. I remained quiet for a moment then told him I needed to leave for work.

When he called again, he started describing the bodies of his brother's daughters, and daughters-in-law.

"Shame on you. They are your daughters, like your own daughter."

He took a breath for a moment. Had I struck a nerve?

"You need to find another woman. One that likes what you're doing."

"I know plenty of women, but I love you, I want you."

"Please," I pleaded. "Stop this. I have my life. You have yours. We are different. Accept that."

"You have to come to Lahore and join us. You will enjoy it."

This time I lost my fear. I didn't care anymore about what he could do. My composure left. "You will stop this rubbish and obnoxious talk," I yelled through the phone. "You are sick. You need to see a psychiatrist. If you call me again, I will go to the police. I will call your wife, and tell her everything. I'll call your daughter, and tell her what you're doing to little children. Don't ever call me again."

After I hung up, I sent him an email, explaining in detail what I would do if he bothered me anymore. The next day his wife Lubna sent me an email. She must have read his email, but I ignored her request. I feared that if I created more conflict with his wife, he would retaliate violently. If he was willing to kill little children in his sex games, I knew he had the potential to hurt me because I had rejected him.

He didn't call me any longer.

Later that year, I was in my clinic early one morning when several men with their faces covered and brandishing Kalashnikovs entered. They demanded that I pay a large monthly bribe, or they would kill me.

"I treat seniors for free. I don't earn enough money from what I'm doing to pay you."

The leader laughed. "Then we will kill you; get ready to die."

One of the men stood up for me. "Leave her alone. She is doing good. My mother watches her TV programs. She likes her and always prays for her."

The leader considered the man's words. "We won't harm you. But you must close this center."

I looked around at all the seniors waiting to be treated. What would they do if I closed the clinic? What would they do if I was killed? Neither of the options were good, but I could work from my apartment—if I were alive. I knew these men were serious. The thugs were well-known for extorting both businessmen and doctors. Occasionally they would drag a doctor or businessman who refused to pay their bribes into the street and execute him in cold blood, leaving the body in the middle of the road as a warning to pay their protection. The government did nothing to protect the neighborhood.

"I will close the clinic. But I need some time to get everyone out." The men made everyone leave, shouting and screaming while waving their weapons as people ran for the exits. I left the clinic with a heavy heart. What was happening to our country that criminals wouldn't even leave the sick in peace?

A few hours later, I walked through my office and clinic for the last time, packed up some papers, and then locked the door.

My heart was broken thinking of all of the seniors who would not receive help. I couldn't sit at home and do nothing. I decided I would begin operating underground. I needed a place to treat patients where these criminals could not find me. I spoke to my father, and he agreed to let me use one of his empty offices as an impromptu clinic. One of the board members also allowed me to use one of his offices to see patients. We operated on a very small scale, but I was able to continue to serve.

After a couple of weeks, I was in my father's office when he received a disturbing phone call. I knew it was a disagreeable conversation because of the tone of his voice. I asked him about the call that troubled him.

"Someone threatened that if I didn't stop helping you, they would kidnap Rafhan [my youngest brother] and kill him. They said I would find his dead body in small pieces. I told them I would never stop supporting you." He looked troubled, but firm in his resolve. "Don't worry, you can continue here." My brother confirmed I didn't need to worry about him.

I decided in my heart that I couldn't put my brother and father in such a dangerous position. The terrorists were determined to push me out of my practice. I feared they would not hesitate to follow through with their threats.

Rafhan had always helped me in my organization's activities, and I loved him very much. So after the threats, I told him I no longer needed his assistance. I knew that if I hadn't been present when my father received that phone call, neither of them would have mentioned it. I loved them too much to put them in any danger, so I no longer saw patients in their office.

Day by day, my activities diminished. The major TV stations that had regularly invited me to speak as a guest on a show would no longer invite me. I began contacting the smaller local channels, newer channels, and talk shows. I knew Mansoor was using his influence to cut me off from the media.

I had an offer to host entertainment programs, but I refused. Despite the fact that my personal finances were diminishing rapidly, I didn't believe that that was the right direction for me to go in. I wanted to stay focused on what I did best. I decided to search for a medical position and to get back on my feet financially. I was very disappointed to have to cease my NGO work, but I was glad both my son and I were safe.

I spent my free time with Taimoor. I knew God would give me strength. I wasn't greedy; I just needed a decent job to take care of my son and me. But after a few weeks of not working, the isolation became intolerable. I knew I had to find a way to continue seeing seniors in their homes while I looked for a job.

Despite the risk, I began visiting senior citizens in their homes. I held meetings in volunteers' houses. I lived a life that I didn't want to live. I lived underground, a secret life of scratching every day to survive. I lived in constant financial stress, which was very strange for me. But I was happy with Taimoor's company.

Traveling through my neighborhood, which had once been peaceful and safe, had become dangerous. In the past few years, the surrounding residential neighborhoods had changed. On one side of my Chapal apartment was the residential area of Pashtuns, and the other side was a Sindhi community. Each of them favored different political parties that were at war with each other. They didn't argue and debate as in Western countries; they took their disagreements to the streets and would shoot each other, killing innocent citizens who happened to get in the way. Stores, shops, and shopping malls were forced to close after the streets became too dangerous. What once had been a peaceful neighborhood now had become a war zone.

One day, Taimoor came home very agitated. "God just saved me now!"

My heart almost stopped while listening to his story. A group of Pashtuns had stopped him and his friends on the way home from school and threatened to kill him. One of his friends, whose father was a member of their party, vouched for him, saying that he was a good boy. So they let him go. But he was shaking he was so frightened. That he would come this close to death on our own street, made me fear to live in my own country.

My once-peaceful neighborhood had been turned into a battleground. MQM party members were breaking into the empty homes and apartments on the streets and taking them over. Families began to leave our street. I wanted to move, but I couldn't afford to live anywhere else. I didn't have the money to buy another house or to rent one, nor did I want to return to my father's house. So Taimoor and I stayed, despite my growing fears.

Once, Karachi was known as the "City of Lights," but now it had been turned into a dark, gritty, violent metropolis. No one knew who would be killed that day through the random acts of terror that had become commonplace.

Leaving my apartment to see a patient or to interview for a job had become a form of torture. Terrorism gripped my beloved Karachi by the throat. Now, I had to hide in my own country while trying to help the most vulnerable citizens.

One day my youngest brother Rafhan came to me, he looked scared and was shivering. Furqan had met him outside his office. He claimed he was performing very strong magic to convince me to marry him. When he explained the bizarre ritual the man was doing, I began to shake inside.

I realized it was too dangerous for me to live in Pakistan. I had no strong political connections, and I had no inclinations to become involved in politics. I knew politics wasn't meant for honest people. But without political connections, I had no protection.

Early one morning, I drove to the Canadian embassy and filled out emigration paperwork. In those days, the process was quick and usually only took three to six months. A few of my friends from medical college had completed their entire Canadian emigration process within six months, so I was hopeful.

After I received the receipt from the embassy for my application, I left the building hopeful that our lives, Taimoor's and mine, would soon change. Canada was a safe place to live and practice my profession. Months later, I followed up at the embassy, and they said my file had just disappeared. I showed them my receipt. They could still not find my file. They had no clue what had happened. Something had happened to the file.

My disappointment was tempered by a call from a colleague, Dr. Nizam. I had met him in New York and again at an international conference in Islamabad a few years prior. He had moved to Pakistan, and he wanted to begin his work with seniors in Punjab. I was excited to speak with him. We had worked together on legislation that was presented to the government to provide geriatric services. It was later passed and signed into law by the president.

I invited Professor Nizam to Karachi. When he visited, I organized small meetings in a board member's office, and invited university students, journalists, and doctors to take advantage of his research. On his last visit, he tried to encourage me. "You are doing good work here in Karachi, all by yourself."

All by myself in so many ways. I had no one at my back. I had no financial resources, and I had growing doubts that it was safe for me to live in the only country I knew as home.

CHAPTER 19

A Narrow Escape

WITH MY STIPEND FROM ASHOKA depleted, my financial situation became cloudy. I still had some savings, but it meant we would have to live very frugally until I felt strong enough to return to work. I still suffered from debilitating migraines every time I thought about the pressures of returning to work and thugs wanting to kill me. Mansoor had ceased his perverse calls, but the effects of his filthy mouth and evil intentions for our relationship still lingered. But I took comfort in my faith in God. He knew my struggle, and I encouraged myself that there was a reward for the righteous, for not succumbing to corruption. And I did feel his *barkat* (blessing)—we were living peacefully; God had returned my son from his dangers, and we both were in good health. At the right time, I would return to work.

I was at home later that year, when I received a panicked call from my brother Rehan.

"Where are you, Raana Baji?"

"At home. Why?"

"Benazir Bhutto, the former prime minister, has been murdered." He knew I lived in my own world these days, and that I needed to pay attention to what had just happened.

"Call Taimoor. Instruct him to come home immediately. There are riots everywhere, and it will only get worse."

He suggested that we both stay inside for a few days until the violence settled down. As soon as I got off the line with him, I dialed Taimoor's cell. He was attending an evening class and didn't answer. I tried several more times, but still no answer. About three hours later, he limped in through the front door. His Sindhi friends had rescued him from a mob that threatened to kill him and carried him home. He was hurt, but safe.

Late into the night, I treated my son's wounds and reminisced on a chance meeting with the slain politician. We crossed paths in the Dubai airport on my return from the US. As soon as I recognized her, I turned and greeted her, "Ms. Benazir Sahiba."

She stopped and scrutinized me. "I don't recognize you. Are you a member of People's Party?"

"No, I am not in politics. But I admire you and your father, Mr. Z. A. Bhutto."

"What do you do?"

"I'm a doctor." I briefly told her about my social work and the geriatric foundation in Karachi, and my activities at the UN.

"You live in Pakistan! You must join us. The PPP needs educated women like you."

"I will consider it."

She was warm and passionate, and I could tell that she cared about what she was doing. Before I left her, she gave me her assistant's contact information, and reaffirmed that she was eager to have me become involved. Then we both had to run our separate ways to catch our flights. We spoke only a few moments, but I remember her face, voice, and her kindness as if we had just met yesterday. She knew that returning to Pakistan would jeopardize her life, but she went anyway.

After the public settled down from the shock of her death, I began receiving emails and phone calls from media outlets asking for interviews. Professionals from different parts of the world that I'd discussed geriatric issues with over the years also reached out to me. Some were interested in joint projects, while others tried to motivate me to return to the struggle for justice for the elderly. In particular, Dr. Erdman B. Palmore, professor emeritus of sociology at Duke University, wrote to me. He was an early pioneer and visionary in research and education regarding institutional and social biases toward the elderly. He wanted me to write a chapter on aging in Pakistan for his book, *The International Handbook on Aging*. He wanted a chapter on programs and issues facing the Pakistani elderly, and he insisted I was the only one qualified to write it.

The chapter would require more research. Just compiling what I had already published in magazines and journals wouldn't do. I resisted the opportunity, fearing my mental fatigue would hamper my effectiveness, and my ability to meet his deadline. But Dr. Palmore was persistent. I finally agreed, and I was able to complete the work on time. The book was published in October 2009.

That October brought to an end to three years of recovery and peace. I had been able to pray five times a day, and I had a routine that made me feel safe. It was time for me to return to work when troubling phone calls started again.

Someone called from New York and introduced himself as Khalid. He stated that he was an admirer of my work with the elderly and asked me if I was available to collaborate with him on a project. He mentioned several ideas—a home for the elderly, a clinic, and other ideas. Since the project would be in Pakistan, I told him that the next time he visited the country we could meet and discuss what he had in mind. He regularly visited Islamabad and Lahore to see his family. On his next trip, he promised to come to Karachi.

After a week, he called again. This time he gave me more information about himself. He was the CEO of a large hotel chain in New York. His full name was Raja Ki Punge, but most Pakistani knew him as Raja Khalid. Americans called him Mr. Punge. He claimed to have friends in influential circles in Pakistan. He offered to help me if I wished to get one of the seats in Parliament reserved for women. I thanked him, but declined his offer. I had no inclination to become a politician. He then complimented me on my work, and while I didn't think much of his political connections, I did appreciate his respect for my work and his kind manners.

Khalid regularly called over the next month. While he was always respectful and complimentary, he didn't make any commitments to come to Karachi, but he kept up his compliments. He had seen me interviewed on Pakistani TV shows and seemed very well informed about elderly issues. It was pleasant to hear someone talk so kindly about my efforts, but I wasn't entirely convinced of his intentions. His calls were always very short, and often were very strange. He said he was visiting Karachi in the next week, and we planned on meeting at my father's office.

This date he had set to meet arrived, and he didn't appear. A few days later, he called from Islamabad, claiming his delay in coming was because of all the interviews he'd been conducting for positions at his hotel in New York. I easily heard several women's voices in the background.

The next time we spoke, he called from the airport in Islamabad. He had to return to New York, and he'd promised his nieces they could visit him in America. I began to wonder if all those women's voices I'd heard in the background on the previous call were his nieces. But they did not sound like the relatives of an educated and wealthy man, but girls from the villages. So far he'd kept none of the promises he'd made to meet me, and this made me suspicious. I did a simple search of Pakistani newspapers online, and his name appeared, connected to two women. A Pakistani politician, Dr. Ms. Tawan, and a Pakistani dancer, who later married his son Nange Punge.

I needed to be very careful with this man. It would be best for me if I stayed away from him.

Then I received a phone call from Mansoor. I had stopped worrying about his calls, so I didn't hesitate to pick up the phone.

"So you were waiting for Khalid, and he didn't come to Karachi?"

I was not only surprised to hear his voice, but that he knew of Khalid.

I tried to play dumb. "Who is Khalid?"

He laughed. "Don't think I'm a fool. I know everything."

My voice caught in my throat. Maybe I was the fool, thinking this man would leave me alone. But how did he know about Khalid?

"You know why he didn't visit Karachi? I met with him, and advised him not to."

"Why would you do something like that?"

"He's too rich and influential. I don't want you meeting a man like that. He'll want to marry you, and then you'll be happy. I can't allow that."

"What's my life to you? I decide whom I'm friends with, not you. Besides we were discussing a project for the elderly, one he wants to help me build."

He laughed hard. "Project for the elderly!" Then he disconnected the call.

Later, I spoke with Taimoor. "I think someone is listening to our phone calls."

"Mom, to tap someone's phone is very difficult. Only intelligence agencies do that. You are not a criminal or spy. You are just an ordinary doctor. Why would someone listen to your phone?"

What he said made sense, but he didn't know what I knew. If you knew the right people or were willing to pay a bribe, then it was very easy to listen to anyone's phone calls.

Khalid continuously called, promising to travel to Karachi to discuss building a home for the elderly. He would fly to Islamabad for a few days, call me from the airport with another excuse why he couldn't come to Karachi, and travel back to New York with more nieces and girls from the family. It was apparent he wasn't a man I could trust. On his last call, I asked him not to call me any longer. I had all the help I needed.

One weekend, I drove to visit my brother at the Naval Colony. I stopped for gas along the road. I spotted a crowd across the way. A group of men had surrounded a woman, they were pushing and touching her, and she was screaming for help. Near me, a group of people had gathered to watch, so I asked a man what was going on.

"I don't know exactly, but I think they are trying to kidnap that woman."

"Why you don't go and help her?"

"No, I can't. It could be their personal matter."

It didn't look and sound personal to me. Her shouting became frantic. Whether she knew the men or not, she did not want to go with them.

"At least call the police." My cell was dead, or I would have done it.

"You go help her." He stood there watching unhelpfully. I refused to watch this happen right in front of me.

One man turned. "Don't put your life in danger for her. She's dressed like a prostitute. Look at her dress."

I spoke louder so they all could hear. "You're not helping her just because you don't think her a decent woman? That's disgraceful."

I crossed the road to the men circled around her. "All of you," I shouted. "Stay away from her."

Those men moved back, and I reached the young women, who cowered on the ground. The men jeered. They were grabbing her clothes, hair, and touching her body.

"Take my hand," I said. She eagerly grasped it. I pulled her to her feet. "Stick with me," I whispered to her. The men were too stunned to move at first, but as we crossed the road, one of them yelled, "Get them both."

We ran to my car, climbed in. One of the men tried to open the door, but she forced him out, slammed the door, and locked it. A few of them stood in front of my car, trying to block me from leaving, while others jumped on the hood and began beating on the roof.

I started my car, gunned the engine, and put it in gear. I shouted, "I will run over all of you if you don't leave." I feared I wouldn't leave here without either killing someone or being killed myself.

I shot forward, and the men dove out of the way. Those on top of my car rolled off by the time I turned onto the main road, where we broke free, and I sped down the road. They must have jumped in their car because one sped up behind me as if to ram us. Just then, I turned into the gate of the naval station, and the men's car continued on up the road, away from us.

We finally reached the Naval Colony gate and pulled up to the guard post. When I told the guard what happened, he wouldn't let the girl onto the base since she wasn't related to anyone stationed there. He wanted me to leave her there before I entered the base.

I called a cab, gave her some fare, and my phone number to let me know she was all right. Later at my brother's house, I received a phone call from the girl's mother. She was very thankful for my help. "You saved her life."

Isn't that my duty as a Muslim, to save a life, and not to allow mindless killing and abuse of our fellow human beings? I felt good for her but bad for those men who would treat a woman worse than they would treat their animals.

Taimoor decided he wanted to study in America. I listened, but I didn't have an answer for him. Not only did I not have the money, but also

I didn't even have a job. He must have seen the disappointment in my face.

"I only need travel expenses and admission fees and my first year's tuition. Then I will take care of myself. After I graduate, I will return here and help you."

"I'm sorry, I can't help you now, but I will find a way to make it happen."

And so, the time had come for me to return to work. Whether someone listened to my phone calls or not, I decided to apply for jobs in person or by email. I delivered my resume myself to Agha Khan Health Services. They needed doctors for the mountain areas in Northern Pakistan. I thought if I could hide out in the rugged north, I would be safe. I could save my money to send Taimoor to the US to study, then his future would be secure. During my interview with Dr. Rozina Mistry, she saw my resume and was pleased to see my expertise in geriatrics. She offered me a position creating a geriatric program at Agha Khan Health Services. And I could work from home in Karachi.

It was an excellent opportunity for me to make a mark in the medical history of Pakistan. She said they had been looking for a competent doctor and researcher for a long time for this program. They had tried a few others, but none of them worked out. She hoped I was the person they had been looking for.

I utilized what I had learned in my own NGO, along with the research I had done around the world, to create a program for Agha Khan Health Services. I collaborated with Professor Steve Albert of Pittsburgh University. I am proud that my contribution to geriatric care has significantly improved the lives of the citizens of Pakistan. I worked on this project for about a year, and successfully completed my work at Agha Khan Health Services in January 2011. It was one of the best experiences of my professional life.

Later that year, an international NGO invited me to attend a conference in Europe for a few days. They paid all of my travel expenses. I renewed my passport, went to Islamabad, and applied for a Schengen visa (a blanket visa that would allow me to enter any EU country), but my application was denied. I was taken aback. I had never been denied a visa before, and I couldn't figure out why now. I was extremely disappointed.

When I came back to Karachi, Mansoor called me.

"You were denied an EU visa. Too bad. You won't be able to renew your US visa either. You will never travel abroad again."

My hand shook as I held the receiver. Why was this devil doing this to me? Was it because I wouldn't join him in his sex games? Was he indeed this powerful? I slammed the handset down on the phone, and I must have stood there for an hour worrying, shaking, and thinking. I was not safe in Pakistan any longer. But I couldn't leave Taimoor on his own.

A few days later, Raja Khalid called me from New York and proposed marriage to me again. He had proposed a few weeks before, but when I refused him, he suggested not to reject him so quickly. He told me that I should take my time and think it over. At the time he first proposed, I was busy completing my program design for Agha Khan Health Services. I believed that my fees would be enough to take my son and myself to the US, where Taimoor could enroll in school.

But now with the refusal of my EU visa, and with my US visa about to expire, I began to believe there was something more to Mansoor's threats. What was his connection to Raja Khalid?

The next time Khalid called I asked him, "Did you meet Mansoor in Islamabad?"

"Yes, and he began talking rubbish about you, so I just ignored him."

"You know," I said, "Pakistani men usually want to marry very young girls. Why do you want to marry me?"

"Every time I speak with you, it's not like speaking to other women. I've made inquiries about your family, and you and your father have an excellent reputation. Most importantly, you are not greedy for my money. You haven't even asked me how rich I am. That's usually the first question out of most women's mouths."

He continued, "If you accept my marriage proposal, I will be the luckiest man in the world. I will take care of your son as a father, and I will arrange for his studies in New York."

These were comforting words at a tough time in my life. They melted all the defenses I'd built up around me. I remember thinking that Khalid was a very kind man. Though I had never met him, he seemed to care. He never used any offensive language like Mansoor, or even suggested he was involved in anything similar to Mansoor. That touched my heart in a way that opened me up to him.

I needed help with Taimoor's education, and I needed someone strong at my back. Living alone, and divorced, was an open invitation to the most perverse men of my culture. If I did marry him, we could leave Pakistan, and I would be free.

I told him we could marry, but only in front of my father. So he would have to come to Karachi. I wanted to take him to my mother's grave, too. He promised with an oath, *Allah Ke Qasam*, I swear to God.

But he never came. In two years of his calling, proposing marriage, and swearing to God that he would keep his promises, he never kept even one. I finally told him not to call me anymore, and to leave me alone.

Around that time, I was invited to Islamabad to speak at a conference on aging sponsored by a federal ministry. After I completed my key-note speech, Mansoor approached. He repeated his same old request: he wanted me to agree to marry him.

I took him aside where I could speak privately. "Mansoor," I said calmly, but thoroughly exhausted by his demands "I have no respect for you in my heart anymore. I can't marry you, please try to understand."

"Don't dream of marrying Khalid. I will never let it happen."

I had already decided in my heart that whoever this Khalid was, he was not the man for me. "Do you know what your problem is?" He gave me a blank stare. "You are a very educated man, a competent executive in the Pakistani establishment, and a renowned bureaucrat with a respectable reputation. But you are talking like an uneducated, stupid man." I turned on my heel and strode away, but in my heart, I had to hold down my fear. He was all of the things I had just said to him, but he was also a powerful manipulator who had friends in high places. He knew so much about me, and I feared he would not hesitate to use it to make my life miserable. He knew I lived alone and was vulnerable. He knew my passport had expired, and that I had applied for the renewal. He also knew my US visa was about to expire. I was in a difficult position.

Despite my fears, I went about attending the conference sessions and collaborating with Ashoka. During one panel discussion, Mansoor walked into the room, striding right toward me. I stood up in a panic. He loomed over me, stared into my eyes, and raised his fisted right palm in front of my face, then opened it flat. He blew a white powder in my face. "My magic spell will chase you over the seven seas. You will never be happy without me." He smiled devilishly and left the room. I could hardly talk, I was so afraid. I could not understand why he wouldn't leave me alone.

I returned home after the conference, shaken and disturbed. Why couldn't this man take no for an answer? I sat on the sofa, my legs pulled under me, with the door and windows locked.

Soon afterward, I received a letter of invitation from the United Nations NGO director, inviting me to visit and participate in meetings on aging. I went online and registered, and updated my information in the UN system. With a formal invitation to attend the UN, obtaining a new visa would be much easier. My passport renewal had finally been approved, and my visa only had a few weeks before it expired. Things were looking up.

It was late in the evening on February 2, 2011, when my doorbell rang. I shouldn't have opened it, but I did. Two men stood on the landing outside my door. I didn't recognize either of them. One asked if I was Dr. Raana. I told them she was not at home right now, and I was not sure when she would return.

He pulled a revolver from his pocket and brandished it. "Tell her Shahid Malik Awan from PTCL came with this," he said. I slammed the door in their faces and ran to the kitchen. Standing by the sink, I caught my breath. They wanted to kill me. Why? Was this Mansoor's doing, trying to convince me I was not safe living alone?

The next morning as I crossed the parking lot to my car, a car drove by the gate. A man leaned out the window and fired a shot my way. I fell to the ground, breathing hard. My heart felt like a hammer against my ribs. As I crouched on the ground, with gravel soiling my knees, I decided to leave Pakistan that same night. I must leave for the US now, or I feared I would never be able to go.

My US visa was set to expire in three days. With the letter of invitation from the UN, I had a good chance of getting through, even though my visa was days from expiring. I at least had to try. As much as I wanted to take Taimoor, his visa had already expired. I had been trying to get it renewed without any success. He would be okay by himself. He was an extremely responsible and competent young man. He had a grandfather and uncles who loved him, and he was a good student. He always told me he could take care of himself. Now he would have to.

I used my neighbor's phone and called my travel agent Imran at Bukhari Travels to arrange a ticket. He had scheduled all my travel for many years, so I asked him for a favor. Would he bring the ticket and meet me at a nearby shopping mall? He agreed.

I sent an email to Beth Lamont. She had become a good friend during my previous visit to the UN. She had offered to help me when I visited the US again.

I packed my suitcases in a panic. When my son came home that evening from college, he was surprised to see my bags packed.

"Mom, where are you going so suddenly?"

"I'm going to a UN conference. Then I will see if I can stay a little longer." I rushed around, gathering things, and he didn't ask any more questions. "I need you to take me to the airport."

"Now?"

"Yes, right now."

"Okay. I know you're not happy here. But don't worry about me. I'm a big boy. You can go and live anywhere you want, as long as you feel happy and safe."

I smiled and gave him a hug. He was such a joy to me, and to part so suddenly would be a shock to both of us. But it would be better to be alive in America than dead in Pakistan. I would be of no use to him then.

He didn't ask any questions during our ride to the airport. He didn't ask me when I would return. Neither did he ask to go with me. I felt a crush of guilt. I knew he wanted to study abroad. He was young, so now was the time for him to travel and explore. As much as I wanted him to be on that plane to America with me, I had to go alone and find my way. Then I could bring him over.

"Please take care of yourself. Go live with your grandfather, even if only for a while. He would love to have you. I know you will be okay."

He assured me he would be just fine.

"If anyone asks where I am, tell them I went to the Northern Area to work with Agha Khan Hospital. Don't tell them I went to the US."

At Karachi airport, when I said goodbye to Taimoor, I didn't know we wouldn't see each other for eight years. I thought after a few months when things settled down, I could return to Pakistan and quietly live in another city. But that wouldn't be the case.

I kissed his forehead, and closed my eyes and prayed to God, *Please take care of my son, he is very innocent.* We parted, but without tears.

I checked in, received my boarding pass, and headed toward the boarding gate. I moved purposely through the terminal hall, toward my plane, when someone grabbed the sleeve of my coat from behind. I turned.

A middle-aged woman in a business suit had her hand on my arm. "Dr. Raana, you can't leave."

"Why not?" I demanded.

"We have orders from a top-level government executive."

I brushed her hand off my arm. We stood in the middle of the busy concourse. Darkness filled the tall windows. My flight left in a few minutes. I didn't have time for these games.

"Show me the orders. I want to see who signed it."

She hesitated. "I don't have anything in writing. But you can't travel."

Half a dozen men surrounded me.

"Please step aside, Dr. Raana," one of them requested. I followed them to the side of the concourse. They circled me and repeated what the woman had told me: I wasn't allowed to leave. I pleaded with the men, but their faces were like stones. They would not budge. I began to cry, "Please let me go. This is my last chance." I knew in my heart that if I were forced to stay, I would never be a free woman.

I closed my eyes and cried silently to myself. Behind me, I heard over the loudspeaker that my plane was boarding. The men wouldn't let me get past them. I stood in their midst, closed off to the world. Someone behind me said the plane was gone. I began to feel faint. I opened my eyes, and the waiting area was empty, the boarding ramp door closed. The flight had departed. I was standing alone.

A man stood by me, "I'm sorry about this mess. I can see you fear for your life."

I nodded.

"If you must leave, please return in the morning. Change your ticket to another airline and speak to the man in charge of the CAA (Civil Aviation Authority), Mr. Haider. He is here in the morning. He is a nice man, and different from the night staff. He will listen to you."

I thanked him, and he left. I decided that I wouldn't return home. I would stay at the airport. I called my friend at the travel agency, and he changed my ticket to another airline. He gave me the itinerary and flight number.

I was too worried to eat or sleep that night. In the morning, I freshened up, drank some tea, and went in search of Mr. Haider. He listened carefully to my story and why I feared staying in the country. He said I shouldn't worry any longer. I was cleared to travel. "Don't worry about the government executives. I will handle them."

He was indeed a saint for me.

I left for the States, with several layovers in between. At Dubai airport, the staff stopped me because the expiration of my visa was so close. I explained to the officer at the counter that I was traveling to the United Nations on official business. I showed him my letter of invitation.

The officer scanned the letter and then said he must speak to his boss. He talked over the phone, and I could tell by his expression his boss would not allow me to pass through. I spoke very slowly and low, "Please allow me to go. This is my last chance to survive."

I could see him thinking behind his steely eyes, considering my words, trying to figure out if I was being truthful or putting on an act.

Finally, he waved me through. "Go. Go. If you are courageous, no one can stop you."

I ran toward the gate, turned and waved to him and shouted: "Thank you!"

When we debarked in New York, I held my breath as I stood in line. Since 9/11, American customs laws had become more stringent. I could be caught in limbo, stuck in this airport with no way to return home. My throat became dry as the line moved forward. I prayed to God not to send me back.

When it was my turn, I placed my passport, UN identification, and my letter of invitation to the conference on the counter in front of the officer. The immigration officer glanced at my UN invitation letter, stamped my passport for six months and said, "Miss, your visa is expiring tonight. Whenever you get a chance, please renew it." Because of the time difference between Pakistan and the US, it was still February 5 in New York. I thanked him very sincerely and praised God. When I was in the line to check my bags, that same immigration officer came by and told the staff they didn't need to check my bags since I was with the UN.

I beamed with pride that I was affiliated with the UN, and I was so thankful to be in America. Now, I had to figure out how to survive.

CHAPTER 20

Seeking Asylum

WHEN I STEPPED OFF THE airplane at JFK, I had no idea what was in store for me. I didn't know what to call myself—a refugee, an immigrant, or just a traveler, here for a time until things settled down at home. I had little clue what lay ahead.

I received an invitation from my friend, Dr. Bill, to speak to his students at Lehigh University. I gladly accepted. I presented the struggle in Pakistan to organize efforts to reach geriatric patients. My visit with the students was invigorating for me and informative for the students, who appreciated the work I was doing.

I attended many events, lectures, and speeches at the UN. One day I sat in on a talk in the Security Council conference hall, given by Mr. Manjeev Singh Puri. He was a senior member of India's Security Council team during his country's tenure on the Security Council. During his remarks, he stated that Pakistan was involved in 9/11. I couldn't believe the blunder. I waited for someone from the Pakistan Mission to speak up, but no one did. They were all there in the front row. But not one of them said anything. I couldn't help myself, I stood up.

"Sir, Pakistan was not involved in 9/11."

He stopped speaking, a look of surprise on his face. "I didn't say Pakistan. I mean to say another country."

"Then you should clarify what you meant, because you did say Pakistan."

A few others in the audience spoke up, confirming he did indeed say Pakistan. He admitted his mistake, but still, I was surprised no one in the audience from Pakistan dared to speak up. After finishing that conference, I was outside the hall, when the Indian official called to me, "Miss, are you from the Pakistan Embassy?"

"No sir, I am a Pakistani doctor here for a conference."

We spoke for a while about India, and I told him about my one visit to his country and the wonderful people I met. Mr. Singh invited me to the Indian embassy to further our discussion. I was very interested, but I wasn't sure where I would live after the conference.

Near the end of my first month in the US, I finally met up with Beth at a UN event. I asked for her help and she promised to pick me up the next day. When her car pulled up at the curb the following afternoon, I stood on the sidewalk with my luggage. Because she was dealing with some personal issues at the time, she had arranged for me to stay with her friend, Rebekah, for two weeks.

Beth also told me about an organization, Scholars at Risk, and counseled me to contact them as soon as I could. They would know how to help me. A few days later, after I settled into my new place, I visited Scholars at Risk. When I told a staff member my story, she advised me to apply for asylum.

I had no idea how asylum worked, but the kind representative explained the process to me. Unfortunately, I wouldn't be authorized to work until my case was approved.

After I understood the process, I agreed to apply for asylum. Scholars at Risk referred me to an organization, that would appoint an attorney and assist me in the process of applying. I wanted to meet with the attorney, but I was forced to move again as my two-week stay expired.

Beth contacted the Pakistani Embassy in New York. She informed them that a Pakistani female doctor needed help. The officer referred me to the ICNA, a women's support center.

After much turmoil, I arrived at the ICNA. The director, Mr. Siddiqi, greeted me warmly. I had moved five times before finally reaching this center. At last, a safe place to stay in America. God was watching over me.

I finally met with Aleks, the attorney referred to me by Scholars at Risk. Aleks was very helpful, and he explained what I would need to do to apply for asylum. He thought my case had a very high chance of being approved.

Shortly after I moved in, the woman who ran the daily operations left the center. Mr. Siddiqi appointed me as the Supervisor of the Women's Support Center. I was very proud and pleased. Living at ICNA was an excellent opportunity for me to meet interesting and influential people. Senators and politicians regularly visited the center. I met Lord Nazir from the UK when he visited the center. I escorted him on a tour, and we were followed by film crews from the BBC and CNN. Reporters came to the center and interviewed us about the work of the center. I didn't think of the consequences at the time, but the articles were published in local papers along with my photo.

The most satisfying part of living at the center were the women who left. They went on to independent and productive lives. It was enjoyable work, and I loved speaking about what we accomplished.

One day Malik visited the center with his wife, and I pretended I didn't know him. After a brief tour, he left with neither of us exchanging a word.

Raja Khalid contacted me on the landline number of ICNA. I was surprised to hear from him. He said that he had seen my photo in the papers. As we talked, he seemed concerned for my situation, that I missed my son and hoped to bring him to the US. He wanted to know about my involvement at the center. I told him about the center and how we helped women from all over the world integrate into life in America.

He was curious about the women at the center, and wanted to know details about them. That alarmed me.

"I can't tell you those things. That would violate their privacy."

"I understand," he said, calmly, and changed the subject. "I'd like to meet you, take you for dinner. Once we get to know each other, then we can talk again of marriage."

I sighed under my breath at the audacity of this man.

"For two years you promised to come to Karachi and meet my father. Yet you never have done what you said you would do. If you couldn't meet me for two years, there's no reason to meet now. I have to go."

I hung up, a little worried that he now knew where I lived. My life was very busy at the center, organizing and settling women as they entered the program. I was surprised by his second call a few days later.

This time he pleaded with me to understand that he was a very busy man with many business interests, and he had intended all along to meet me in Karachi, but the circumstances of his busy schedule never permitted. He apologized, and I again fell into the trap of extending forgiveness where none was warranted. Only time would prove that to me.

I agreed to meet him, but was clear: I would never marry in America—only in Pakistan in front of my family. He backed off marriage, and we agreed to meet.

I went to meet him in Ronkonkoma on Long Island. When he picked me up at the train station, he showed me to his car. A woman sat in the front seat—another surprise—and he opened the rear door, so I could slip inside. For the first time in more than two years, I now studied this mysterious man. In the car, he watched me in his rearview mirror as I watched him. He introduced the woman next to him as his secretary, Tuntana. Instead of his home, he drove to a hotel. Inside the room, I took a seat. In my naivety, I had no idea what we were doing here.

I took a seat at the table. He stood over me.

"Your photos don't do you justice. You are beautiful."

Tuntana scoffed and slumped onto one of the beds. He spoke to her, bantering about her salary and other meaningless things I didn't care about.

"You said you'd take me to your home to meet your family."

Tuntana laughed so hard she almost howled.

"Next time, Baby. Not this time. Now we need to get to know each other."

The air in the room drew suddenly close, uncomfortable. What was he talking about? Raja nodded, and Tuntana sauntered over to a table with glasses and liquor bottles. She poured three drinks and brought me one.

I waved the glass away. "I don't drink."

He looked startled. "I was told something different."

"You have the wrong information about me from Mansoor."

Tuntana held the glass in front of me as if I hadn't told her the truth.

"Don't bother her."

She set the drink down on a side table and began to undress. Kahild held out his hand to me.

"Come, join us. This is your training," he said, smiling.

I was so disgusted. This was the true Khalid. He and Mansoor were precisely the same men. All the phone calls with empty promises, the offers of marriage; they were nothing but an enticement into his games. I became heated inside, but I couldn't move. He sensed my refusal, went to the phone, and spoke to a woman, calling her to join them.

In short order, another woman entered, didn't hesitate to undress, and lay on the bed. At the same time a man entered. Raja greeted him and introduced him to me as Lucky Sing. He was surprised that I was sitting on the sofa, and not participating in the group sex. Raja told him I didn't want to party with them, and Mr. Sing became angry, telling him that I was part of the deal. Raja again ordered me to undress and join them, but I refused.

"I cannot force her," he said to Mr. Sing. The man turned in a huff and left the room, slamming the door. Raja was upset, but Tuntana gave him another drink, and he settled down. The three of them began their orgy right in front of me.

For a moment, I thought I was dreaming. This couldn't be happening to me. But these were flesh and blood people. Every motive of Khalid's calls became crystal clear to me in that moment—he was a pervert like Mansoor. He didn't want me as a wife, but as one of his playthings. In disgust, I rose and headed for the door. I swung it open, stepped into the hall, and it slammed behind me. I had been so stupid to listen to this man's excuses and not my own sense. He proved he was a man who had no intention of keeping his promises. He had only wanted to deceive me from the beginning. How many vulnerable women had he forced into his scheme?

Alone in the cold hall, I crossed my arms in front of me to ward off my shivers. I thought of these women from Pakistan in the room, and the other women that no doubt were innocent village girls, brought here by this monster for his sex business. Was he a human trafficker? What about those people who whisked me off to an empty house and wanted to take my phone? They all were in some sordid business I knew nothing of and never suspected. I simmered at the treachery and evil of these men, as I waited, praying to God I would get out of here safely. I don't know how long I stood there, waiting, before a fully clothed Khalid came out. I demanded he take me home. We drove to the train in icy silence. At the station, I told him not to ever contact me again.

He faced me. "I know where your son lives, remember that. You are alone in this country, and anything can happen."

I wanted to claw his eye out, but I jumped out of his car instead. As he sped off into the night, I hoped that would be the last of him.

A few days later, he started calling, pleading with me for forgiveness. I told him I was shocked at his behavior. He could do whatever he wanted with his life. But that's not the life I wanted; why did he keep bothering me since we had different lifestyles?

He began swearing by Allah that he would change his ways. He would sponsor my son to come to America. After we were married, he would go on *hajj* and live the rest of his life as a devout Muslim.

I had heard these same promises from another man, and I was in no mood for his lying. I told him that under no circumstances would I ever marry him, and that he should never call me again.

Before we hung up, he claimed I was jeopardizing my son's future. He would never be able to come to the US because I had applied for asylum. I didn't believe him. His only goal was to fill me with fear. The man was a fraud. I read one day in a Pakistani newspaper that circulated in my neighborhood, that Raja's son, Nange Punge, was being openly ridiculed for marrying a nude dancer who at one time had dated Raja for several years. I saw it as a form of judgment by God that an infamous girl he once dated was now his daughter-in-law.

Seven months had passed since I had last seen Taimoor. We hadn't talked much on the phone, but now was the time to act. He needed to come to America. I reached him at work, and he was excited to hear from me. We caught up, and I told him I had applied for asylum, and wouldn't return home until it was approved. I told him that he should apply for a visa to come to America. If he applied for a tourist visa, we could be together much sooner.

The day of his interview at the US embassy, I lay awake the entire night. When he called with the sad news that he had been rejected, I tried not to cry until I was alone. Gaining permanent residency in America and having my son with me would have been a dream come true. Now I felt defeated in all of my dreams. I began complaining to God. *Why was life so cruel to me?* I grew bitter and skeptical. Maybe I should return to Pakistan and move secretly to another city.

I stopped answering Khalid's calls. Then he began calling from a blocked number. Before I could hang up, he said, "If you want your son to be safe, you better listen to me. Do you know he is attending political rallies, and it would be easy for us to kill him?"

That struck terror in my heart. I called Taimoor, and demanded to know why he was attending political rallies.

He was very reasonable with his answers. "Mom, if the young people of this country don't think for Pakistan, then who will? Besides, I'm only out listening to Imran Khan."

I understood his feelings. I could not ask him to become a hermit, but I did plead with him to move to his friend's house for the time being.

From then on, I blocked Raja's calls.

A few days later, the director of ICNA received a call on the office phone. When he came to me, he had a concerned look on his face.

"The call was from Pakistan, and it was for you."

The caller threatened that if I didn't return to Pakistan, my son would be kidnapped and my father would be jailed. I became very scared that this harassment would go on until something terrible happened.

One of the center's directors said I should contact the police. Another director said it was an empty threat and I shouldn't take it seriously. Besides, what would the police do if the caller was in Pakistan? I asked for the number of the caller, and after dialing it went to Khalid's voice mail. It was his Pakistan number. Not only was he a sexual pervert, but he wasn't any better than the terrorists who used violence and intimidation to get what they wanted. I called my attorney, Aleks.

He advised me that it wasn't best for me to return. I wouldn't be any safer and my chances of obtaining asylum would be over forever. I could never reapply. The threat against my father was most likely empty, and it would be best for my son to go into hiding. I agreed with his assessment.

After this episode, Taimoor applied again for a US visa, and was turned down. Evidently, with my asylum request, family members were barred from entering until my case was resolved. I didn't know that beforehand. Alone in my room at night, I cried. I became angry at God. I stopped praying because I couldn't focus during prayers. I felt God wasn't my friend anymore. He wasn't at my back.

The next time I spoke to Taimoor, he tried to console me.

"Mom, think of it like this. I feel God will give me a better reward, and the sooner you are granted asylum, the sonner you could travel to meet me in any country. Now you are in the safest place."

As much as I was distressed to be apart from him, I had to agree with him. But when I had left home, I thought I would be away for a few months, things would quiet down, and then I could return. Now I was on a completely different path, one I could not step away from without jeopardizing my chances of a permanent residency in the US.

Finally, the day came for my asylum interview. Aleks had called me the day before to prepare me. He met me at the immigration office (USCIS), where the interview was to be conducted. I was agitated, and he tried to calm me. He wanted me to keep it simple in the interview, and not to seem more intelligent than the immigration officer. I answered everything truthfully about my situation, but still, the officer seemed suspicious. She said she'd have to forward my file to Washington, DC, for further investigation. My case should have only taken a few months to approve, but instead it took six more months.

Aleks told me that my case took so long because I was an educated woman from Pakistan. At the time of my interview, the US government was prosecuting a Pakistani scientist accused of involvement with the planning of terrorist activities related to 9/11. Dr. Aafia Siddiqui was an American-trained neuroscientist charged with aiding terrorists. It was a bad time for me, but it was also a bad time for Dr. Aafia and my country. Aleks said if I were an uneducated housewife, my application would have been approved quickly.

Eventually, my asylum was approved, and I thought that I could now sponsor Taimoor. When I told him, he was very excited that we would finally be together. When I asked Aleks about the process, he laid out the steps. I had to first apply for a green card. After a waiting period, I could apply for citizenship. Then I could sponsor Taimoor to come to America. When he told me that the process could take another ten years or more, I was very disappointed. I didn't tell Taimoor, but he is a brilliant young man. He did his own research, and told me it would take a long time for him to come to America.

Our separation was beginning to wear on him. I realized he was heartbroken. He knew for a fact that now he had to live alone for a long time, which was causing him pain. Citizenship seemed so far away, and so many obstacles seemed to stand in my way.

A wave of sadness came over me. I prayed to God that all of those who had played a hand in my leaving the country that I loved would leave me alone. I felt the pain of my son, of my father, of my brothers, and nieces and nephews. I didn't know when I would see any of them again. My anguish became so real, I had to cover my mouth with my hand to stop from crying and cursing out loud.

With a work permit, I now could work like any other American. It was time to move out of the center and make it on my own. Walking the streets of New York, the reality hit me that I was now an immigrant, building a new life. It was time to start.

I found a room with Mumte, a Pakistani woman. I applied for a position in customer service at a CVS pharmacy. I was hired and began working weekends. Everything was so new and fast-paced that I felt excited. But this was my life now, and I decided to do my absolute best. A contact from ICNA referred me to Pakistani orthopedic doctor who hired me as a medical assistant.

With a new place to live and a weekend job, and working full-time during the week as a medical assistant, my life was busy. I hoped and prayed all of my troubles were behind me.

In my free time, I returned to attending meetings and conferences at the UN. Khalid kept calling my cell phone, but I refused his calls. I could hear his threating messages, saying I should go back to the center and shouldn't continue jobs. This went on for a week or two, and then one day, the orthopedist told me he no longer wanted me to work for him. I was crushed. He didn't give me a reason. He insisted that he no longer needed me.

I knew that wasn't true. He had a hectic office. I was very hurt, and that night I could hardly sleep trying to figure out in my mind what I might have done to cause my abrupt dismissal.

The next Wednesday morning, I awoke to loud conversations outside my bedroom door. It burst open, and a group of men and women rushed in. I tried to jump out of bed, demanding to know what they were doing. I grabbed for my phone, thinking to call 911 for help. Someone slapped it out of my hand, and it clattered to the floor. One of the women pushed me down on the bed and clamped her hand over my mouth and nose, and the other grabbed my neck and started strangling me. I gasped for breath. Her hands were so tight I couldn't even scream. I feared she would kill me. Fearing I would black out, I prayed for help. The thought came to me to fight for my life. I bit her hand and I pushed as hard as I could at the lady with her hands around my throat. And she backed off.

I screamed at them, "Why are you doing this?" I backed away from them.

"Just leave her," one of the men said.

Mumte and other women grabbed my arms, pulled me from the room, and pushed me out the front door of the apartment. One of them threw my purse outside on the sidewalk, and then slammed the door. I was too dizzy to think straight. The day before I had lost my job, and now I stood in the road with no shoes and in my nightdress.

I went back to the apartment door and banged on it. I shouted through the door for my shoes and my jacket. I was freezing. I kept beating until the door opened, and a woman threw my shoes and coat at me.

"I need my clothes."

She slammed the door in my face. I found the nearest subway and used my MetroCard. I had very little money in my bag, but I had enough in the bank to rent a room. I had to find a new place to live with someone Khalid wouldn't know. New York was a big city; he couldn't know everyone or be everywhere.

All that day, I searched. I read classifieds and used pay phones. I spent the night at a kind woman's apartment I knew from the center. I left her apartment early the next morning to continue my search. That night I stayed with an Afghan lady and spent all day Friday searching again. By Friday night, I was so exhausted I could hardly walk when I saw a room advertised that might work. Finally, I found a tiny room, but the landlady couldn't have it cleaned and ready for several hours. I was able to crawl into bed at 2 a.m. I slept so soundly on a mattress with no sheets or pillows. The kind landlady put a comforter on me, so I slept well.

Saturday morning I needed to be at CVS for work. I didn't have anything to eat, and I rushed in, hungry and dizzy. My manager, Angel, at first was angry with me that I wasn't prepared to work. He threatened to fire me if I couldn't work.

"Please don't fire me," I pleaded. "It's the first and last time I will ever come to work like this. I'm just exhausted. Give me some time to straighten out my living situation, and I'll be ready to work." Angel turned into a true angel. He agreed, and said that I could return tomorrow, ready to work.

I went across the street to Citibank, requested a new bank card, ate breakfast in Jackson Heights, and bought a new cell phone with a new number. Perhaps I should have changed my phone number long ago, but I feared losing contact with my son and family in Pakistan. That night, I slept for ten hours, and went to work refreshed and excited about my job.

After work, I went to the police station and filed a report, asking for help retrieving my belongings. The police met me at Mumte's apartment, and I was able to pack my bags and leave. I saved my job, and with a new place to live, I called my son to tell him I was fine. A week later, a new store manager, took over my CVS location. He complimented me on how hard I worked, and how well I treated customers. When customers turned in their surveys, they were always satisfied.

Within a short time, he increased my hours to full-time. After three years, I moved to a Duane Reade Pharmacy near the UN as a beauty consultant.

Over time, Taimoor met a girl at his job, and I allowed him to celebrate his engagement. He applied for a student visa for a European country, and received a scholarship and moved to a safe country. He kept asking me to visit him. In June 2016, I flew to meet him. On my long flight I kept thinking about him, how I missed seeing him happy and grown. I regretted that I had left him alone to face uncertain dangers. It had been five-and-a-half years since I'd seen him. I felt like weeping, I missed him so much, but I kept myself together on the flight.

When I landed, cleared customs, and greeted him for the first time after half a decade, I searched his eyes—he was glad to see me. I held his hand. When I had left him, he was a skinny teenager; now he was a grown man. He was so polite, kind, and gracious. He was the man I had raised him to become. I was very proud of him.

He drove me to his apartment in a nice part of the city. As we talked and got reacquainted with each other, he spoke of his surprise.

"Mother, you look so weak and fearful."

I had to admit, I was weak. I had lost weight through all the ordeals of the last five years, and my struggle to establish myself in a new country. I began to miss all the years we weren't together. But here he was, a full-grown responsible adult. He had learned to manage his own life well, working and studying abroad, and taking care of himself.

He wanted to know what had happened to me in New York that I would come to him so tired, worn out, and full of fear. I told him about Khalid and Mansoor, but he stopped me.

"Mom, these men are harassing you because you're a good person. You need to realize they are more afraid of you than you are of them. If the only way they can get women to be with them is bribery and intimidation, they are small and mean people. You are an exceptional woman in Pakistani society. I've always admired your bravery and independence and how confidently you went about your life in a Pakistani society that degrades women to second-class status. Men in our country don't like women like you. They are afraid of you."

I felt so proud of him at that moment that he knew my struggles were always against a society that didn't honor women.

"My son, I am sorry that I didn't leave any money for you."

He sat next to me, and took my hand. "Mother, you have given me so much. You've taught me the right way to live. I can live confidently and take care of myself. No parent can give their children more than that. If you had left me a lot of money and never taught me anything, I would be nothing but a spoiled child."

"When did I teach you all of that?"

"I witnessed everything you went through, and how you always fought for what was right. I am very thankful for the education and teaching you've given me. You are the best person I've ever seen."

My heart was filled with gratitude to God. I could not think of any better reward in my life then the word of my son.

"Mom, here is what I suggest you do. Stay here with me for a few months, and be at peace." He wanted me to pray again, to regain my peace and happiness.

For the next three months, I stayed in his home. I prayed every day, I took walks, and cooked for my son. After all the running from trouble and the difficulties of my life, I began to relax and find some peace.

Living with my son, I observed that he had become a responsible and practical young man. All the hard and difficult times I had while raising him didn't come into our conversation. He seemed to only remember the good things, the pleasant times, and the humorous events that made our life easier to bear.

During my stay we celebrated Ramadan. I began again to pray, to read the Quran, and to fast. I spent the whole month reading the Quran, and my faith in God became strong again. My hope for my son and for my own life revived.

In thinking about my life and all my troubles, I knew that I had to leave all of the troublemakers, those who had made my life miserable, to God. One day, we will all stand before God on Judgment Day. God will judge them.

Now is the time for me to be at peace and to be happy that my life has not been in vain. My son is here with me, and he is safe, and he has become a real man, one who knows how to treat others justly and kindly, especially women.

Now I know, God is at my back.